$\mathcal{N}$IGHT $\mathcal{C}$OME $\mathcal{S}$WIFTLY

$\mathcal{P}.\mathcal{B}.$ $\mathcal{W}ilson$

New Dawn Publishing Co.
Pasadena, CA 91102

Cover by Koechel Peterson & Associates, Minneapolis, Minnesota

NIGHT COME SWIFTLY
Copyright © by P. B. Wilson
New Dawn Publishing Company
Pasadena, California 91102

Library of Congress Cataloging-in-Publication Data

Wilson, P. B. (P. Bunny), 1950-
        Night come swiftly / P. B. Wilson
            p. cm.
        ISBN 0-9621408-7-2
        1. Afro-Americans—North Carolina—History—19th century—fiction. I. Title
PS3573.I4646N54 1997
813'.54—dc21   97-6334
                                                                          CIP

Printed in the United States of America

97   98   99   00   01   02   / BC /   10   9   8   7   6   5   4   3   2

To my Father and Mother,
Clifford and Elisabeth

Acknowledgments

To Bill Jensen, who planted the seed in the writing of a novel. To Dr. Patricia Williams, professor of English at Texas Southern University, who watered the seed and provided editing assistance with the slave dialect.

To Meaalofa Lafaialii, who enabled me to finish this work by dedicating a year of service to our family. You were more than an assistant; you are my friend. To my daughter, Fawn, and niece, Azzure, who served unselfishly in supplying administrative and clerical support.

To those who gave their valuable critiques. I will be forever grateful to my sister, Elenor Ashe, Sandy Snavely, Marilyn Davis, Michelle McKinney and Mary Dumas. I would also like to thank Christy Joy, Priscilla, Susan, Arlene, Peggy, Tanya, Barbara, Karen, Carrie, Rita, Andrea, Yvonne, Helen, Renee, Katie, and Lainie. Also to my editor, Lela Gilbert.

And, saving the best for last, to my dear, wonderful husband, Frank. Thank you for helping me cross the finish line.

Part 1

1

May 1851
Raleigh, North Carolina

"Massa Jack? Massa Jack?" Sadie haltingly repeated. Eyes fixed on endless yesterdays, Master Jack Douglas stood at the open terrace window. The baby continued to cry, but still he made no movement.

"Massa Jack? Da baby is hungry. Let me take 'er, suh. I has plenty o' milk seein' I jes' had my baby, Tilly, two weeks ago. Please, Massa Jack."

An hour passed with the baby cradled in his arms. Sadie took courage and walked in front of her owner; she just barely reached the middle of his chest in height. She tried again.

"Mis' Becky ask dat I take de baby now, Massa Jack."

Sadie hoped the sound of Becky's name would summon her master's mind from its hidden sanctuary. His steel-gray eyes fastened on the frightened slave before him. Sadie reached ever so slightly for the infant, and Master Jack lowered the baby into her arms. He wondered aloud if he had told Sadie that the baby's name was Meredith. Sadie told him he had not, but assured him that it was a most important name.

Then Sadie scurried to the bedroom door with the little bundle, silently praying that he wouldn't change his mind. Half turning before leaving the room, she saw Master Jack once again, a statue, not moving. She thought if he'd had his way, he wouldn't be breathing either.

His sensitive, beautiful wife, Becky, lay motionless beneath the white sheet just a few feet away. Soon her body would be removed, but for now Master Jack would stand guard. Perhaps her soul had lost its way and would find the path back to him before they came to take her away. Perhaps.

August 1861

The spray of river water seemed to stop midair. Captured by the glistening summer sun, it turned into liquid, sparkling diamonds. Snapped to reality by gravity, the water caught Meredith across her high-flushed cheekbones. Sputtering with watery laughter, she exclaimed, "You're in trouble now, Tilly!"

Meredith's aqua-blue eyes flashed toward the ebony back of her assailant who was escaping quickly toward the river bank. Meredith pushed through the shallow river, her ivory hands extended to catch the culprit. Tilly scampered up the embankment squealing with delight.

"It serves you right, Meri!" shouted Tilly over her shoulder.

Meredith pulled her slim, ten-year-old body out of the water. Her long, soft-auburn curls clung to her skin as she dashed toward Tilly. Nothing mattered—not the lateness of the hour, or concern about the civil war, or care for the clothes they had shed before diving into the gently flowing river. She was with her best friend.

Tilly hid behind a giant oak tree trying desperately to pant softly so she wouldn't be detected. A crackling twig alerted her to Meredith's nearness. Before she could turn to run, a hand grabbed her arm.

"I got you!" shrieked Meredith.

Tilly reached for her ticklish side, and Meredith let go long enough for Tilly to run to where their clothes lay waiting.

Exhausted, she collapsed on the rich green grass with Meredith quickly dropping down beside her.

"My, my, my," said Tilly, as she pulled on her undergarments and looked at Meredith with concern. "What will your daddy think when he sees you, Meri? The last time you come in with that red skin and tangled hair, my momma licked me something good. Said it wasn't proper for a genteel-bred southern girl to come home looking like that—and she thought it was my fault."

Meredith adjusted her white stockings and promised she would be ever so careful to slip in without being seen. "I'll pretend to be sick tomorrow so everyone will think my red cheeks are due to fever. I don't want to get my friend in trouble. Oh, and Tilly," Meredith suddenly changed the subject, "for the last time, it's 'came' in—not 'come' in."

Tilly rested her body on her hands behind her and sighed. "Meri, I'm not a white girl. I'm a slave. My people make fun of me when I talk proper. Not Momma, of course. Sometimes I even think she's a little proud of my talking. But I can see Aunt Susie going back and forth in her rocking chair saying, 'Who ya t'ink ya are li'l mis' missy wid all dat fancy talkin'? You jes' gonna end up pickin' cotton like de res' of us. Ya bettah not be forgittin' who ya is!' "

"That's silly," responded Meredith.

Tilly continued. "Aunt Susie also said that some masters give their child a dog to play with, but Master Jack gave me to you. And when you get tired of playing with me, I'll be just another slave girl."

Meredith was visibly upset and raised her voice. "What does your Aunt Susie know anyway? You're gonna always be with me—not because you're a slave but because you're my best friend. Besides, you're just as smart as me, and even smarter in arithmetic. And don't forget, I need you to help me with my numbers tomorrow. Miss Martha is going to make me write standards. By the way, did you bring it?"

Meredith had dismissed the subject, and Tilly's heart had been reassured. She hesitated for a moment and heard Meredith ask again, "Did you bring it?"

"Uh huh," answered Tilly as she pulled out the neatly folded paper from the pocket of her brown burlap dress. "Miss Martha would die if she knew I wrote this. I can see her now, standing straight as an Indian's arrow and speaking in that voice that puts a whining mule to shame. 'Good Lord, Miss Meredith, you know slaves aren't capable of learning to read or write. That's why I don't mind when Tilly sits with you at your lessons although your father, bless his heart, thinks it's an abomination!'"

Meredith found it hilarious that her friend could imitate Miss Martha so perfectly. As she lay on her back in the warm grass giggling and looking up at the blue sky, she suddenly pointed and exclaimed, "Why, Tilly, look!"

Tilly lay on her back and followed Meredith's finger.

"I see the man I'm gonna marry," gushed Meredith.

"Oh, I see him too, Meri. It's that big white puffy one on the right!"

Meredith playfully nudged Tilly, "No, silly, look a little to the left. It's that handsome cloud. See him? He's tall and dressed in a uniform with a sword at his side. Why, he's just the most beautiful man that ever walked the face of the earth and he's all mine!"

"I know, I know, Meri," sighed Tilly, reciting what she knew would be Meredith's next statement. Tilly jumped to her feet, twirling around in the arms of an invisible man. "I will meet him at my coming-out ball. One look and he'll be swept off his feet by my beauty and charm. He'll propose, and by the following spring I will walk down the bridal path in my beautiful garden."

"And how did you know that?" Meredith inquired indignantly.

Tilly smiled, flashing teeth so perfect and white that Meredith thought an angel must have once possessed them. Only her deep dimples could upstage such an inviting smile. Her dark, chiseled features and large, round, black eyes often captured Meredith's imagination as she thought about the stories Tilly told of her grandfather before he was captured and taken on the slave ship. He had been a tribal king, and she guessed that was why Tilly walked like a princess. Meredith knew her father would punish her severely if he found out she allowed Tilly to speak of her family's history in Africa. That was strictly forbidden . . . and slaves could never speak in their native language, either. Meredith just didn't understand why.

Tilly broke into Meredith's thoughts. "I read first last time."

"But yours are always better."

"Says who?"

"Says me!"

Tilly sighed, "I do declare, Meri, I'm sure the war would be over by now if you were in charge!"

"I'm sure you're right—so read on."

"O.K., but you have to close your eyes so you can see the words."

Meredith heard the paper unfold. Tilly cleared her throat and spoke softly. "The title of my poem is, 'My Friend to Me.'"

Powder sweet
Powder white
Powder soft
Powder light
Is my friend to me.

Put it on
See it blend
Now we're one
On my skin
Is my friend to me.

God saw two
Made them one
Knew we'd shine
As the sun
Is my friend to me.
Is my friend to me?
Is my friend to me.

Meredith lay completely still and then asked, "How do you do that?"

"Do what?"

"Write a poem like that? Every time you write one I want to cry."

Tilly whispered, "That's because you're powder soft."

Meredith opened her eyes and saw her friend sitting in front of her. Thoughts began to flood her mind, *Why does Tilly have to be a slave? Why couldn't she just be a friend who lived down the road? Why are there so many rules that tell us how to act when we are around other people? And why do I always ask myself the same questions when I can never come up with any answers!*

"That was beautiful, Tilly. I'll keep it always. Now it's my turn." Meredith stuck her hand into her frilly, white pocket and brought out a neatly folded paper.

Tilly opened it slowly and then caught her breath. "Meri! This is better than the last one."

Meredith had once again drawn a beautiful picture. She said she wanted to be an artist one day. Tilly looked at two girls—she and Meredith—diving into a river.

"I not only drew a picture, I wrote a story. So take your seats, ladies and gentlemen, while the Meredith Story Theater opens its curtains!"

A rustling in the bushes behind them caused the girls to jump. A pair of black, piercing eyes could be seen through the leaves. "Don' be 'fraid chil'ren. It jes' me, Auntie Ruth."

Meredith and Tilly rushed behind the bush throwing their arms around the short stout woman with a blue bandanna tied around her head.

"Hold it! You two gonna squeeze de life out o' me."

As Meredith buried her face in the tired woman's apron, Tilly searched her face for an answer. When Auntie Ruth smiled brightly you hardly noticed her two front teeth were missing. She winked her eye and Tilly knew: Ben had made it.

≋ ≋ ≋

Tilly yawned and stretched in the canopy bed until she felt she was two inches taller. Meri was still asleep. Every morning just before the sun came up, Tilly instinctively woke up. She eased out from underneath the white embroidered quilt, tiptoed to unlock the bedroom door, then lay down on the floor pallet that was really her bed. Meredith had raised a fuss with her daddy when she was five years old and said she wanted Tilly with her because she was afraid of the dark. Master Jack said it would be all right if Tilly slept on the floor. So every night Meri locked the door in case anyone tried to come in. Then she and Tilly crawled into bed and told stories until they fell asleep. But Tilly knew she'd be in bad trouble if she got caught, so she guessed fear is what woke her up every morning.

Soon she would need to help her momma prepare breakfast for Master Jack, Meredith, and Pastor Duncan. The reverend came every Sunday, except when it rained so hard the wagon wheels wouldn't turn. But that wasn't often. Most Sundays the three of them left together and went to the beautiful white church down the road a bit. Tilly went once a year when the church had a picnic and Sadie helped cook the food. She even saw inside the big church doors, which happened to be standing wide open at one picnic. She wondered if heaven looked like that. The pews were polished so bright she could comb her hair while looking at the reflection. Colored glass windows had pictures of important people, and she even saw a picture of Jesus on the cross. At first she thought He was looking at her, but that couldn't be, could it?

Sundays were the days when Tilly wore her special dress to help her momma serve the food. She slipped on the long gray dress that fit her thin body so snugly. Momma said every time she let the dress out it seemed Tilly's body knew it and just filled in the empty spaces. Her crisp white apron was slipped over her head and tied around her waist. She combed her hair in the early morning light and reckoned she looked just fine.

Tilly opened the door quietly so she wouldn't wake Meri, then giggled silently at the silly thought. She had to drag Meri out of bed every morning—there was little chance of disturbing her. As soon as the door opened, she was engulfed by the smell of freshly picked magnolias. They were arranged in a vase on a neatly polished hallway table. She called it a picture vase because it had people dressed in fancy clothes painted on it. Meri said it was from England and was made in the sixteenth century. Tilly couldn't figure out why anyone would want something so old, but it was useful for holding beautiful cut flowers from the garden.

Tilly eased down the long corridor. Jim and Cory, two of Master Jack's house slaves, had shined the floors until they seemed to sparkle as pretty as the dinner crystal. The hardwood peeked out on either side of the floor runner. She loved the red carpet with its swirls of gold and deep blue that seemed to chase each other to the end of the hallway as if they were racing to Master Jack's dark bedroom doors.

Approaching the staircase, Tilly paused for a moment, closed her eyes, and held the sides of her dress as if to curtsy. She and Meri had practiced often, walking up and down the double winding staircases that met in a highly polished black-and-white square floor. Miss Martha said it was never too early for a southern belle to practice for her coming-out ball. With books balanced squarely on their heads, Tilly and Meri would gingerly glide up and down the stairs. A large sparkling chandelier hung between the stairs, over a large round table. It was here that George, the gardener, placed his most beautiful flower arrangements.

The ritual of Sunday morning beckoned Tilly to the top of the stairs. This was the only time during the week she was alone. As she descended the stairs, an imaginary crowd of people waited below with admiring eyes—eyes not intended for Meri. They stared intently at Tilly, who seemed to float to the landing at the bottom of the stairs. Then she curtsied in front of a handsome young gentleman who looked upon her with adoration. As she lowered her eyes so that he would not think her too forward a deep, stern voice shattered her dream.

"What are you doing?"

Looking toward the top of the stairs, she saw Master Jack glaring down at her.

"I . . . I . . . I was just . . ."

"Stop your foolishness and get to your work!"

As Tilly scurried across the foyer through the dining room and rushed into the kitchen, Master Jack looked toward Meredith's bedroom door. He was slowly beginning to believe Agatha was right.

Bertha, one of the cooks, was sitting at the table peeling potatoes. "Goodness, chile, even a tornado don' move dat fas'. Somebody chasin' ya?

Sadie stood at the stove stirring the grits. She put her spoon down when she saw the strange expression on her daughter's face. "Whut's wrong, Tilly?"

Taking a deep breath, Tilly responded, "Nothing, Momma."

"Don' lie to me, chile."

"I'm not, Momma. I was just excited about seeing you."

Sadie paused. "Well, I hope ya're jus' as excited 'bout gittin' me some fresh eggs from de hen house."

"Yes, Momma." As Tilly rushed out the back door and across the yard to get the eggs she wondered why Master Jack was awake and dressed. She had never seen him up so early.

Once Meri had tried to talk her father into allowing Tilly to eat with them in the formal dining room. He had firmly let her know that it wouldn't be permissible and that she was never to ask again. Seeing her unhappy expression, he'd picked her up and given her a big hug.

"I declare, Meredith, you are just like your mother," he'd said. She had buried her face in his neck, wanting to pout but loving him too much to do so. She didn't want to add to the sadness he wore on his face.

Tilly would always stand across from Meri's chair so they could talk to each other with their eyes. Each believed she knew what the other was thinking. Then, after Meri's return from church, they would go out to play. Going over the early morning breakfast conversation, they always discovered they were right. They really did know each other's thoughts.

This morning, Tilly stood in her usual place after she helped serve breakfast. Pastor Duncan, dressed in his Sunday-go-to-meeting black suit, blessed the food. During the prayer, Meri looked at Tilly and rolled her eyes as she moved her head from one side to the other. Tilly stifled a laugh. She knew what Meri meant. They had given Pastor Duncan a nickname: Old Crow. Just like the crow that flew over the plantation making a cawing sound, so the pastor's voice resembled the big black bird. It raised and lowered as if pulled by a string.

As the pastor took a bite of bread and dug into his eggs he remarked, "Jack, I was sorry to hear about your slave running away. What was his name? Ben?"

Meri glanced at Tilly. Oddly enough, she was looking at her mother, who appeared not to notice.

Meredith's father froze at the pastor's words. Before he could answer, Meri jumped in, "Ben? Daddy, why would Ben run away? You were always so kind to him—just like you are with the other slaves. Why would he run away from here?"

Meri looked at Tilly for confirmation, but her friend's eyes were fastened to the floor.

Her father forced a smile and looked at Pastor Duncan, who was uncomfortably shifting in his chair.

"This is not the kind of conversation we should have at break-fast."

Pastor Duncan cleared his throat, "You're most certainly right, Jack. I wasn't thinking."

Meri's eyes were centered on her father's face as she waited for an answer. He squeezed her hand and gently replied, "We'll talk about it later."

"No, we'll talk about it now!" announced Meredith.

"Meredith!"

Meri knew she had crossed the line. "I'm sorry, Daddy. But I loved Ben. As long as I can remember . . ."

"That's enough!" her father scolded. Breakfast ended in silence.

A short time later, as the carriage rolled through the arched entrance at the end of the driveway and onto the main road leading to the church, Tilly could see Meri sitting erect inside. She was still upset. Bertha and Sadie were washing dishes when Tilly returned to the kitchen. They didn't see her in the doorway.

Sadie sighed, looked at Bertha, her long-time friend, and said with a troubled expression, "Massa Jack left while it was still dark. Had a group of men wid dogs. I hope Ben done made it."

"He did," Tilly stated quietly.

Both women turned and stared down at the small-framed girl.

"Why ya say dat?" asked Sadie.

Tilly knew she was going to get into trouble but didn't want her mother and Bertha to be worried. Sadie slowly dried her hands and sat at the kitchen table covered with a red-and-white checkered tablecloth.

"I saw her the other day."

"Who? Where?"

"Auntie Ruth."

Sadie slammed her hand down hard upon the table. "Ya went back to de rivah didn' ya?"

Tilly nodded her head.

Bertha moved her heavy round body close to Sadie. She put her hand on Sadie's shoulder and said encouragingly, "Let de girl talk, Sadie. Go on, Tilly."

Tilly clasped her hands in front of her and recounted, "We . . . I mean . . . I saw Auntie Ruth."

"Whut do ya mean *we*, Tilly? Does Mis' Meredith know 'bout her?"

Tilly nodded slowly.

"How could ya, Tilly?" stormed Sadie.

"But Momma, she doesn't know what Auntie Ruth does. And besides she loves her."

Sadie looked up at Bertha in disbelief, then back to Tilly. "Chile, ya could be de death of Auntie Ruth!"

"Oh no, Momma! Meri is my best friend. She would never do anything to hurt Auntie Ruth!"

The slap stung Tilly's face. She recoiled in shock and pressed her hand against her cheek.

Sadie shouted, "How many times I got to tell ya, Tilly? Mis' Meredith owns ya. She don' know no bettah right now. But one day her eyes gonna grow up an' ya'll be jes' another slave. Ya done a terrible t'ing!"

Tilly trembled as she gathered enough courage to continue her explanation. "Auntie Ruth smiled and winked at me while Meri was hugging her. Meri didn't even see it. But I knew Ben had made it to the first safe place."

Sadie sat at the table slowly shaking her head.

"Momma, I'm sorry," said Tilly.

Extending her hand, Sadie motioned Tilly to come. She pulled her in her lap and rocked as she held her tightly. Tilly's mother began to mumble to herself, "Oh, Tom, please he'p me to teach dis chile dat she's a slave and he'p Ben be a free man."

Sadie was talking to Tilly's father again. She always did that when she felt helpless. Tom had died in the cotton field after stumbling and falling under a heavy wagon wheel—this had happened when Tilly was just two years old. How Sadie missed his strong, wise companionship.

Tilly instinctively knew what was coming next. Her mother had told her the story so often that Tilly knew exactly what she would say before it was said. But she had no choice; she listened to her momma tell it one more time.

"When de slave traders come into our village der was loud cryin' an' fightin'," Sadie recalled as if in a trance. "I woke up so scared I thought de life inside me would jes' get up an' leave. My fo' younger brothahs and two sistahs got in a corner and jes' held each othah. We could heah Na-Na—that's what we called yo' grandpa; it means 'fathah.' He was screamin' an' tryin' to break free of de ropes dat was a holdin' him. I ran out of de hut toward him. He grab me and held me tight. I felt him put somet'in' in my braid at de top o' my head 'fore some men come an' tore him away."

Sadie laid her head on Tilly's shoulder and continued, "Dem slave traders marched us to de ocean where a ship was waitin'. We was stacked on dis ship, layin' down side by side, not bein' able to move. Der was people above an' below me. When dey would bring us out ever' couple days der was enough room in my ropes to reach up and tighten my braid. I didn' know whut Na-Na had put der but I was goin' to protect it wid my life. De las' time I saw yo' gran'pa he was on de slave block. Dey wanted him to open his mouth to check his teeth, jes' like an animal. He fought so hard dat dey whipped him til' he was on his knees. Den he looked up an' saw me. I reached toward my braid an' nodded my head so he would know whut he gave me was safe. I don' know why but he stopped fightin'. He got to his feet, opened his mouth, an' some white man bought him. I never seen him, Momma, my sistahs or brothahs ag'in. I was seven years old. When I finally looked at whut he put in my hair, I seen it was de small, smooth, black stone with our tribal name marked on it. He wore it 'round his neck and mus' of tore it off when I come close to him."

Sadie rocked back and forth a long time. Finally she said, "An' dat's why no white person is gonna do us no good—evah! Can't ya see dat, Tilly?"

Tilly nodded her head, but in her heart she knew Meri was different. Sadie held her a moment longer and then said, "Tilly, me an' Aunt Bertha will finish de kitchen. You go on outside an' play."

Sadie heard the kitchen door close and then dropped her head in despair, "Don' say it, Bertha. I know I was wrong an' shouldn' a-told Tilly 'bout Ben. I jes' gits so lonely without my Tom and I gits to talkin'.'"

Bertha patted Sadie's hand, "I understan', Sadie. I loved Tom too. But you jes' have to keep some things to yo'sef. Dat gal would be in a heap o' trouble if Massa Jack took to askin' questions."

Sadie stared off in the distance and softly replied, "I know, I know."

"Why didn't you tell me?" stormed Meri.

"Tell you what?" Tilly asked with a blank expression.

"About Ben."

"What about Ben?"

"Tilly, you're hiding something."

"No, I'm not."

"Yes, you are. I thought you were my best friend. I thought we didn't have secrets!"

Meri stretched out on the grass and began to cry under the weeping willow tree. This was their favorite spot; they came here every day to talk and play. Tilly sat motionless, not knowing what to say. Finally she reached over and touched Meri's shoulder.

"Meri, you are my best friend. But if I had told you, I would have been in terrible trouble."

Meri looked up with tear-swollen eyes and asked, "Trouble with who?"

"I can't tell you."

Meri jumped to her feet. "Well, as of this day, I am no longer your friend!" She turned on her heels and raced to the house—then through the front door, up the winding staircase, into her bedroom and threw herself across her bed, crying hysterically.

Tilly lay on her back in the grass and stared at the cloudless blue sky. She felt like a big hole had burst open in her heart. She held her chest, breathing hard, feeling as if she'd explode. The sun was going down when she returned to the house. Slowly opening Meri's door, she saw her sad friend lying still, having cried herself to sleep. As she approached the bed, Meri stirred as if sensing her presence.

"Tilly," she said without looking up, "I'm sorry. I didn't mean it. You'll always be my best friend."

With tears streaming down her face, Tilly responded, "Meri, what's happening? We never fight. Let's promise never to talk about this again or about anything else that will make us cry."

Meri sat up in the middle of the bed.

"I promise."

After a moment of silence she suggested, "Let's make a pact that we'll always be together."

Meri slid off the bed, went to her chest of drawers, and pulled open the bottom drawer. She reached toward the back and took out a box. Inside was a locket encasing a picture of her mother. Tilly had seen it many times. They would stare at the sweet, lovely face in the locket and imagine what she must have been like. They sometimes spent the day playing out scenes that might have depicted a day in Meri's mother's life.

Meri lifted the locket, opened it, and stared at her mother. She unclasped the lock on the chain and walked over to Tilly.

"Turn around," she instructed her friend.

Tilly obeyed and Meri fastened the locket around her neck. "I want you to have this. There is nothing more dear to me. I think a part of my mother lives in this locket. That is how you will know that I will never leave you—because I will never leave my mother."

Tilly clasped the locket in her hand. "Wait here!"

Tilly ran from the bedroom, into the backyard, and moved a brick that was a part of the house's foundation. She fumbled in the dark hole and brought out her buried treasure wrapped in burlap. Carrying it in both hands, she returned to Meri's room.

This, too, was not new. Meri knew the story. Sadie had given the stone to Tilly on her seventh birthday. Tilly stretched out her hand and extended the stone to Meri. She rolled it over and over again in her hand. Tilly and Meri sat on the floor in the light of dusk staring into each other's eyes. They could hear Jim on the back porch playing his harmonica. The low, moaning tones seemed to usher in the ominous dark clouds overhead, pregnant with rain. A warm wind caused the white eyelet curtains to slowly rise and fall. Tilly unfastened the locket and handed it back to Meri.

"Why are you giving it back?" Meri asked, looking a little hurt.

"Because now it belongs to me and I'd like you to have it. From now on it's called 'Tilly's locket.'"

Meri slowly placed the stone in Tilly's hand, "And this is 'Meri's stone.'"

"I'll take good care of it, Meri."

"And I'll take good care of yours too, Tilly."

That night they slept, one holding the locket, the other holding the stone. Now they knew—they would always be together.

2

"eady, set, go!" shouted Meri.

Tilly and Meredith descended each of the winding staircases two or three steps at a time. The front door had been purposely left ajar to assist in their quick escape. As Meredith reached the bottom of her staircase, Sadie unexpectedly came around the corner. She was caught and swung around quickly by the rambunctious ten-year-old.

"Well, I' be! You two slo' yo'sef down now. Do ya heah me?" Sadie said breathlessly, trying to take charge. All she heard in return was laughter. Tilly jumped down the four stairs leading from the porch. Meredith ran between the two white pillars, then leaped over George, the gardener, who was kneeling over the flower garden just below the porch wall. Chuckling, he raised up, took off his straw hat, and wiped his brow with his white handkerchief.

Sadie slowly closed the front door as she watched her daughter and the master's daughter scale the white fence leading to the green pasture beyond. Her heart felt heavy. Soon Miss Meredith would blossom into a young woman. As the front door closed firmly she knew that when that day arrived, Tilly would be shut out of her mistress' life forever.

Miss Martha, Meri's tutor, stood at the study window watching the girls through the lace curtains. Meredith's lessons were over and, as usual, they celebrated with their daily race. Meredith's teacher looked forward to this part of the day as much as her student. Each day she stood in the shadow of the lace curtains watching Meredith running with all her might to beat Tilly to Sleepy Hollow—their sacred playing ground. A lump formed in her throat as, in her imagination, she ran with Meredith, feeling the warm wind flowing through her hair.

Martha had missed her childhood. Her younger years had been spent raising her six brothers and four sisters. Her mother had been forced to eke out a living at the local laundry after her father took sick of lung disease. But she constantly reminded herself of how fortunate she was to have a father who had forced her to do her studies. Without his encouragement, she wouldn't have a job as a teacher. Nonetheless, during this one moment of the day she was able to capture a taste of her childhood long gone, never to return.

Slowly a frown began to crease Miss Martha's brow as she remembered a perplexing incident from that morning. She turned and looked at her student's desk recalling how Meredith had read from the literature book that still lay open. Meredith was always insistent that Tilly have the same book even though she couldn't read. But today they were sitting together. As Meredith approached the bottom of the page, Tilly had turned the page first—appearing to be reading ahead. Miss Martha saw Meredith glance quickly at Tilly with what seemed to be a reprimanding look.

Surely she'd been wrong. Just the other day she had read another article about the inability of slaves to learn to read and write. It was even mentioned that some were known to have tails like monkeys. *No, this morning's situation must have been a coincidence.* Miss Martha shook her head quickly, clearing away any possible thought that Meredith's slave could comprehend the lesson.

While Miss Martha pondered the incident, Jack Douglas leaned against the upper-balcony column watching his daughter and Tilly light out across the lush green grass and down a slope until they were out of sight. He sighed deeply. How could he have allowed such a friendship to blossom between Meredith and a slave girl? His grief over Becky's death had caused him to lose sight of the painful future such a friendship would confront. *For-tunately,* he thought, *Agatha will help me resolve this dilemma. She is smart and decisive and attractive in her own way— although not at all like Becky.*

Jack's heart pounded at the memory of his first love. He allowed his mind to drift carelessly back through time. The music of her coming-out ball rehearsed itself in his mind. The smell of perfumed women, swishing by as they waltzed with men more rhythmically gifted than he, lingered in his nostrils. His eyes were fastened on the most beautiful girl at the ball. She threw her head back in delight as she twirled in the arms of Carl Winston. It seemed every woman there wanted to be with his handsome counterpart. Then it had happened! Becky had turned her head slightly and her dark-brown eyes met his. Jack shifted his weight from one leg to the other just as he had done that night the moment she looked at him. He remembered his embarrassment when he felt the color rise in his cheeks.

Do I dare think she could have an interest in a gangly, awkward young man such as me? he thought.

The dance was over and Becky walked over to a young woman, raised her decorated fan to cover her mouth, and whispered into her friend's ear. All of a sudden Jack became very thirsty. When he turned around from the punch bowl, crystal cup in hand, Becky was standing in front of him. Her red-haired, freckle-faced friend made a formal introduction. Becky curtsied, and Jack bowed, spilling the majority of his punch on the floor. The two girls giggled, then Becky took his arm. She asked if he wanted to get some fresh air and began walking him toward the garden as two maids scurried to clean up his embarrassment.

It was in the courtyard with the full moonlight caressing Becky's face that he fell in love. There was something about her that could not be captured in words. A free yet tamed spirit; a quick, yet gentle wit; an undaunted pride and confidence. He found himself laughing aloud as she chatted about her dance with Carl and the colorful characters who filled the room.

Jack sat on a marble seat and gently pulled Becky by the hand so she would join him. With reservation he said, "You could have come into the garden with any young man in the room. Why me?"

"Well," Becky said slowly lifting her fan to her face, "your eyes were calling me."

"And what did they say?"

"Come away with me, my fair lady."

"Will you?"

At that moment Becky's girlfriend appeared to whisk her back to the party. His love—his life—glanced over her shoulder at him before entering the ballroom. He made up his mind that night: She would be his wife.

He could hear the sound of Meredith's laughter every time he shared that story with her. Then Agatha's face, superimposed over his dreamy memory, would pull him back to reality. He felt compelled to spend equal time thinking about her, considering his plan to propose marriage. No, she didn't make his heart skip a beat when she walked into a room, but he was older now. There were more important things to consider: a mother for Meredith and a stately woman who could manage the house. She came from good stock and he would be content. He would make himself content.

Jack pulled at his royal-blue waist-jacket that rode proudly over his white pants. His black boots were polished. Soon his guests would arrive; he was expecting fifteen plantation owners from as far as a hundred miles away. Today they would develop a plan to stop the runaway slaves. He had lost Ben; he wasn't about to lose another.

Sadie bent over the basin of wet clothes and began hanging them up, one at a time. She loved this solitary task because it allowed her to be alone with the warm breeze and the clothesline.

She did some of her best thinking here. The plantation owners had begun to arrive. Henry, the butler, would be there to greet them. He and the other servants were all dressed in their best uniforms. Master Jack had left special instructions that only the male servants handle the service of the food. That was a strange request, but she was happy for the unexpected relief. She and Bertha had prepared all the little delicacies, and now she was alone in her haven. As she clipped the end of a sheet to the line, a firm breeze caused it to lift gently. Slowly it drifted down again but not before Sadie's attention was drawn to an elderly man leading a horse toward the barn.

She assumed that he was the driver of one of the elaborate carriages arriving at the front of the mansion. His head was bent and he walked with a limp; there was nothing else remarkable about him. Sadie leaned down to pick up another piece of clothing and felt the same strange sensation she'd experienced the day Tom died. It was as if something were pulling on her.

She carefully eased toward the barn, looking over her shoulder often to make sure no one was watching. The barn was dark, even though it was noon. One of the wooden planks was missing, allowing sunlight to stream through as though someone was holding a lantern to shine on one particular spot. The old man was standing in the light with his back to Sadie. Suddenly she felt an uncontrollable inner quaking. Time had altered the face and stature of the man, but there was no doubt in her mind who he was.

"Na-Na," she breathed quietly.

The old man turned, lifted his head, and stared at the tiny woman standing in the doorway. Her father whispered her name, "Ama," as if no time had passed.

"Oh my!" Sadie softly exclaimed as she rushed into his outstretched arms. They held on to each other for what seemed forever. She wanted to savor the strength of his arms around her, to hear his heart beat, to linger in the smell of his being. Knowing this was all she would have to hang on to when they were forced to part again, Sadie made each moment a memory to treasure.

The old man took a deep breath and slowly released it, saying, "O' sweet Jesus, t'ank ya!"

He felt Sadie's body tighten slightly. Pushing her away with both hands and holding her shoulders firmly he studied her for a long time. Finally he asked, "Whut name do dey call you by?"

"Sadie . . . Sadie Douglas."

"I see. Well, mine's James Poole. I been waitin' a long time fo' dis day. I ax de good Lawd to he'p me fin' my family so I kin make sho ya'll know Him," he said pointing his right finger toward the heavens.

Sadie's face revealed her stark disapproval. Only in her dreams had she ever dared to hope that one day she would once again see her father. But in none of her imaginings had she heard a statement like the one she had just heard.

"Whut's wrong, chile?"

Sadie hung her head, shamed by her feelings. "I sorry, Na-Na. I jes' didn' . . . well . . . it jes' dat I don' wanna believe in no white man's God."

Her father lifted his left hand and rested it on the neck of the brown horse. Looking down at the ground, then up to Sadie's eyes, he chuckled and stated, "Why, gal, Jesus is de only t'ing a white man don' own. Oh, he t'ink he do but he don'. When dey took me off dat ship, I say I die firs' befo' I be a slave. But when I wuz standing on that auction block an' looks up an' see ya, I say to mahse'f I wuzn gonna stop til I fin' all my family. I runned away two times but got caught. Den one day as I star' to learn mo' on how to speak like white folk, I begin to lis'n when my massa was readin' de Bible. Dem massas loves to read dat Bible. It was in de Good Book dat I fine out I a free man."

"Whut you sayin'?" questioned Sadie.

"I means dat Jesus died fo' us all so we can be wid Him in heaben one day. When dat time come, we nevah has to say goodbye agin. Dat's whut I tell yo' sistah."

Sadie clasped her face between her hands with eyes wide in amazement. "My sistah . . . who . . . where . . . which sistah?"

"Araba."

Sadie sat down on a bale of hay next to her, shaking her head in disbelief.

Her sister Araba was only one year older than she was. As a child, her father had nicknamed Sadie "Little Shadow" because she was always just one step behind Araba. They would sit for hours in the family's hut, weaving baskets and singing songs. Without thinking, Sadie began to sing one of the tunes she had not sung since leaving Africa's shores. Stopping abruptly she questioned, "Whar's my sistah?"

"I see'd huh in Waynesboro when I drive de massa fo' a meetin'. I know me chillun when I sees dem. We cud only speak for a short while but when I tell her 'bout de good Lawd, she smile an' say she wud see us in heaben."

"Whut name do she go by?"

"Hannah Richardson."

Sadie mouthed the name silently then looked up quickly. "And Momma?"

For the first time Sadie saw her father's eyes cloud over. He hung his head and shook it sadly.

Tilly slipped on the grass and grabbed for Meri's ankle, causing her friend to tumble down. Meri had won the race yesterday, and Tilly was determined not to allow it to happen again today. The birds in the weeping willow tree took flight as the girls continued to struggle toward their goal, laughing so hard they could hardly catch their breath. The wooden swing hung on ropes from the tree, and soon one of them would claim victory by being the first to have a seat. Tilly made it to her knees, and with one final thrust caught hold of the swing, pulling herself to a sitting position. Meri collapsed with her face in the grass, heaving with gleeful disappointment.

"Alas fair maiden, tomorrow is another day," Meri recited from her literature reading that morning.

"I'm surprised you got to that part of the story 'cause you were reading so slow."

"Well, Miss Martha knew just how slow I was reading because you turned the page before I got to the bottom. I thought I'd fall off my chair. I do declare, Tilly Douglas, you gave me a scare."

"I know . . . but the prince was just about to save the princess and you were taking too long."

Meri rolled on her back and looked into the thousand eyes hidden in the leaves on the tree. At least they looked like eyes, and they seemed to all be looking at her. She wondered what they were thinking. Did they know how happy she was? Two weeks had passed since her fight with Tilly and not one bad word had been said since they promised always to be together.

Tilly broke into her thoughts, "So what are we going to play today?"

Meri thought of two games right away and when they got through, it would be time to return to the house for lunch. She remembered that her daddy was having a party, and there were sure to be lots of goodies left over when his friends left. So for two hours, they played and frolicked and chased each other until they lay exhausted.

"Do you wanna race to the house?" Tilly asked.

"No, not today. I'm too tired."

"Me too, but I'm hungry. Let's get going."

"Gentlemen, I consider it an honor that you have graced the Douglas Plantation," Master Jack stated, looking around at the dignified men in his parlor. "As you know, the invitation was extended so that we might discuss the serious nature of the problem many of us have been having with runaway slaves. I experienced my first loss two weeks ago, and I don't plan to let it happen again."

Master Jack glanced at his male servants, who were standing at attention with expressionless eyes. He wanted them to hear of his plans to stop the flight of any more slaves so the news would spread quickly around the plantation.

"I am opening the floor for any suggestions to discuss. Then we can decide our strategy." At that point, the men began expressing their ideas fast and furiously.

Master Jack interrupted, "Gentlemen, gentlemen, we seem to be full of possible solutions; however, we don't need to hear them all at one time."

The suggestions went from the sublime to the ridiculous. Then Lawrence Poole, a short, plump, dark-headed man who always seemed drenched in sweat, stood and waved his hand dramatically. "My friends, I believe we should appeal to the *entrepreneurial* spirit of the slaves."

There was sardonic laughter throughout the room.

"And just what does that mean exactly, Mr. Poole?" asked Master Jack.

Mr. Poole looked at each of Master Jack's slaves before answering with a smirk, "Well, if it's freedom they want, let's agree to give it to them right here."

The room buzzed with curiosity.

"What I mean is this," Mr. Poole continued, "we need to stop the Underground Railroad—but no one is coming forward as to its location. There needs to be some incentive. Let's offer a piece of land to any slave who gives us information that uncovers this hideous group of people. The land will be something they own free and clear. They can move their families on it and grow their own crops. They would still work for us, but it would give them something they've never had—a chance to be a landowner."

Master Jack surpressed a smile as he saw his slave Jim look quickly at Cory and then back at the wall. Mr. Poole had indeed touched a nerve. Master Jack quickly made a motion to accept the idea. It was seconded without debate, and for the rest of the meeting every possible detail of the plan was carefully worked out.

≈ ≈ ≈

Sadie was shaken out of her reverie by the sound of Tilly's voice. The children had returned.

"Na-Na, I have somebody dat wan's tuh meet ya. I be rat back."

Sadie hurried out of the barn, up the dirt road, past the partially hung laundry and through the back door into the kitchen. Bertha was preparing a meal for the two hungry playmates. After whispering something into Bertha's ear, the jovial woman turned to Master Jack's daughter and said, "Mis' Meredith, hit's time tah be takin' a bath so ya can say goodbye to yo' pappa's people. I know Tilly gets yo' bath but her momma wan's to speak tuh huh for a bit. I be doin' it, if'n ya don' min'.'"

Meredith studied Sadie for a moment. She was trying to act like nothing was wrong, but something was different. Meredith shrugged her shoulders and said, "O.K."

Sadie took Tilly by the hand and pulled her toward the back door. "But Momma, I'm not through eating my food."

"I know, I know, Baby, but I jes' need to see ya fo' a bit."

Sadie hurried to the barn with her daughter in tow. There was no introduction necessary. As Tilly stood in the open barn door, her eyes fell on an old man standing next to a brown horse. He wasn't big like the warrior she had pictured in her mind so many times before, but his eyes told her who he was: They were Sadie's eyes; they were her eyes.

Tilly walked slowly toward the strange, yet familiar person. A tear rolled down her grandfather's cheek. For one timeless moment he was looking at Ama. This was the way he had remembered her during his long nights of bondage. Bending his tired frame until his eyes were even with Tilly's, a thousand words were spoken in the silence.

At last he spoke. "I t'ink dees old eyes has nevah seen a mo' happy sight," he said. Reaching out, he picked Tilly up and held her in his arms. "I'm yo' gran'pa."

"I know."

"And jes' how dos ya know dat?"

"Because I've seen you here," said Tilly, pointing to her head.

"Peoples call me Preacha Man 'cos I loves to tell of de good Lawd."

Tilly glanced at her mother. Knowing her mother's thoughts about "white man's religion," she expected a reaction, but it wasn't as big as she thought it would be.

Tilly's grandfather put her down and reached for a book lying on a pile of hay. "Dis heah is de Good Book."

Tilly held the Bible in her hand. So many pages had been turned down at the top that it fell open to the book of Psalms. Tilly read aloud, "The Lord is my light and my salvation; whom shall I fear? The Lord is the strength of my life; of whom shall I be afraid?"

Her grandfather took one step back and put his hand over his heart, eyes full of stunned disbelief. "De chile kin read. How? Who?"

"I taught her," said a tiny voice behind Sadie.

They all swung around quickly and saw Meredith; Bertha stood beside her in frustration. Meredith walked past Sadie and Tilly and approached the old man. "You're Na-Na, aren't you?"

Sadie's father tried to move his mouth but no words came out. Then Meredith caught the sides of her dress and curtsied. "I'm not sure what I'm supposed to say to a tribal king because I've never met one," she announced.

When Meredith realized Tilly's grandfather was in the barn, she had rushed to the secret hiding place and removed its treasure. Now she stretched out her arm, opening her small hand. "This belongs to you."

Sadie gasped and her father fell to his knees as he took the smooth black stone from the young girl's hand. His withered palm held the stone as if it had been placed on an altar. Leaning his head back, his eyes fixed on the ceiling, he appeared to be in a trance. For a split-second, he was traveling back to his village, surrounded by family and friends. He could smell the African soil after a rain and, for a brief instant, he celebrated his marriage to his beautiful wife who served him faithfully as his queen. Slowly he brought his head forward and took a deep breath. He had not taken that trip for many years—and never before without the anger of the past. Now he knew that he really was a free man.

Sadie moved to Tilly's side, her eyes scolding and reprimanding her daughter for showing her white mistress the precious black stone. Her father raised his other hand to stop her reaction.

"Come heah, chile," he beckoned Meredith.

"Why you teach my gran'chile to read?"

"Because she's my best friend."

Embarrassed, Sadie lowered her head. Then her father spoke. "Dis chile has de heart of an angel. You kin trus' her. Don' be 'fraid, Ama, dis chile don' mean ya no harm. De good Lawd done showed me."

He motioned for Tilly to stand next to Meredith then untied the yellow bandana around his neck and tore it in half. "From now on ya'll always have a piece o' me," he said, smiling broadly and pointing to the sky with one finger. "Bring it wid ya to heaben."

Tilly's grandfather laid his hands on each of their heads. "De Bible say, 'Love is stronga' dan death.' Nobody can take away de love you have fo' each othah." He gathered them in his arms and held them.

Just then, one of the house slaves rushed into the barn. "James, Massa Poole is done wid his meetin. He wanna go." Sadie's father took the reins of the shiny brown horse and turned it around. He looked at his granddaughter, seeming to take in every fiber of her being. "I don' eben know yo' name."

"My name is Tilly."

He bent down, hugged her, placed the smooth black stone in her hand, and then stood to face Sadie. "Ama, der is good white folk an' bad white folk. Some of our peoples is good an' some bad. Don' forget it was our own peoples dat led dem slave traders to de village. Dey sold us, too. An' it's white fo'k dat be helpin' slaves run no'th to a new life. Don' let yo angah make ya mis' de Lawd. I sees ya in heaben."

Sadie grabbed her father and wept silently against his chest. Maybe if she held onto him time would stop, and they would be carried away to another place free of pain and separation. Sadie gripped tightly but soon felt two strong hands pull her back. She didn't have to look. She knew it was Bertha—the same friend who had pulled her away from Tom's body when they took him away to his final resting place. Then she watched her father lead the horse out of the barn toward the front of the mansion. Quickly she hurried inside the house, with Tilly and Meredith following closely behind. They stood by a front window to take one last look.

Master Poole was standing on the front porch with Meredith's father. He saw James approaching but almost didn't recognize him. The old servant's head was up; his shoulders were back. He looked twenty years younger. It was his ongoing conversation with Master Jack that kept him from continuing his observations. As James approached, he overheard Master Poole say, "You see this here slave? Finest one I have on the plantation. Faithful as can be. Now, the next time you have a runaway slave," he said as he moved toward his carriage where James was standing at attention, "all you have to do is fix his leg a little bit."

He laughed as he tapped James' broken leg with his cane. "Ain't that right, James?"

James kept his eyes fastened to the ground. "Yea, suh, Massa Poole. I know you's right."

"They call James 'Preacher Man' because he loves the Bible. Can't read, of course, but seems to have a good understanding of what's read to him. And he loves to sing. Why don't you sing a tune for Master Jack, James."

"Why sho', Massa Poole."

James lifted his eyes toward heaven. His deep baritone voice seemed too powerful to be coming from just one man. All the plantation owners standing on the porch stopped their conversation and turned to look at the old man standing beside his owner and the exquisitely decorated carriage. James sang the words to a song he shared every Sunday with the other slaves on Master Poole's plantation.

> Climbin' up d'mountain, chil'ren,
> Didn' come here fo' to stay,
> If ah nevah mo' see you ag'in,
> Gonna meet you at de judgment day.

James sang the verse and another chorus and then, as he lowered his eyes, he saw Sadie, Tilly, and Meredith standing at the window. Sadie placed her hands on the glass and was leaning forward in silent anguish. He saw her call his name.

James helped his master into the carriage, closed the shiny black door with the plantation crest on its side, and lifted himself up to his seat. He firmly slapped the reins on the horse's back and steered the carriage around the circular driveway and down the road.

Tilly felt her mother's pain, but she shed no tears. Her large, round, black eyes blinked slowly, losing sight of a grandpa she had seen so briefly. Meredith looked at Tilly, up at Sadie, and then to the end of the road where the carriage disappeared from sight. Why was she feeling so sad? What did Master Poole mean when he tapped Na-Na's leg with his cane? Something was wrong, very wrong. She just didn't know what it was.

3

This was Tilly's favorite part of the day. As the sun was about to say goodnight, it blasted the sky with a fiery red. She thought it seemed angry. The clouds declared their agreement as they reflected their rage in brilliant oranges. Had the sun seen what had happened today? Maybe that's why it was so outraged.

Meredith and Tilly sat in their usual evening place—the white rocking chairs on the front porch. They moved back and forth in silence. A horse-drawn carriage could be seen at a distance. Meri recognized the driver and glanced at Tilly, who returned her look with a sigh. The carriage came to a stop directly in front of the stairs. Willie, the driver, jumped down to open the door and Agatha Stanton stepped down. Lifting the bottom of her emerald dress ever so slightly, she ascended the stairs to the front porch. Her red hair was swept up to the top of her head, crowned with a small, matching emerald hat. The loose curls around her face seemed to highlight her green eyes. Agatha turned her long neck, looked to her left, and said, "Good evening, Meredith."

Meredith put on her best face and responded, "Good evening, Miss Stanton."

"Please, do call me Agatha."

Meredith continued to look at her and rock in her chair but did not reply. After a short pause, Agatha went into the parlor. She never seemed to notice Tilly at all, and she ignored Henry, the butler, who was standing in the doorway. She could hardly wait until she would rule the house. There were some things she would immediately put in order. Not only would she remove the little brat (or should she say brats) from the front porch, but she would definitely redo the parlor. It was so very stifling.

Agatha had come from a good family, but her father was completely out of money. Of course, there was no reason for Jack Douglas to know about that. Once she married him, she would have enough money to take care of herself and her family.

After the air seemed to clear with Agatha's entry into the house, Meredith and Tilly smiled at each other and said simultaneously, "You want to?"

They both nodded their heads and slipped carefully from the rocking chairs. Easing their way to the side of the house, they hid behind the big bush just outside the open parlor window. They couldn't be seen because of the large statue that stood next to the fireplace. It was supposed to represent Meredith's grandfather, although Meri didn't know if it actually looked like him because he died before she was born. All she knew was that he looked unhappy about being left to stand there for so long.

Jack entered just as the girls crouched down.

"Agatha, darling."

Meredith looked at Tilly and mouthed the word "darling." Tilly's hand went to her mouth to stifle her laughter.

Jack kissed the back of Agatha's hand and led her to the sofa near the open window. *She looks lovely in her green dress with its matching hat. She will add a lot of class to my plantation,* he thought. Henry brought in cool drinks and then dismissed himself quickly.

"Jack, dearest, you look tired. How was the meeting?"

"Surprisingly good. I believe we came up with a plan to help us uncover the location of the Underground Railroad. It was suggested that we offer any slave who comes forward with information a piece of land. The land would be his to own."

Agatha smiled ever so slightly and noted, "Why, Jack, that's superb! I do believe there is greed in everyone, even a slave."

Jack touched her hair and asked, "And how was your ride here?"

"Long and tedious. I will be ever so glad when I no longer have to take that drive."

"Don't worry, my dear, it won't be long. I will be talking to Meredith shortly about my desires."

"And what might those desires be?" she asked coyly.

There was a long silence and the girls tried to get a peek, but Meredith's grandfather was in the way. Finally Jack said, "Agatha, I need to talk with you about something that has been troubling me. It appears you were right: The relationship between Meredith and Tilly has become most unhealthy. Why the other morning I saw her slave descending down the spiral staircase as if she owned the estate—even pretending to curtsy at the bottom of the stairs in front of who knows who."

Agatha gasped, *"No!"*

Jack continued, "I just don't know what to do. Meredith would be outraged if I tried to separate them."

Again there was a moment of silence and then Agatha spoke. "I do have a suggestion, dear. Doesn't your sister live about four hours from here?"

Jack nodded as she continued. "Send Meredith to her Aunt Beatrice for a week. While she is gone, sell Tilly. When Meredith returns, there won't be anything she can do about it. In time she will forget. Soon she will be a young woman and will become consumed with endless balls and activities."

Meredith started to jump up, but Tilly held her down and put a finger to her mouth, warning her to be quiet.

"Agatha, you are so very wise."

"Of course I am, dear. I chose you."

Alarmed and afraid, Tilly led the way around to the back entrance of the house, and they made their way up to Meredith's room without being seen. The oval, upright mirror, which rested on a walnut wood base, reflected two frightened faces as the girls paced back and forth like caged animals. Nothing was said for a long time, then Meredith finally shouted, *"He can't do that!"*

Tilly stopped walking and responded, "Yes, he can."

"No, he can't! I won't let him!"

"Meri, there's nothing we can do."

"Yes there is! He can't sell you like you were a cow!"

Tilly sat on the edge of the bed. It was getting dark, and the lighted candles gave the room a soft glow. She looked deep into Meredith's eyes and said, "How do you think all the slaves got here—except those who were born here like me? Your daddy bought them. And, yes, he can sell me."

Meredith did not move. Slowly she opened and closed her eyes trying to take in what had just been said. She'd never before thought about how the slaves had come to be on the plantation. Even when Henry went to town and brought back new slaves, their origins never crossed her mind. She remembered Tilly telling her how someone had bought her grandfather off the slave block, but what did that have to do with her daddy? He wasn't like that person.

Now it was Tilly's turn to be surprised. How could Meredith not know that the slaves on her plantation were bought? Yet Tilly knew Meredith was surprised. In all of their time together it had never been discussed. All they'd ever wanted to do was laugh and play.

Meredith said quietly, "One day I remember saying to Daddy that the slaves seemed to work so hard. From the time I got up until I went to bed they never stopped working. He told me their happiness came from working on the plantation. God made them to work. I believed him. I thought it must be true because the slaves were singing all the time, and they were all so nice. Especially Bertha. When she laughs, everyone laughs—even Daddy."

Bertha had been Meredith's grandfather's slave and had helped raise her dad. Bertha could make Master Jack smile whenever she wanted. It was like she knew just what to say. No other slave on the plantation could talk to Daddy like Bertha.

Meredith stated firmly, "We'll run away."

"Where would we go, Meri? How would we live?"

"I don't know and I don't care! He can't take you away from me."

"Meri, we have to tell my momma. She'll know what to do."

Sadie was sitting in her room holding one of Tilly's garments in her hands. She sat perfectly straight in the high-back chair, her mind intensely focused on repairing the torn dress with a needle and thread.

"Momma?"

"Not now, Tilly. I'm busy."

"Momma?"

Sadie looked up in frustration and then saw Meredith standing beside her daughter. She forced her face to look pleasant.

"Now whut kin I be doin' fo' ya two gals?"

Tilly approached her mother and took the sewing out of her hands and laid it on the bed. That got Sadie's attention.

"Momma, I have something to tell you," Tilly said nervously. Glancing up at Meri, Tilly continued, "Master Jack doesn't like me and Meredith being friends."

Sadie had always known this day would come. Of course the master was going to put a stop to the girls' everyday activities. Well, she agreed with him. It was time for Tilly to start working in the kitchen. Sadie knew it would be hard for her at first, but she would get used to it.

"Momma, Master Jack is going to send Meri to her aunt's house next week and while she's gone . . ."

"Go on, chile. While she's gone . . ."

"He's going to sell me."

"Whut?" Sadie exclaimed and then quickly lowered her voice to a hush. "Why, he can't sell my baby!"

Sadie leaped up from the chair and started walking in circles. The agony on her face caused Tilly to start crying.

"Firs' my daddy an' now my baby!" Sadie dropped on her bed and began to weep.

Meredith walked over and laid her hand on her back. "Don't worry, we'll think of something."

Sadie glared at Meredith with all the hate she felt for Master Jack in that moment. She spat out the words, "Ya can't sell my baby!"

Tilly quickly moved to Meri's side and said, "Momma, Meri wants to help. She doesn't want me to leave."

Sadie realized what she had done and reached for Meredith's hand. "I' sorry Mis' Meredith. I didn' mean no harm. But whut I gonna do? Tilly, we can't stay heah!"

"We, Momma?"

"Yes 'we,' Tilly. You all I gots in de world. We gotta git away."

Sadie stood holding the high-back chair, not moving, not speaking. She mumbled softly under her breath, "Auntie Ruth . . . Auntie Ruth. She'll know whut to do. Tilly, she knows, but I don' know where Auntie Ruth is."

"Meri and I can go to the river tomorrow, Momma, and wait for her."

Sadie nodded her head slowly. It was their only hope.

When the girls returned to Meredith's bedroom, Tilly told her all about Auntie Ruth. How she helped slaves escape to freedom through something called the Underground Railroad. Tilly wasn't sure how it worked, but maybe Auntie Ruth could give them some answers.

Meredith slid off the bed and stood in front of Tilly. "That's what happened to Ben, isn't it?"

Tilly nodded her head.

"Why did he leave? I thought he was happy here. When I saw him fixing things around the house, he would look at me and smile so big I would think that no one was as happy as he was.

And he told the funniest stories. Do you remember the one about the jack rabbit and the fox?" Meredith asked.

Even the seriousness of the moment couldn't stop the two of them from laughing. But it was short-lived. Meredith asked once again, "Why did he leave?"

Tilly lay back on the bed with her hands stretched over her head and stared at the ceiling.

"Meri, why does your daddy tell you never to go past the barn?"

Meredith pondered the question and then replied, "He says the other part of the plantation is prettier. That he fixed it up just for me to play and there's nothing to do past the barn. That's where the animals get fed and cleaned and I'd get all dirty. We have so much fun at Sleepy Hollow, I didn't care about going down there."

Tilly sighed. "Well, I think if you go down there one day you'll know why Ben left."

"Mis' Meredith?" Henry called out as he knocked gently on the bedroom door. "Mis' Meredith, yo' fathah is axin' fo' ya downstairs."

"All right, Henry. Tell him I'm coming."

Meredith began to pace anxiously once again. "What am I going to do?"

Tilly answered, "Don't tell them we know, Meri."

Meredith glanced quickly into her mirror. She stuck her out-of-place hair down by licking her hand and smoothing it over the top of her head. Then she rushed downstairs. Agatha was now sitting in the chair to the left of the fireplace, and her father was standing beside her. As Meredith entered the room her father smiled brightly and went to meet her.

"Well, well, well," he said, "don't you look beautiful today? Come and sit with us and have some lemonade."

Only Agatha's eyes moved as she watched Meredith walk to the chair opposite her. It occurred to Meredith that Agatha's smile looked painted on by an artist who was having a bad day.

"It's so lovely to see you again, Meredith," said Agatha.

"Thank you."

"And how has your day been?"

"Fine," said Meredith mirroring Agatha's fake smile.

Her father didn't notice, but Agatha did. Her father went on to reveal the exciting plans for her visit with Aunt Beatrice. He was leaving in a week for Hampton, and she would leave for Sommersville the day after he left. They were only about an hour apart and, when he finished his business dealings, he would join her the following morning for breakfast at Aunt Beatrice's house. They would spend the afternoon shopping for some beautiful dresses and a new baby doll. Meredith, lightly kicking the bottom of the chair with the back of her shoes, wondered if he was going to buy some slaves.

"That sounds like fun, Daddy. I'll tell Tilly to pack our clothes."

"Our clothes?"

"Me and Tilly's clothes. She always goes with me."

Meredith's father tried desperately not to look disturbed. Agatha knew he was at a loss for words so she hastily added, "This trip, Meredith, is just for you. Your Aunt Beatrice is looking forward to spending time alone with her precious niece. It's about time you got to know each other better since you're beginning to blossom into a beautiful young lady."

Agatha looked up at Jack and smiled assuredly as Meredith fumed.

Now Meredith remembered what Agatha reminded her of: the green snake she and Tilly had chased through the tall grass by the river the other day.

"It sounds like fun," Meredith recited.

"Good! Then it's settled." Master Jack beamed. "I'll ask Bertha to prepare your luggage, and Cory will drive you there next week. I'm looking forward to spending time together with my beautiful daughter."

He glanced at Agatha and smiled. Their plan was in place. Meredith would be taken care of, Tilly would be gone, and Agatha would be his wife. Asking to be excused, Meredith slowly climbed up the winding staircase to her room where Tilly was waiting.

Meri leaned her back against the door and heard it close. "Meri?" called Tilly. But there was no answer. Suddenly Meri rushed to her closet and pulled out a piece of brown luggage. She unfastened the straps and then went back and started pulling out her clothes. All the pain in Meredith's heart began to erupt as she grabbed clothes from her closet and drawers, stuffing them wildly into her suitcase. Tilly walked to the closet and firmly put her hands on Meri's arms.

"Meri, stop. What are you doing?"

"He can't sell you, Tilly. We have to leave!"

Meri crumpled into a heap on the floor sobbing. Tilly put her arm around her friend's shoulders. From that day on, neither one of them could ever remember how long they sat that way. It seemed like an eternity.

4

The school lesson was over. Meredith and Tilly closed their books, stacked them neatly on the desk, and headed out the front door. Miss Martha took her position at the window and watched through the lace curtains as the young girls walked slowly, hand in hand, toward Sleepy Hollow. She thought they were acting a bit too melodramatic, considering the fact that they were going to be separated for only a week. This trip would be good for Meredith. Mr. Douglas was wise to begin putting distance between her and the slave girl. They were much too close.

Tilly and Meredith turned to the left when they were out of sight and headed toward the river. In two days Meredith would be leaving. And within a week, Tilly knew she would be separated from her mother, her extended family, and her best friend—savagely ripped from the only home she'd ever known. The one thing that gave Tilly a faint ray of hope were the few words she could remember reading from her grandfather's tattered Bible: "The Lord is my light and my salvation, whom shall I fear?" But with each passing day, that light seemed dimmer.

They had gone to the river every day since Meredith learned of her father's plans, but they still hadn't seen Auntie Ruth. She just had to come today. Never knowing when she might appear, they began their wait, hoping against hope to see her.

Auntie Ruth watched the girls approaching from behind a thick bush. She had studied them the day before but hadn't gone near. The news had spread like wildfire: The masters were giving a piece of land to anyone with news of the Underground Railroad. She knew that some slaves would sell their kinfolk just to have a place of their own, and that meant her life was in serious danger. As sweet as these girls were, they could be used to set her up for capture. Today she selected a spot close to where she knew the girls would be sitting.

Meredith and Tilly flopped down on the grass. They sat in silence for a long time. Even the river was still. The hot sun reflected off small darting insects that swarmed over the water's surface as if playing tag. The birds were singing a symphony, but no one was listening.

"Tilly?"

"Huh?"

"What if she doesn't come today?"

"She'll come. She knows we're in trouble."

"How does she know?"

"I don't know. She just does."

That was all Auntie Ruth needed to hear.

The girls continued to stare down at the grass, methodically pulling up slender blades as they spoke. Then Tilly glanced up and gasped. She hadn't heard a sound, but there stood Auntie Ruth beside a giant oak tree.

The older woman put a finger to her mouth and motioned for them to come. As they came near, she turned and began to move into the woods, nervously peering into the shadows. She sat down on a tree stump as she pulled the girls close to her. Meredith was quietly crying, and Tilly was trembling.

"We gots to be real quiet chil'ren," whispered Auntie Ruth.

Meredith and Tilly simultaneously whispered back, "Why?"

"Dat ain't impo'tant rat now. Tell yo' Auntie Ruth whut's wrong wid ya."

Meredith told the whole story, with Tilly looking on nodding her head in agreement. Auntie Ruth picked up a stick while the young girl was talking and started drawing in the dirt. For some reason, her thoughts came more easily when she was scratching on something. When Meredith finished, Auntie Ruth remained quiet, considering how best to respond.

"Tilly, you an' yo' momma can't stay heah. If'n ya do, ya massa is gonna sell ya. But t'ings done changed. De massas got de slaves lookin' fo' me. Said dey would give dem some free land if I git caught. It ain't safe right now."

Auntie Ruth kept drawing in the dirt and then asked, "Mis' Meredith, where ya say yo' auntie live?"

Meredith gave her the information, then Auntie Ruth dropped her stick and said, "Dis is whut we gots to do."

Meredith's father picked her up and gave her a final hug. His horse, Fury, stomped and snorted, ready for the long journey ahead. Mounting his ride, he looked down at the only person in the world he truly loved and announced, "Don't forget, young lady, I will meet you at your Aunt Beatrice's house on Thursday morning for breakfast. Everything is ready for your trip tomorrow; Cory will take you. We're going to have a good time!"

Meredith forced a smile. She waved goodbye as he turned his black stallion and galloped up the dusty road into the late afternoon sunlight. Bertha, who stood beside her, took her hand and walked up the stairs to the house. Tilly met Meredith at the front door, and they headed for her bedroom where they spoke quietly together for hours.

The candles had just been lit throughout the house when Tilly went to summon Henry to Meredith's room. He came quickly.

"Mis' Meredith?" he inquired.

"Henry, my father gave this letter to me before he left and asked that I give it to you. Tilly and I started playing and I forgot."

Meredith handed the letter to Henry who looked at it in stark disbelief. He recognized his master's letterhead right away, but wondered why his master would leave him a letter knowing he couldn't read.

"Do you min' readin' it to me, Mis' Meredith?"

Meredith took the letter from Henry's hand and read, "Henry, my sister has asked that Miss Meredith be brought by Sadie and Tilly. She is having a party and will need their help. Sadie can drive the carriage."

Had Henry been able to read, he would have recognized the handwriting of a ten-year-old and would have quickly noticed the misspelled words.

"But Mis' Meredith, why de massa didn' tell me fo' he leave? Dis don' seem right."

Meredith looked as if she were considering his question and then replied, "When my daddy left he said it was time I started doing grown-up things. Then he handed me this letter. See, he signed it right here."

Henry was sure something was wrong, but he felt totally helpless. Against every instinct within him he said, "Dat will be fine, Mis' Meredith. I gonna tell Sadie to git ready."

Closing the door, Henry walked quickly down the corridor, still fighting off his intuition. When he knocked on Sadie's door, she acted quite surprised to see him. His news seemed to take her aback. Henry heard her murmur something about it seeming strange that Master Jack had asked Meredith to give him the letter after he left. But then her job wasn't to think like her master; only to do what she was told. She began packing her clothes and Tilly's.

Sadie could hear Bertha moving around in the kitchen. She tried to be nonchalant as she took a seat at the kitchen table. That was the first curious thing Bertha noticed. Sadie always seemed to be strung so tightly. Finally her small, tense friend spoke up.

"Ya know, Bertha. I was jes' wonderin' if ya know how t'ankful I am fo' all you's done fo' me. I mean, lots of times peoples don' say it. Dey t'ink it alots but dey don' say it."

Bertha laid her washrag on the sink and sat across from Sadie.

"Sadie, whut's goin' on?"

Sadie shifted nervously in her seat. Auntie Ruth had sent strict instructions with Tilly for Sadie not to tell anyone of their departure—not even Bertha. It wasn't safe to trust anyone.

"I don' know whut ya mean, Bertha."

"Yeah ya do! Mis' Meredith sayin' dat Massa Jack wan' you an' Tilly to take huh to huh aunt's house. I nevah hear of such carrin' on. You know dem gals done fixed up a plan to be togethah. De massa sho' gonna be mad!"

Sadie breathed a sigh of relief when she realized Bertha hadn't figured out their plan. "I know but whut kin I do? If'n Mis' Meredith is speakin' de truth, we would be in bad trouble if we don' go. I gonna takes dat lettah wid me so if Mis' Meredith done somet'ing wrong de massa will speak to her 'bout it. If she be tellin' de truth den no harm will come. If Mis' Beatrice is havin' a party an' need mo' he'p, I bettah be der."

Bertha patted Sadie's hand and got up to go to her room. Sadie wanted to follow, wanted to keep telling her over and over again how much she meant to her. Knowing she wasn't the easiest person to be around, Sadie had always appreciated Bertha's love for her. Bertha was devoted to Sadie in spite of all the anger Sadie felt toward the world. But now she couldn't tell her. Maybe she already knew. That was the most Sadie could hope for.

Bertha stood by the carriage looking uncomfortable. "I tell ya Sadie, somet'ing is wrong! Dis is not de way de massa do t'ings."

"I know, Bertha, I know," replied Sadie.

Meredith and Tilly came down the stairs and got into the carriage. Meredith looked down and said, "Goodbye, Henry. Goodbye, Bertha. I'll bring you something back from town."

Bertha gave Sadie a big hug. She glared at Meredith and Tilly as if she wanted to pull them out of the carriage and administer a good licking. Sadie hoisted herself into the carriage and gazed fondly at her closest friend. She slowly turned the carriage and headed up the driveway and through the archway displaying the Douglas Plantation sign then onto the main road.

"Momma, wait," Tilly said.

Sadie pulled the carriage to a halt, and Tilly stared up at the house. Sadie saw Bertha standing in the doorway.

"Whut ya lookin' at, chile?"

"It's pretty, huh Momma?"

"Yea chile, it is pretty," Sadie agreed slapping the reins on the horses' backs. As the carriage moved forward, Sadie and Tilly looked over their shoulders once more. The red brick mansion with the white pillars stood at attention against the rolling green hills.

Yes, Tilly was right. It was a pretty house.

Bertha walked into the kitchen to start lunch. Sadie's scarf was lying across the chair. She picked it up, went into Sadie's room, and opened the closet door. Taking a step back, she stared with disbelief at what she saw: Sadie's uniform—the one she wore for serving special affairs. Bertha sat on Sadie's bed and looked at the unfinished sewing on her small table. She remembered their strange conversation the night before. Somehow Sadie was trying to tell her something. Bertha didn't even want to think about what it could be. Sadie would never leave her uniform behind. She would never leave without saying goodbye, either. Or would she?

Two hours passed and Sadie pulled the carriage to the side of the road. Jumping down she announced, "It's time we stop an' take a li'l res'. Bertha made some fried chicken an' some othah good t'ings."

Sadie laid out a tablecloth on the grass and began unpacking the food. After eating lunch, the girls ran into a field across the road and picked some berries for dessert.

As they started gathering together the remains of the picnic, Meredith went to the carriage and pulled out a small red velvet purse with a gold pendant on the front. She handed it to Sadie.

"Whut's dis, chile?" Sadie questioned.

Meredith replied, "It belonged to my mother. It was the purse she carried to her coming-out ball. Every year on my birthday, my daddy adds a gold coin. He says it's for my ball."

Tilly ran to Meredith's side. "You can't give us that, Meri. You're going to meet your husband at the ball, remember?"

"Don't worry, Tilly, my daddy has more money. Anyway, you will need money to eat and get a place to stay."

Sadie didn't say a word. She was listening to her father's voice telling her not to be afraid and to trust this white child who was standing before her. Reaching out, Sadie took the red purse and got down on one knee. Pulling Meredith close, she hugged her and remembered how she had nursed her at her breast. *Isn't it strange,* she thought. *Even though I held dis baby in my arms, dis is de firs' time I've evah hugged her.*

Sadie whispered, "Na-Na was right. Matta' a fact, he was right 'bout a lot of t'ings. I will fo' evah be beholdin' to ya, Mis' Meredith."

"Call me Meri."

Sadie looked up at Tilly then back to Meredith and stammered, "Well, al . . . alright, Meri, I t'ank ya."

Sadie and Meri looked into each other's eyes. Meri had never noticed how beautiful Sadie's eyes were—so much like Tilly's.

Suddenly Sadie took note of the position of the sun and nervously shuffled the girls to the carriage. "We must be gittin' on to town befo' dark," she said.

≈ ≈ ≈

"Is this my little angel?" Aunt Beatrice said pinching Meredith's cheek. "Come in, come in. I am so happy to see you, and look how you've grown! My goodness, it's a good thing you arrived. Just look at those black clouds. We are in for a storm."

As Meredith entered the house, she thought how strange it was that nothing seemed to have been moved since her last visit. Everything was just as it was. The familiar smell of the house enveloped her. She thought that if George were to fill up their basement at home with fresh cut flowers it would smell just like this. There were two things her aunt loved: the color pink and flowers—flowers in vases, flowers in pictures, white lace flowers in the white tablecloth on the large dining room table. It seemed that all the furniture was covered in various colors of rose or pink with just an accent of white and blue added here and there.

After Aunt Beatrice finished inspecting Meredith, she turned her attention to Sadie and Tilly. "Meredith, I thought your father said Cory was bringing you."

Meredith didn't take her eyes from the figurine she was studying on the living room end table. "Cory got sick this morning, and Henry asked Sadie to bring me."

Fortunately, her father had not included any details in his letter to Aunt Beatrice concerning his plans for Tilly. Aunt Beatrice hesitated slightly and then ordered her butler to take Meredith's luggage to her room and to direct her slaves to their quarters. After dinner was completed, Tilly followed Meredith to her room and began getting her ready for bed. Sitting at the dressing table after her bath, Tilly began brushing her friend's hair.

"Meri?"

Meredith looked at Tilly in the mirror. So far their plan had worked. If everything went well it would mean this would be their last time together.

"Yes, Tilly?"

The sound of a large hoopskirt in the hallway interrupted them.

"Well, aren't you a clean and pretty one! That will be all, Tilly."

"But Aunt Beatrice, Tilly and I were just . . ."

The look on her aunt's face said it all. Tilly laid the brush down and began to leave the room. Meredith swung around in her seat toward her; Tilly stopped in the doorway, turned and took one last look at her best friend. The door closed softly.

The rain began slowly but, like a train picking up speed, it began to beat heavily against the window. It was dark outside, very dark. Everyone in the house was asleep except Sadie and Tilly, who sat on the bed in their room. The only sound was the ticking of the grandfather clock in the hallway and the pounding of their hearts. A light rap on their window startled them. It was time to go. Quietly lifting the window, they eased themselves to the ground.

"Take my han' an' folla me." They couldn't see Auntie Ruth, but they knew her voice. Coming quickly around the corner of the house, they all stopped abruptly at the figure of a person in white directly in front of them. Lightning filled the sky. It was Meredith standing in the pouring rain.

"Tilly, I couldn't let you leave without saying goodbye."

The two girls fell into each other's arms. Taking one step back, the sky lit up once again and Tilly saw the tears streaming down her friend's face, mingling with the rain.

"We have to go, Tilly!" urged Auntie Ruth.

Tilly reached for Meredith's hand in the dark. "Meri, take care of my locket."

"And you my stone."

"I will."

Meredith couldn't see Tilly leave. She just knew she was gone.

5

*J*ack stood on the front porch looking stately in his black raincoat and hat. The hard downpour had eased into a gentle rain. The large, dark-brown door with beveled glass opened deliberately.

"Good morning, Beatrice," he beamed as he kissed his sister's cheek. Jack breezed past his older sister not noticing the concern on her face. Walking into the parlor toward the large white stone fireplace, he asked cheerfully, "Where is Meredith?"

As he turned on his heel, he saw Beatrice nervously moving her dainty white handkerchief from one plump hand to the other.

"What's the matter?" he questioned.

"Your slave is gone, Jack."

Jack's face was blank. "What do you mean?"

"I mean gone. Last night . . ." Beatrice held her breath.

Jack hurled his riding gloves against the fireplace shelf, nearly toppling a piece of crystal. He fumed at the thought of losing Cory, one of his best slaves. First Ben, now Cory. It was infuriating!

Beatrice interrupted his thoughts. ". . . and she took her daughter."

Jack froze. Her words began to sink in. He spun around quickly, and began to question her. She explained that Cory had become sick, and that Sadie had driven Meredith to her home. The blood was pounding in Jack's head. He could barely see. None of this made sense. If Cory had gotten sick, Henry would have sent one of the other male slaves. He would never have asked Sadie to drive the carriage four hours to Sommersville.

"Your slave must have dropped this. I found it on the floor in her room," Beatrice said, holding a letter in her shaking hand.

Charging up the stairs three at a time, Meredith's father made his way to his daughter's room and burst through the door. Meredith stood leaning against a window that overlooked the backyard. In what seemed like only one step he crossed the room. Reaching for her shoulders he began to shake her.

"Where are they, Meredith? *Where are they?*"

"Daddy, you're hurting me!"

He let his daughter go and took a step back.

"I'll ask you one last time. Where are they?"

By now, Meredith was crying uncontrollably. Aunt Beatrice had made her way up the stairs and rushed to her side.

"Jack, calm down!" Frightened by her brother's rage, she shielded Meredith with her arms.

Once again her father asked about Sadie and Tilly's whereabouts. Meredith shook her head, whimpering, "I don't know."

"Did you write this?" her father asked holding up the letter.

Meredith nodded.

"Why would you do such a thing?

"Because you were going to sell Tilly."

"And what made you think that?"

"I overheard you talking to Agatha."

Her father's face turned blood-red. "You had no right to meddle with my slaves. They belong to me!" he shouted.

Meredith rose up and shouted back, "No, Daddy. They don't belong to you. You can't buy and sell people like animals. Tilly is my best friend!"

Aunt Beatrice gasped at her niece's assertion. Jack felt dizzy. He stood staring at the shadow of someone he knew long ago. *Becky? It was as if she were in the room listening. Had Meredith heard their conversations while being formed in Becky's womb? Was that possible?* He couldn't allow himself to think about it. Pulling himself together, he fixed his eyes on Meredith, seething with an erupting, deep anger he'd never felt before. "Well, I'm going to find your 'best friend.' And when I do, I'm going to sell her and put her mother in the cotton fields!"

Meredith drooped back into her chair, sobbing in her hands. Aunt Beatrice sat in stunned disbelief. She had never heard of such things. Just what was the world coming to?

Jack disturbed her thoughts with stern instructions. "I want Meredith taken home today. Give your driver instructions that none of the house staff is to tend to her when she returns. If she wants to help her slave run away then she can take care of herself!"

"Jack, you don't mean that. Why, she's just a child! Who will see to her bath, get her dressed, comb her hair?"

"That's her problem now. Just do as I say!"

Jack jumped on Fury and headed for the Poole Plantation just outside of town. The heavy rain the night before had coated everything along the road in thick, sticky mud. David Poole was standing on his front porch giving his children a goodbye kiss. James, his slave, was bringing his master's gray stallion to the front of the house when he caught a sight of a black horse in the distance. He couldn't remember seeing anyone run an animal so hard. James stopped in front of Master Poole, holding the reins of his horse. Jack rode up and dismounted even before Fury came to a stop.

"David, one of my slaves ran away last night and took her daughter with her."

Out of the corner of his eye, Jack saw the old slave standing next to Master Poole look up at him and then back toward the ground. Had he not been distracted, he would have stopped to ask why.

Master Poole cursed under his breath and gave instructions to James to fetch his two older sons and prepare their horses. As James hurried away he overheard Master Jack tell his master how important it was to get the two slaves back. The little girl was his daughter's slave. Glancing back over his shoulder, James happened to see Scully, one of the yard servants, speaking to Master Poole. He was holding his old brown hat in his hand whispering something in his ear. James felt as if the bottom of his stomach had fallen out.

When Master Poole's sons were ready to ride, the four men thundered up the road. Scully was walking past the shed when James grabbed him from behind and threw him to the ground.

"Whut did ya tell him?" demanded James.

"Who? Whut?"

"I said, whut did ya tell him?" James repeated his question.

"Nothin'. I didn' tell him nothin'!"

James jumped on the man's belly, put one hand around his throat and raised his fist.

Scully winced and shouted, "O.K., O.K., I tol' him 'bout the Rutherford's house, how dem runaway slaves go der firs'. Don' be mad, I jes' wanna git me some land. Ya understan' don' ya?"

"Dat was my daughtah an' gran'baby dat runaway!"

"I didn' know."

"It don' matta dat ya didn' know. It would still be somebody's chil'ren. Ya ain't no bettah dan Judas. Sol' ya own peoples for a piece of land. Now I'm gonna go pray an' ax de good Lawd to he'p my chil'ren be safe. An' you need to go an' t'ank de Lawd dat I loves Him mo' dan life 'cause if I didn', ya'd be dead."

The slaves on Master Poole's plantation talked about it for a week. They had never seen Preacher Man get that upset before. And they never saw it again.

"Bertha, there's someone comin'," said Henry, pointing toward the end of the road. Bertha peeked through the front window, then went out to the porch. When she realized the passenger of the carriage was Miss Meredith, she rushed down the stairs and pulled open the door. She could tell the girl had been crying. She immediately feared for Sadie and Tilly.

"Why, Mis' Meredith, whatevah is de mattah?"

Meredith cried uncontrollably as Bertha helped her up the stairs. She saw the driver talk to Henry, who was frowning and shaking his head.

Bertha guided Meredith to her bedroom and sat her in the rocking chair. Henry stood at the hallway door motioning for Bertha.

"Mis' Meredith, I be rat back," she said as she made her way into the hallway.

"Bertha, de massa sent word dat we ain't s'pose to tend to Mis' Meredith."

"Whut!" exclaimed Bertha as she quickly pulled the door closed behind her. "It mus' be some kin' of mistake. Dat driver ain't heahed right."

"No, he was real clear. Say Mis' Meredith he'p Sadie and Tilly run away, an' Massa Jack say if she wanna he'p her slave git away, den she kin takes care of huhse'f."

Bertha slumped against the door, and Henry caught her in his arms.

"Oh my, she don' passed out. Cory, come he'p me!"

When Bertha came to she was lying on her bed. Henry was standing over her, his eyes alight with concern. For a moment she forgot about what had caused her to faint and focused instead on the face of the only man she had ever really loved.

"Bertha?" called Henry gently. The look on her face startled him. He hadn't seen that look for many years. Just as quickly as it had come it disappeared.

Bertha snapped out of her stupor and sat up.

"Whoa, not so fas'. Ya gave us a scare," Henry said.

Bertha put her hand to her head and began to remember the shocking events that had just taken place. *Sadie an' Tilly were gone fo'ever. Mis' Meredith is in terrible trouble with her fathah, and I don' know whut to do. No one has evah give' me an order not to he'p someone in de hous'. Poor Mis' Meredith . . .*

Bertha rose to her feet as Henry asked, "Where ya goin'?"

"I'm gonna see 'bout Mis' Meredith."

"I can't let ya do dat. When Massa Jack ain't here, I runs dis hous' an' he say no one is to tend to huh."

"Henry Douglas, if ya don' git out of my way somebody gonna git hurt—an' it ain't gonna be me! Dat gal can't cook for huhse'f, an' she's gonna be needin' some food aftah dat long trip."

Henry had seen Bertha's stubborn resolve before. That was all he needed to know. She was a force to be reckoned with—he stepped to the side. Bertha went in the kitchen, put some hot soup in a bowl, and made her way to her mistress' room. Meredith was sitting in the same chair, not rocking, just staring into space.

"Well now, Mis' Meredith, it's time you git a little somethin' to eat. How ya gonna grow if ya don' eat?"

Bertha sat the tray down on the small table next to the chair and scooped up a spoonful of soup. Meredith mechanically opened her mouth, but as she swallowed the delicious soup her eyes went to Bertha's face. It was a kind, loving face.

"I thought my daddy didn't want anyone to help me." Meredith softly said.

"Well, sometimes people git a little mixed up and says t'ings dey don' mean. Yo' daddy loves ya."

"Not anymore."

"Oh no, Mis' Meredith, he always gonna love ya. Ya his pride and joy."

"She couldn't tell you."

"Who couldn' tell me?"

"Sadie. She couldn't tell you she was leaving. Auntie Ruth made her promise. She said nobody could be trusted since land was being given to the slaves who turn in people for working with the Underground Railroad. Sadie cried when Auntie Ruth made her promise not to tell you."

Bertha stopped and put the spoon down. She got up and walked to the window and looked outside. She wondered how it was possible that there could be so much pain in a world that

God had made so beautiful. The sun cast a golden shadow through the trees as its rays cascaded down into the valley. Somehow she had understood that Sadie was forbidden to say goodbye, but hearing it was like putting a warm compress on her heart.

Sadie was sitting on the ground with her knees pulled close to her chest. She was so scared, all she could think to do was rock back and forth. Forgetting for a moment that she had a child that needed tending to, she thought about their journey through the night; not knowing where they were going; not being able to see a foot in front of her; hearing the imaginary sounds of people following them. But they were safe now. A white family had taken the six of them in, given them a change of clothes to wear, food to eat, and had led them into a cellar to wait until night—the only time they could run for freedom.

Sadie lifted her head and looked at the cold, dark, underground shelter. There was a little light coming in from some splintered boards around the foundation. Tilly was using the light to read a book she carried in her pouch. The pages were soaked with rain but that didn't deter her. She turned the pages carefully so as not to tear them. Tilly told Sadie it was called *Pilgrim's Progress,* but the title meant nothing to her illiterate mother.

Auntie Ruth had fallen asleep in the corner, resting peaceably on the cold dirt as if it were a warm feather bed. Sadie wished she could do the same thing. The others in their group were Adam, a twelve-year-old boy, who was huddled next to his mother and his uncle. He couldn't—or wouldn't—talk. They weren't sure. His mother said it seemed his tongue got stuck to the top of his mouth when his master beat him one day for picking cotton too slowly. She said there was hardly any skin on his back when he got through. His uncle, Gus, made Sadie nervous. There was something about his eyes and the way he looked at her that made her skin crawl.

Tilly put her book down and made her way over to her mother. Sadie took her in her arms and held her close. Auntie Ruth stirred and began to sit up. Sadie thought this was a good time to talk to Tilly.

"Tilly? " she said.

"Yes, Momma?"

"When we gits up no'th, you gonna be able to go to school. Dis money dat Mis' Meredith give us will he'p ya learn mo' an' git a good job. Why you kin be a teacher or even a nurse."

Tilly shifted to look up into her mother's face, almost invisible in the dark. She asked inquisitively, "How do you know that, Momma?"

"Oh, I heah t'ings. Someone say dat slaves, I mean ex-slaves, even buy der own home in de no'th."

"Really? But why didn't you tell me?"

"I see ya gittin all dat learnin' and I t'ink dat if I tell ya maybe it would make ya sad to live on de plantation. But now ya gonna be free, Tilly. We gonna use dis money to send ya to a school dat gonna teach you to git a job. Whatevah ya do, Tilly, keep studyin' 'cause nobody can take ya learnin' away. Promise me."

"I promise, Momma."

The sound of rapidly approaching horses shattered the silence in the shelter. Mrs. Rutherford went out on her porch. She assumed that the riders were looking for runaway slaves. Usually that didn't trouble her, but she had recently heard about slave owners offering a piece of land to anyone who helped uncover the Underground Railroad.

A tall, rangy man on a black stallion was the first to arrive at her doorstep. It was a hot day, and by the looks of his horse, he had been riding a long time. Three other men pulled up along side him.

"Good afternoon, ma'am," he said, "We're trying to find some runaway slaves. Have you seen anyone?"

"No, I haven't seen any runaway slaves."

"Well, now that's mighty strange Mrs.—what did you say your name was?" said the short, stout man. Mrs. Rutherford thought he might have been attractive if he hadn't looked so mean.

"I didn't say, but it's Rutherford. Mrs. Rutherford."

"Well, now that's mighty strange, Mrs. Rutherford. Rumor has it that you hide runaway slaves."

"That's ridiculous!" she stammered as her heart began to pound powerfully against her chest.

The short man dismounted. Walking toward her, he announced, "Well then, you don't mind if we look around."

"I most certainly do! This is my house and you're trespassing. My husband will be home soon, and he doesn't take kindly to this sort of thing."

Master Poole stopped and spoke in a raspy voice, "Well, you betta pray, little lady, that your husband don't come home."

Master Jack went with the three men. Opening the door to the cellar, he began his descent down the dark stairs. It took a moment for his eyes to adjust to the darkness, but it was obvious that no one was there. As he turned, something caught his attention. He walked to the corner of the room and picked up a book lying in the dirt. When he reached the top of the stairs he spoke to the three men walking through the house, "There's no one down there, and if there was, it surely wouldn't be a slave."

"Why do you say that?" asked David.

"I found an open book," chuckled Jack, *"Pilgrim's Progress."*

David laughed, and the men walked out of the house.

Auntie Ruth jumped to her feet and peered through a small crack in the wall. Immediately she recognized Master Jack's horse. With a wave of her hand and a signal to be quiet, the freedom leader motioned for the group to follow her.

Tilly wondered where she could be going in such a small dark place. Then, she heard the sound of something being lifted. There was a slight shove on her back pushing her forward. Two other people were making their way down a ladder, to another cellar. There was just enough room for them to stand side-by-side. Auntie Ruth was perched on the ladder trying to hear the conversation going on outside. As the cellar door was opened, she moved the overhead covering into place.

After a short time had passed, two thumping sounds resounded above their heads. Auntie Ruth pushed up the heavy piece of wood. Mrs. Rutherford helped each person out.

"Ruthie, it's very dangerous right now. Maybe you should stay another day."

"T'ank ya, Mis' Rutherfor', but we gots to be gittin' on. It ain't gonna git no safah. We gonna leave w'en it git dark."

It seemed the sun would never go down. Just before it was time to leave, Auntie Ruth gathered everyone in a circle for prayer. She looked around the group and said, "I wan' each of ya to ask de Lawd for somethin' an' den we gonna pray."

Tilly felt uncomfortable because this was the first time she had ventured to ask God for anything. The squeeze from her mother's hand let her know that it wasn't going to be easy for her, either. Realizing darkness was their only cover of escape, Tilly whispered, "Lord, I pray that night come swiftly so we can be safe from the people who want to hurt us."

Adam's uncle Gus snickered. Tilly didn't know why. She didn't know that he had never heard a slave talk proper and had no idea what "swiftly" meant. She also didn't realize that jealousy of her knowledge made him despise her.

Sadie cleared her throat and said, "Lawd, please let whut Na-Na tol' me 'bout ya be true."

Tilly looked up quickly, but it was too dark to read her mother's face. She hadn't spoken of God since she had seen her grandfather. Tilly could still remember him pointing to the sky and saying, "I see ya in heaben."

≈ ≈ ≈

The house was dark, and Bertha couldn't sleep. She had taken some food to her master's daughter but dared not defy his orders entirely. Before leaving her bedroom, she helped her mistress take off her clothes and put on her nightie so she could get some rest from her long trip home. When she left the room, the girl was staring at the wall, rocking back and forth in her chair. It troubled Bertha greatly to leave the child unattended.

I have to check on huh, she thought later that night. Bertha eased out of her bed and lit a lantern. Making her way up the winding staircase, she kept hoping that Henry wouldn't hear her. Slowly turning the doorknob and easing into her room, she walked softly toward the bed. Lifting the light, she gasped. *Mis' Meredith gone! Maybe she is still sittin' in huh rockin' chair?* But the soft light proved that to be untrue. Her heart began to race within her, and she didn't know what to do.

Turning quickly to leave the room, her eyes caught a slight movement. Tiptoeing in that direction, Bertha saw Meredith lying on Tilly's mat on the floor. She raised the light over her, and a great well of love rose within her for the precious child. As she moved the light close, Meredith appeared to be clutching something in her hand. Bertha reached down and eased her fingers open. A black rock fell to the floor. Meredith must have picked it up from the road. Bertha knew what it meant; she had been in the barn when Meredith had presented Sadie's father with the smooth black stone. This wasn't it, but Bertha understood its significance.

Placing the lantern on the nightstand, Bertha bent down, scooped the girl up in her arms, and sat down in the rocking chair holding her close to her breast. They had each lost a best friend, and Miss Meredith had made it possible for Sadie and Tilly to start on their freedom road. As Bertha rocked back and forth, she made a silent commitment: She would serve and protect Meredith until the good Lord saw fit to take her old body home.

Meredith sighed gently as she nuzzled into Bertha's chest, sensing the safety of these arms. The exhausted child didn't awaken. As Bertha laid her in the bed, leaning down to give her a kiss, she heard Meredith whisper a single word in her sleep: "Mommy."

6

The heavy rain had covered the tracks of the runaway slaves, and after a day of searching the pursuers gave up. Jack slowly rode toward his mansion. Looking up, his eyes were drawn to the top floor of his house. His bedroom window silently called to him—the window that once would have allowed the moonlight to filter through as Becky lay in his arms every evening. He could still smell her long brown hair and the fragrance of her soft skin. He relived the warm kisses that enveloped him night after night, covering him, and for a moment nothing mattered more to him than the remembrance of the love he so painfully missed.

After a long, hot bath, Meredith's father sat at his formal dining room table waiting for his dinner. Meredith was late coming down, and his heart sank when she finally entered the room. Clearly the slaves had obeyed his command not to assist his daughter. Her hair looked like it had been combed with a rake from the garden. Her dress had been buttoned to the top, but somehow had been started in the wrong place. The top button stood alone, as if looking for a friend.

"Bertha."

"Yes, Massa Jack."

"Take my daughter upstairs and get her ready for dinner."

"I be glad to, Massa Jack."

A tear rolled down Meredith's face as Bertha took her hand and led her up the stairs. Her father got up from the dining room table and walked into the parlor questioning himself unmercifully: *How could I have allowed my daughter to be shamed in front of my slaves? Have I lost the affection of the most important person in my life? Will she ever forgive me? I'll speak to her tonight.*

Meredith returned to her room immediately after a silent dinner. Her father had thought it strange that during the meal she'd sat opposite her usual spot at the table. But Meredith had prepared herself well. She knew that her heart would break if she looked up from her plate and saw the empty space where Tilly had once stood. Now, with the dinner ordeal over for the night, she was preparing for bed when her father came in.

"Bertha, you may be excused. Come back later and finish preparing Meredith for bed. And tomorrow select another girl to attend to her needs."

"Yes, Massa Jack," said a relieved Bertha as she quietly eased out of the room.

Jack paced slowly back and forth, glancing up at Meredith every so often. He wasn't sure how to begin, and she wasn't helping him. Sitting at the vanity table with her back to him, she focused on the floor.

"Meredith, I want you to know . . ." her father said in a soft voice that made her want to run into his arms. Jack paused and leaned against a tall oak closet, his hand resting on the top. His fingers touched a piece of paper. Instinctively he picked it up, opened it, and began to read. Meredith could see him in her mirror, and she felt panic rising within her. Whenever Tilly wrote her letters, she would climb up on a stool next to the closet and put them on top where no one would ever find them.

"What is this? " questioned her father.

"A . . . a . . . letter."

"This is not your handwriting. It's signed by . . . Tilly?"

Meredith nodded her head.

"What does this mean? How could Tilly write this letter? That's impossible!"

"She learned to read and write, Daddy. I taught her."

Whatever Jack had determined to tell his daughter was swept away in his anger. He reached for another piece of paper on top of the closet, and then another.

Tearing the papers into shreds, he threw them on the floor and stormed out of the room, slamming the door behind him. Meredith picked up each tiny piece of paper and gathered them all into a jewelry box that she had been left by her mother. She sat on the floor and held the container close to her heart, remembering Sleepy Hollow, the swing, the river, and the laughter. Memories alone would have to be her company now.

The next morning Miss Martha sat at her desk in the study waiting for Meredith to arrive. She was very late and entered the room without Tilly. "Meredith, I have spoken to you before about your tardiness. This puts you behind in your studies. You must try harder. Where's Tilly?"

It was the first time Meredith had been asked the question. Everyone else in the house already knew. She tried to form the words but they wouldn't come out.

Miss Martha interrupted before Meredith could respond, "Well, it doesn't matter. Let's get started on your English. I believe you were reading from *Pilgrim's Progress,* is that correct?"

Meredith nodded.

"Before we begin, however, you were to study a poem from your literature book while you were away. Come and stand next to your desk and recite it, and then you can read from your book."

Meredith walked to the side of her desk with her head down.

"Come now, Meredith. Look at your posture. Lift your head, shoulders back, and speak clearly."

Meredith obeyed, cleared her throat, and looked directly at Miss Martha. She began softly.

> Powder sweet
> Powder white
> Powder soft
> Powder light
> Is my friend to me.

She paused, fighting back tears. But when she began again her voice was stronger.

> Put it on
> See it blend
> Now we're one
> On my skin
> Is my friend to me.

> God saw two
> Made them one
> Knew we'd shine
> As the sun
> Is my friend to me.
> Is my friend to me?
> Is my friend to me . . .

Miss Martha wanted to stop her halfway through the poem, but it was so beautiful she decided to let her finish.

"That was very nice, Meredith. But it was not your assigned piece. Who wrote it?"

"Tilly."

"Who?"

"Tilly wrote the poem."

"That's not possible."

Meredith slammed her hand on the desk. "Yes it is! Tilly could read and write and do arithmetic. She is smart—just as smart as me! She is nice and kind and pretty and . . ."

As the rage stored inside Meredith was at last unleashed, she began throwing papers and books across the room. Miss Martha sat motionless in her chair, too stunned to move. Finally Meredith stormed out of the room, ran out the front door, and across the driveway, weeping loudly as she went.

Miss Martha rushed to the window looking through the lace curtain. For the first time, she was sorry for having allowed herself to share in Meredith's feelings. It had been safe before because she was always happy. But now it was too late. Miss Martha was swept away. Like a mighty rushing wind that swept through her mind, she remembered the day she had fled from old man Dugan's place. Her mother had asked her to deliver his laundry. When she'd arrived, he'd asked her to put it in the back room. Setting the laundry basket down, she'd heard a door shut. When she turned around, he was blocking her way out. When his desire was satisfied, she, too, had run sobbing from the house.

No one had ever known—she had been too ashamed. Sam never understood why she had turned down his marriage proposal. But she was certain that after they were married, he would find out and come to hate her. Her only safety, she had decided, was in being alone.

"What is going on?" demanded Master Jack, shattering her contemplation.

Miss Martha jumped at the sound of his voice.

"I . . . I . . . don't know, Mr. Douglas. Meredith became very upset and stormed out of the house."

"Did you know that Tilly could read?"

Nervously, Miss Martha began picking up the papers and books that Meredith had thrown across the room. "Well, no, I didn't. Meredith just told me. I didn't see any harm in them both having a book when she did her reading."

"What are you talking about?"

Miss Martha assumed that if he knew about Tilly's reading, he must also know about the extra books. "Well . . . Meredith asked if Tilly could have the same books while she studied. I didn't see any harm because I knew she couldn't . . . "

"You were wrong, Martha Grant, and from this day forward you are no longer in my employ!"

"Oh no, Mr. Douglas. Please listen. I need my job. You see my father . . . "

"Gather your things. I will leave your salary with Henry when you are ready. Good day, Miss Grant."

As Master Jack turned to leave the room, a book that Miss Martha was holding caught his eye. He reached over and took it out of her arms. *"Pilgrim's Progress,"* he recited. "Is Meredith reading this book?"

Miss Martha nodded.

Master Jack asked if there were two copies. When Miss Martha said yes, he asked to see the other one. She searched frantically and couldn't find it. Without explanation, he shouted for Henry to prepare his horse.

Just before sunset, the Rutherfords stood in front of the home that Mr. Rutherford had built for their wedding day thirty-seven years earlier. The fierce flames reached high into the air as if trying to call back from the embers a lifetime of memories.

The Rutherfords had known something was terribly wrong when the four horsemen returned. Going back into the basement with a lantern, Master Jack had discovered the hidden cellar and a few articles of clothing left behind by the runaway slaves. Mrs. Rutherford didn't want to tell them the route Ruthie had taken, but when they put a rope around her husband's neck and began leading him to a tree, she surrendered the information. Giving up Prentice was too great a price to pay. All they could do now was pray that the slaves would make it.

Auntie Ruth had walked her five runaways all night long. They took a couple of short rests, but it was beginning to get light and the next safe house was on the other side of the river. As they came around the last bend, she stopped abruptly and stared at the raging water in front of her. It had never been that high before. Sadie trembled at the sight.

"Auntie Ruth, we ain't gonna cross dat rivah, is we?" Sadie asked. "I can' swim!"

Ignoring Sadie's question, Auntie Ruth told Gus to look inside a large fallen log and take out the rope that was hidden inside it.

"Make a loop an' throw it 'cross de rivah, Gus. Take hol' of a branch and fasten de othah end to dis here tree."

While Gus was working with the rope, Auntie Ruth turned to Ruby, Adam's mother, and instructed, "I wan' you to go firs', an' den Adam. Den I go wid Sadie, Tilly, an' Gus behind. We gots to go now or de light is gonna catch us!"

Sadie knelt down in front of Tilly. She couldn't let her see the fear that was screaming inside her body. "Tilly, now I don' wan' ya to be afraid. We's gonna make it."

Sadie took the long cord from the red velvet pouch and lifted it over her head and across her shoulder. She pulled on it slightly to make sure it was snug to her waist. Then she drew Tilly close and whispered in her ear. "On de day ya was born, I say to ya daddy dat I hope my eyes see de day when my baby is free. He smiled an say, 'Don' worry, Sadie, God gonna make a way.' Yo' daddy an de good Lawd is watchin' ovah ya, Tilly, so don' be afraid, O.K.?"

Tilly nodded. She had swum in the river at home many times without her mother's permission, but it had always been still— never like this. The water here seemed to be boiling in anger, rushing toward some terrible confrontation. Before Tilly had any more time to think, Auntie Ruth was calling them to the shore. Ruby, a tall thin woman, reached for the rope. Adam followed.

The water was cold, and Tilly tried to make sure her foot was securely on a rock before taking a step. She was almost on the other side when a hard rush of water hit her in the face, and she lost her grip with one hand. Gus could have helped her, but he looked the other way. Tilly heard her mother scream her name, but her other hand couldn't hold on any longer. Sadie watched

Tilly being swept downstream and, with love overpowering her fear, went after her. As she reached toward Tilly, the water continually tugged and dragged Sadie under. She gasped for air each time she rose to the surface.

Tilly was sure she was going to die, then the current seemed to lift her for a moment and she saw a fallen branch hanging in the water. With one desperate move, she reached up and caught it. Using every ounce of her strength, she swung one leg across the branch and began to pull herself up. Looking around, she saw her mother coming toward her. She reached out and caught her by the wrist. Sadie locked her hand around Tilly's wrist trying to keep her head above water. But by inches, Tilly was sliding off the branch. Sadie knew they would both be washed downstream. The water pounded against them unmercifully. With all the might she could muster, Sadie grabbed the red pouch by her waist, lifted it over her head, and placed it in Tilly's hand. Then, with one last look at Tilly's face, she let go.

"Momma!" screamed Tilly as she watched the water carry her mother away. She clung tightly to the branch and sobbed her mother's name over and over again.

"Hol' on, Tilly!" shouted Auntie Ruth. "We comin' fo' ya!"

Ruby, Gus, and Auntie Ruth formed a human chain. Auntie Ruth put her arm around Tilly's waist and said, "Let go, Tilly, I got ya!"

Tilly clutched the red bag as she was pulled from the river, dripping and choking. Auntie Ruth held the limp girl in her arms and made her way to the shore. Looking up she saw four men on horses on the other side. She knew that one of them was Master Jack.

Tilly raised her head and she, too, saw horses across the river. It was the last thing she remembered before she fainted. As her head fell back, the red bag dropped out of her hand. Fortunately, the long purse cord caught on a branch from a fallen log on the way down.

≈ ≈ ≈

"We'll have to shoot them, Jack!" shouted David Poole.

The big slave had cut the rope, ending the possibility of their following on foot. The horses would never make it in such a swift current. Master Jack knew David was right. If they didn't shoot them, they would get away.

"I'll give the order! " Master Jack shouted over the sound of the roaring river.

Master Jack raised his gun just as the short, round woman pulled Tilly from the water. He had watched as Sadie was swept downstream. Tilly was in his sights when she appeared to collapse, and he saw something fall from her hand. The red purse caught on a branch and swung back and forth, its gold pendant glistening in the newly risen sun. Jack recognized it immediately.

"Hold your fire!" he demanded.

"What?" questioned Master Poole. "No, Jack, I'm gonna kill me some slaves!"

Master Jack turned his horse and pointed his gun at the three men. "No, David, put your gun down!"

Master Poole looked down the barrel of Jack's gun and lowered his weapon. "Have you gone mad, Jack? They'll get away!"

Then they turned to look across the river. The slaves were gone. So was the red purse.

Jack's horse walked along at a deliberate pace. He was close to home, and Fury knew the way without the help of his master. The scene continued to rehearse itself over and over again in his mind. *Why didn't I shoot? Why couldn't I shoot? Now I'll be the laughing stock of every plantation owner in the county.* He could already hear David Poole sharing the story over a glass of wine at one of his elaborate garden parties.

But Jack knew why he couldn't pull the trigger. If he had, he would have shot Becky. He saw her standing there, holding the red purse just as she had ten years before. It seemed like just yesterday when he'd seen her reach up and feel around on the top shelf of their closet. Pulling down the red purse, she'd settled her eight-months-pregnant body on their bed, opened the purse, and dropped in a gold coin. Her face had been radiant.

"Jack?"

"Hmm," he replied from the other side of the bed, where he was propped up on pillows reading a novel.

"I know this baby is going to be a girl. And this purse is for Meredith. Every year on her birthday we'll put in another gold coin for her coming-out ball."

"Is that all you think her coming-out ball is going to cost?"

"Of course not. It's just to get her excited and looking forward to that big day. You remember what happened at my coming-out ball don't you?" Becky sheepishly smiled, and Jack put his book down. He reached over and put his hand on her stomach just as Meredith decided to kick. Pure delight spread across his face. It was to be short-lived. Becky stood up and turned around to face him. She was holding the red purse in front of her, and Jack was mesmerized as it swung back and forth.

"And Jack, I need to talk to you about something else, too."

The change in her expression told her husband this was not going to be a pleasant conversation. She explained how she had been down to the slave quarters and had watched Sadie's baby being delivered. Jack sat up in bed, and she could see he was upset. He had asked her not to go down there, but she enjoyed visiting with the slaves so she had disobeyed. There was something very special about them—an incredible peace, a genuine laughter, and the gift of song. She asked Sadie's husband, Tom, to tell her when it was his wife's time. She'd arrived just as the baby girl was being eased into the world from her mother's womb.

"Jack, I saw the way Sadie looked at her baby—just like any other mother would do. These people are just like us, Jack. They are born, fall in love, bear their children, and try to live as best they can. I tell you there is something wrong with buying another human being. Yes, their ways are different than ours, but they come from another country. That doesn't make us better than them."

"Stop it, Becky! You don't know what you're saying. Those people are not anything like us. They are incapable of learning. We did them a favor when we brought them here."

"A favor?" Becky asked incredulously. "You did them a favor by snatching them unwillingly from their homeland? By bringing them to a foreign country and buying them like cattle? If they can't learn, how are they able to speak our language without going to school? You can communicate with them, can't you? If they can't learn, how did Billie draw out that building to store the cotton in, and then instruct some of the other slaves how to go about building it?"

Jack hated it when Becky contended with him. She was always so darn logical.

"The Bible says that slaves should obey their masters," he reminded her.

"Don't you go using the Bible on me, Master Jack Douglas. I read it, too. The slaves in the Bible were the result of unpaid debts or wars being fought, with those who were defeated becoming slaves. We weren't at war with these people. We took them from their homes and their country so we wouldn't have to pay someone to work the land."

"Our land, Becky . . . our land!"

"Jack, dearest, let's pay these people. Or, if that would not be practical, we could give them a piece of land—something they would own, and they could still work for us. They would be able to build their own houses."

"Becky, my father would turn over in his grave if he could hear what you just said!"

"But you're not like your father, Jack! You're thoughtful, kind, and compassionate—that is, until it comes to the slaves."

Jack walked around the bed and took Becky's hands in his. Pleadingly he said, "Listen, Sweetheart, you have to think with your head and not your heart. When it comes to the slaves, it's about business and reputation. What would the other plantation owners think or do if they found out we were paying our slaves with money or land? It could endanger all of us."

"Jack, I just think . . . "

"What you think doesn't matter!" Jack thundered.

Becky looked crushed. "You're being cruel. I tell you, Jack, I just don't know how I can ever live if we don't do something about the plight of these people."

Fury continued to put one hoof in front of the other. Becky's last statement echoed in Jack's mind with each step. *Is that why Becky died? Had her death been some sort of a punishment? What if I had done what she asked? Would she be standing on the porch today when I ride up to the house?*

He sat up straight in his saddle and shook his head. *"Stop it, Jack,"* he told himself. Then he rehearsed his familiar response to the question "Why?" concerning Becky's death. The answer was clear: *There was nothing he could have done. Meredith had been born in a breech position, and the delivery had been too difficult for Becky to endure. It wasn't anyone's fault.*

Aroused by sudden feelings of panic, Tilly woke up. She was in another cold, dark basement. She reached out for Sadie. "Momma?"

Someone was trying to comfort her, but it wasn't her mother. "It's gonna be O.K., Baby. God is always by yo' side," said Ruby.

Tilly shut her eyes quickly, fighting back the surge of tears. She was only vaguely aware of the small hand finding its way in the darkness, then resting gently on her back. It was Adam. He didn't say anything; his hand spoke for him.

Then Tilly remembered the river. She saw her mother's last look, and she sobbed into Ruby's chest. In the quiet solitude of the night, Tilly struggled with the waves of pain that engulfed her, then left her drained and aching with memories. At one point, Auntie Ruth started to sing.

Swing low, sweet chariot,
Comin' for to carry me home,
Swing low, sweet chariot,
Comin' forth to carry me home.

Tilly cried until she fell asleep again. Twice she sat up, startled by the horror of her loss. Each time, Ruby recited her words of encouragement and Adam put his hand on her shoulder. He just sat there quietly in the dark—watching, protecting. She was awakened again shortly before it was time to go. Frantically she began feeling around her.

Auntie Ruth came over and asked, "Are you lookin' fo' dis?"

She pointed to the red purse stuffed deep in her pocket. She asked Tilly if Miss Meredith had given her the money. When Tilly said yes, Auntie Ruth patted Tilly on the head and told her what a blessing it was to have a good friend like Miss Meredith. Auntie Ruth promised to give her the purse when they reached Chicago.

Auntie Ruth forced Tilly to eat some food so she'd have enough strength for the journey. Soon they were on their way again. They walked all night long. Tilly was vaguely aware that Adam never left her side. When the sun began to rise, Tilly panicked. Why weren't they rushing for cover? Auntie Ruth turned around and smiled at the group. They had made it! Tilly saw a sign that read Stanton. She would later learn that this city was the border town between the north and the south. Everyone started laughing and singing—everyone except Tilly.

They walked for another hour and came to a gently flowing stream. Auntie Ruth encouraged everyone to find a spot and take a bath. Tilly walked a little further, shed her clothing by the side of the stream, and waded into the water. It was warm. She closed her eyes and thought she could hear Meri laughing.

"Well, well, dat wata' mus' sho feel good."

Tilly spun around and saw Gus standing next to her clothing. She remembered the first night Ruby, Adam, and Gus had joined them in their escape. When the sun rose the next morning, Tilly saw Gus clearly and shuddered. There was a deep gash down the left side of his very dark face, and he had a lazy eye that made it seem like he was looking in two different directions. She had tried to stay as far away from him as she could during their flight to freedom.

Gus picked up her dress and said, "Ya lookin' fo' dis? I takes care of it. As soon as ya git washed up, I be here holdin' it fo' ya."

Tilly began to tremble. *Why was he looking at her like that?* She didn't know what to do. Just then she saw someone step from behind a tree and hit Gus across the back with a piece of wood. He fell to the ground, crying out in pain. Auntie Ruth stood over him.

"I seen whut ya did at de rivah. If I see ya near dis chile ag'in, ya gonna meet ya maker an' I don' t'ink He gonna be happy to see ya. Do ya understan' me?"

Gus winced in pain and nodded his head. Auntie Ruth helped Tilly from the stream and into her clothes. Then she led her back to the group. Tilly found a large rock nearby, crawled up on it, and sat down with her legs crossed. The sun was setting, and she was startled to hear the sound of footsteps. She turned her head and saw that it was Adam. He sat beside Tilly in silence. She felt him looking at her several times. Finally he stammered, "I-I-I sor-sorry b-b-bout ya momma."

For a moment Tilly forgot her pain. *Adam could talk!*

Adam continued, "I-I has a . . . a gift fo-fo' ya." He raised his hand out in front of him, palm side up. Adam squinted one eye toward the setting sun and looked as if he were holding something. Then he opened one of Tilly's hands and placed it on top of his. As Tilly turned her eyes toward the sky, she saw the bright orange sun sitting in the palm of her hand.

"D-d-de sun b-b-belong t-t-to me. Now I g-g-gives it to ya. It will k-k-keep ya warm."

Tilly smiled, took the imaginary sun in the palm of her hand, and placed it against her heart. Ruby stood at a distance, tears streaming down her face. Two miracles in one day: First they had reached freedom, and now Adam had spoken.

Miss Bridges was a lot younger than Miss Martha, and prettier too. The top of her long, blonde hair was pulled back from her face, clipped together at the top of her head, then falling to her waist. But it was the twinkle in her eye that caught Meredith's attention the first time they met.

Diane Bridges thought she had never seen a sadder girl than Meredith Douglas. She had heard rumors that Meredith had helped her slave run away, and Diane was looking forward to meeting such an unusual child.

It had been two months since Meredith's former teacher had left. Day after day Diane had observed Meredith going through the motions of doing her lessons. When they were finished, the girl immediately disappeared into the kitchen. There she sat for hours watching the kitchen-help prepare meals. She seemed especially attached to the older slave, Bertha.

One day, Diane saw Meredith doodling on a piece of paper. Trying not to invade her peaceful mood, Diane moved nonchalantly behind her student. Even from a distance she could see that Meredith was talented. Hoping that she had discovered the key that would unlock the door to Meredith's heart, the next day she arrived on the scene with paper, pencils, paints, and brushes.

"Today our lesson is going to be outside." For just a moment Diane thought she saw a glint of pleasure in Meredith's expression.

"Can you take me to one of your favorite places?"

Meredith nodded and led her teacher across the driveway, over the fence, and down to Sleepy Hollow. The ten-year-old walked over to the swing and pushed it as if someone were sitting there. She hummed a tune that Miss Bridges had never heard before.

"That's a pretty song. What is it?"

Meredith shrugged but didn't speak. Diane sat with her back against a tree and moved her hand adeptly across the paper. After a while, Meredith sauntered over and slowly walked around to stand by her teacher. She gasped faintly as she saw herself on the paper pushing a swing from the weeping willow tree. With real interest, she now sat down and watched the emerging portrait. Diane asked Meredith if she liked to draw. Meredith nodded and went to the log where she kept her drawings. She handed Diane the picture of her and Tilly diving into the river.

"Is this your friend?"

"Yes, it's Tilly."

"And who is Tilly?"

"My best friend."

"Come and tell me how she looked."

As Meredith began to describe Tilly, Diane's fingers moved to capture her.

"No, her eyes were bigger and rounder," explained Meredith.

Finally Meredith looked at her teacher and said, "That's her!" Meredith took the picture and held it gingerly.

"You must have loved her a lot. Did you come here often?" Diane asked.

"Every day."

"Would you like to come with me again? I can teach you to draw like this."

Meredith smiled. It was the first smile Diane had seen from her, and she marveled at how pretty she was. Bertha saw Miss Meredith and her teacher walking up the road as they returned. One look at her mistress' face said it all.

"T'ank ya, Lawd. Ya done sent somebody to he'p her pain," Bertha whispered.

Meredith couldn't stop talking after she returned.

"What's for dinner, Bertha?"

"Somethin' jes' for you, Mis' Meredith."

"Bertha, please call me Meri."

Bertha looked up at Meredith sitting at the kitchen table. "Yo' daddy would have my hide if he heah me calls ya Meri."

"Daddy? Oh, you can do anything you want with him. He loves you."

"He don' love me dat much. I knows jes' how far I kin go wid him and dat is too far."

"Tilly called me Meri."

Bertha nodded, kept kneading the bread dough, and then said, "I tell ya, Mis' Meredith, whut ya had wid Tilly was jes' for you an' huh. It like puttin' dos good t'ings ya'll had in a box. Ya kin open it up an' t'ink 'bout it anytimes ya wanna."

"Do you miss Sadie?"

Bertha turned the dough over into a bowl and put a light cloth across the top. She washed and dried her hands and poured two glasses of lemonade—one for her and one for the master's daughter. Taking a seat across from Meredith, she sighed and nodded.

Meredith reflected upon her time with Miss Bridges earlier that day. She thought about Bertha and realized that the slave's smile was gone just like her own. Meredith reached over and put her hand on top of Bertha's hand.

"Remember when Preacher Man said he'd see us in heaven?"

Bertha nodded her head up and down.

"Do you really think there's a heaven?" asked Meredith.

"If I didn' t'ink der was a heaben, I don t'ink I could make it."

"What are you gonna do when you see Sadie in heaven?"

Bertha got a faraway look in her eyes and then started to laugh, her heavy chest bouncing up and down. "Dat Sadie was a sad-lookin' woman—had a rat to be. But when I sees her in heaben, I gonna tickle her till she can' stop laughin'. Den I gonna give my son Ben a big hug."

Part 2

.

7

Nine months later
Chicago, Illinois

"Tilly!" shouted Ben from the upstairs window.

Ben disappeared momentarily, then he rushed out the front door. He lifted Tilly from the wagon and swung her around. It was the first time Auntie Ruth heard the girl laugh since she'd been with Meredith at the river. Ben held her close as his eyes searched the wooden transport holding the other runaway slaves. He was looking for Sadie, but one look at Auntie Ruth said it all. Sadie hadn't made it.

Seven days later Tilly sat in the weather-beaten third-story window, her eyes riveted on a red-shirted boy playing in the middle of the street. The stick lying on his shoulder was poised to hit a ball, which was about to be pitched by a lanky, determined girl. Shouts of laughter from the other children reached up as if to beckon her down.

Turning from the window, Tilly glanced over her shoulder and saw Ben standing near the door, a worn suitcase in his hand. Her eyes downcast, Tilly pleaded, "You're my only family now, Uncle Ben. I wish you didn't have to leave."

Ben didn't respond.

Tilly had always called Ben "uncle" even though they weren't related. Her momma had said it wasn't right for her to call grown-ups by their first names, so she had to add aunt, uncle, miss, or mister to show respect. Tilly sighed and knew it was time to go.

For the first three days after her arrival, she didn't think she'd ever stop laughing. It seemed everything Uncle Ben said was funny. And the weather helped cheer her up too. Tilly was happy that winter was finally over. The hot humid summer had not yet arrived, but warmth was beginning to dole itself out in small doses as spring continued to settle in.

Last evening, while relaxing in their small, crammed apartment, Ben had handed Tilly a piece of paper. He cleared his throat and wondered how to break the news. In the meantime, Tilly was trying to make sense of the flyer. It was asking colored men to join the Union Army. He quickly began explaining, "Tilly, I signed up befo' I knew ya was comin'. I'm sorry. I has to go . . . "

"But what about me?"

Ben smiled broadly and said, "De good Lawd has been kind to ya, Tilly. Ya get to stay at Harriet Dawson's Home fo' Girls!"

Ben made the announcement as if Tilly would know who and what he was talking about. He went on to explain that Tilly would pay for her keep by working for Miss Dawson, and when she was older the money in the red purse would help her go to school. Meanwhile, there would be girls her age at the home and she would have a good time.

Tilly, however, was not convinced. In just a short period of time, she had said goodbye to her best friend, lost her mother to an angry river, and now the last link to her life as she had known it was about to walk away from her.

Tilly looked at the boy in the red shirt one last time, then eased off the windowsill, picked up the paper bag with her few belongings, and made her way out the door. The walk to her new residence was a long one, and the noonday sun seemed to be shining only on her and Ben. There were fifteen stairs up to Miss Dawson's double doors. Ben knocked; Tilly waited uncertainly.

When the doors opened, a full-bodied woman with gray streaks in her black hair welcomed them. Her warm smile seemed genuine, but her eyes looked as if the shades had been drawn so no light could enter. Tilly wanted to turn and run, but knew there was no place to go. Compliantly, she followed the two of them into the hallway. Ben and Miss Dawson spoke briefly, then he came and knelt in front of Tilly.

"Tilly," he said nervously, "Der is still lots of our peoples not free. I joined de army to go an' he'p dem. I'm strong and ya gots to be strong too."

Tilly nodded and then put her hand on Ben's cheek. As a tear rolled down her cheek and dropped onto her scuffed brown shoe, Ben took her in his strong arms and held her close.

"When I gits back, Tilly, we gonna have a party. Would ya like dat?"

Tilly nodded as she remembered it was her birthday. Ben didn't wait for an answer. He stood quickly, then tipped his hat to Miss Dawson. Walking onto the front porch, he turned, looked at Tilly, then shut the door behind him. Tilly blinked hard one time, hoping she would wake up finding herself in Meri's room. Maybe this was a bad dream. She quickly realized that yes, it was—and she was living in it.

"Mis' Meredith, if ya keep lickin' de icing in de bowl, der won't be none to put on de cake. An' yo' poppa gonna sho be mad," Bertha chided.

Meredith slid off the kitchen stool and kissed Bertha on the cheek. "O.K., Bertha, but it's the best you've ever made."

"Dats whut ya say every time I makes it," chuckled Bertha as Meredith walked out of the kitchen.

Bertha finished icing the lemon cake and put it on top of the large straw basket. This would surely be enough food to last the four of them until they reached Sommersville. Just hearing the name of the town reminded Bertha of the last trip Miss

Meredith had taken to Aunt Beatrice's. Fortunately, things appeared to be getting back to normal.

This time Jack, Agatha, Meredith, and Diane would be making the journey. Meredith's father had invited her to travel with him and Agatha, and Meredith had insisted that her teacher join them. Bertha suspected that her little Meredith had more in mind than just having a traveling companion. Meanwhile, Agatha was going to see a seamstress to get her dress made for the engagement party—and that was reason enough for a carriage ride with her intended.

The journey had just gotten underway, but already Jack felt as if he had been riding for a lifetime. Agatha seemed to think everyone needed to be entertained because she had been talking incessantly since their departure. He secretly admired the way Miss Bridges continued to look interested in Agatha's comments—*how could she be?* Meredith started rolling her head from side to side against the coach's royal-blue cushions. She wondered if Agatha would ever stop her chatter.

Meredith closed her eyes and imagined Tilly sitting next to her. Then she envisioned the two of them tossing this worrisome lady out the carriage door. The fantasy caused her to erupt in laughter. Agatha stopped talking, and all eyes in the carriage turned to Meredith.

"Oh, please excuse me, I just had the silliest thought," giggled Meredith.

"And what might that have been, dear?" asked Agatha.

Meredith put the end of her braid in her mouth and looked at a loss for words. "I . . . I thought . . . what if the lemon cake melted and everything in the basket tasted like lemons." Meredith turned to look out her carriage window, but not before she noted the three blank expressions on the others' faces.

"Are you hinting that you're hungry already, Meredith? We won't be stopping for another two hours." Her father sounded worried.

"No, no, it was just a thought."

Agatha disregarded the cake comment and continued to talk to Diane. "I was just thrilled when Jack offered to pay for my engagement dress. He is always so full of surprises!"

Jack pretended to smile as he searched his mind, trying to remember when he had consented to purchase her engagement attire. He was sure the father of the bride was supposed to bear that responsibility. No, he was unable to recall any such conversation but refused to allow himself to believe it wasn't true. After all, he had been quite busy lately and seemed to be continually distracted. Just then his eyes fell upon Diane. Suddenly uncomfortable with her poise and quiet charm, he forced himself to look in another direction.

As the coach continued up the road, Meredith caught a short breath as they rode past her and Tilly's river. The sun had found an opening in the clouds, and its rays spilled down upon the quiet water. A fish broke the surface and the ripples lazily floated to the shore. Meredith tried to block out the thoughts of the last trip she and Diane had taken to that favorite place, but they made their way through anyway. It had seemed like a bad dream.

Against her will, Meredith's mind drifted back. Just two months earlier, Diane had been sitting on a rock near the river, teaching her how to sketch trees, when an unusual sound had caught Meredith's attention. Most people would assume it to be a bird, but Meredith had learned its special pattern.

"Diane, I'll be right back," Meredith nonchalantly said with a quick little smile.

Her teacher assumed nature was calling and nodded. Meredith walked into the woods toward the stump where she had last met with Auntie Ruth and Tilly. There was no one there, but two folded pieces of paper lay on top of the fallen tree. Meredith looked in every direction but saw no one. Just as she tucked the papers in her apron pocket, she was startled by the sound of running.

A man's voice shouted, "I see her!"

In dismay, Meredith watched three men with guns in hot pursuit of a darting, shadowy figure. Without thinking, she began to follow the men while screaming at the top of her lungs, "No . . . don't! Stop! Stop!"

A shot rang out, causing the birds in the treetops to rise in terrified flocks. Meredith froze as if she had been shot herself, and then started running again. As she came into a clearing, the three men were standing in a circle staring at something on the ground. Meredith ran between them. There she saw Auntie Ruth lying face down in the dirt.

When Meredith collapsed on top of Auntie Ruth's body, sobbing and screaming, the three men had looked at one another in bewilderment. Just then Diane arrived and pushed one of the men to the side. She stood in shock looking at the lifeless woman, and at Meredith lying on top of her, weeping with all her heart.

Diane's eyes had flashed at the men as she yelled, "Why did you do this?"

"Do you know this woman, ma'am?" one of the men demanded.

"No."

The man shrugged. "She's been helping slaves run away to the Underground Railroad. She's no good."

Diane instantly made the connection. She walked over to help Meredith remove herself from her fatally wounded friend, sensing the danger to both of them if she did not react properly.

"No, we don't know her. The girl is just stunned to see anyone killed like this. Come, Meredith, we must go."

Diane had been grateful that Meredith was sobbing so loudly that she hadn't heard her deny knowing the woman. Meredith hid her face in her teacher's skirt as Diane led her back through the woods.

After completing a search of Auntie Ruth's body to see if she was carrying any information on the Underground Railroad, one of the kneeling men paused and looked up at his male friend and said, "I knew I'd seen that little girl before. That's Jack Douglas' daughter. She's the one who helped her slave and her mother run away last year. As sure as shootin', she knew this woman."

A heavyset man with a gun tucked under his arm and a straw hanging out of his mouth looked toward the woods where the woman and child could no longer be seen. He drawled, "Well, I guess they'll never know how fortunate they were that you have a bad memory."

Diane was out of breath when they stopped halfway to the house. She had continued to look over her shoulder while ushering Meredith along, hoping those terrible men had not followed them. Collapsing in the grass, Diane had reached up and pulled a distraught Meredith onto her lap and rocked her gently in her arms. There was so much Diane didn't know about Meredith because she had been careful not to pry. But today she felt Meredith needed to talk. After a little prodding, Meredith opened up and told her the whole story: meeting Na-Na, Agatha deciding Tilly should be sold, the trip to Aunt Beatrice's, and the escape with Auntie Ruth.

Meredith sobbed as she reached into her pocket pulling out the two pieces of paper, "And now look what happened to Auntie Ruth for bringing this to me!" Diane took the papers as the young girl cried on her shoulder. She carefully opened a letter from Tilly, read it quickly, and tucked it away.

Meredith was so grief-stricken that she forgot to ask for them back. Diane didn't mention them either, as they walked to the house. Meredith asked Diane not to tell Bertha what had happened. It would hurt her too badly. When they returned home, Meredith went to bed while Diane told Bertha she had an upset stomach.

The next day had been a beautiful Saturday morning. Meredith woke up realizing she had given Tilly's letter to Diane. Now she would have to wait until Monday to read it. When Monday arrived, Diane refused to give it to her until she finished her lessons for fear she would become upset. At last, when they were finished, Meredith quickly opened the first piece of paper and read:

Dear Meri,

I miss you so much. Tomorrow I will go to Chicago and stay with Ben. I spent the whole day thinking about Sleepy Hollow. Sometimes I just see us sitting in the swing and singing our favorite song over and over again. Momma died in the river. I'm so sad. I wish you were here. Please write me at this address: Ben Douglas, 444 Wyatt Street, Chicago, Illinois. Write soon.

Tilly

Meredith opened the second piece of paper, got up slowly, and walked toward the kitchen with her head hung low. Bertha was checking the meat in the oven. She blew the hot gravy on the spoon and took a sip. As she closed the oven door she said to Meredith, "Um-um, yo' stomach gonna sho be happy tonight!"

Then Bertha noticed the expression on Meredith's face as she sank down into the kitchen chair. Bertha sat beside her and asked what was causing her face to be so long. Meredith handed her the letter.

"Why, chile, ya know I don' has my readin' glasses," Bertha laughed.

Meredith had forgotten for a moment that Bertha couldn't read. "It's a letter from Tilly. She's in Chicago."

"T'ank de Lawd! I know Sadie is dancin' in de streets."

Meredith's eyes welled up with tears, "Sadie didn't make it, Bertha. She died on the way. And after Auntie Ruth left these papers for me Friday she was . . . "

Bertha asked, "She was whut, chile?"

"You see there were these three men . . . they had guns . . . "

Bertha got up and walked to the sink, looked out the window, and mumbled, "If it be all rat wid ya, Mis' Meredith, I t'ink I be goin' for a walk now."

Bertha didn't wait for Meredith to reply as she walked out the back door. That night at dinner Master Jack asked for Bertha but was informed she was ill. He told Henry to make sure to look in on her and then asked Meredith why she kept pushing the food around her plate. Three days passed before they saw Bertha again.

"Meredith Douglas, whatever are you thinking about?" asked her father firmly. "I have called your name at least five times with no response."

Her father startled Meredith, diverting her from the memories of her last trip to the river. She turned from the carriage window and looked at Diane, who always seemed to know what she was thinking about. Sensing her pain, she took her hand. Meredith thought that next to her mother, Diane was indeed the most beautiful woman she had ever seen. Her hazel eyes sometimes appeared to be the same color as her blonde hair. Her gently sculpted nose graced her soft full lips. She was especially stunning today in her ivory lace-covered dress. It reminded Meredith of a wedding gown. As she looked from Diane to her father Meredith noticed that her daddy was watching her closely. *Does he know what I'm thinking?* Meredith wondered. She smiled faintly and closed her eyes, pretending to doze.

As Miss Dawson led the way up the dimly lit wooden stairs, Tilly's eyes scanned the immaculate house with its big airy rooms. It was hard to believe a colored woman could own such a house. She was soon informed that the first door on the right at the top of the stairs was to be hers. A fair-skinned girl about Tilly's age sat on the bed holding on to the post. She rose to her feet as Tilly and Miss Dawson entered.

"Tilly, this will be your new home and your new friend, Patsy. Patsy, this here is Tilly."

Patsy smiled and Tilly nodded her head.

"Show Tilly where to put her things," Miss Dawson instructed Patsy before leaving the room.

Tilly noticed a quilted-covered bed against the wall on the opposite side of the room and saw that the colorful bed covering went well with the small red roses in the wallpaper. Patsy walked to the dresser and pulled out a drawer for her. Tilly placed her few items inside; the red purse holding her coins and the black stone wrapped in Tilly's grandfather's yellow bandana were pushed to the back of the chest and covered with her clothing.

Just then, out of the corner of her eye, Tilly saw someone standing in the doorway. A large girl, around fifteen years old, was blocking the door with her hands on either side, leaning forward a bit.

"So dis is de new lost chile," the girl remarked. "How's it feel to share ya room wid a high-yella' gal?"

Patsy rolled her eyes and said, "Tilly, this is Rose. Rose this is Tilly."

Tilly and Rose stared at each other.

"Well, dis is gonna be good, Patsy. She don' talk and ya nevah stop."

Tilly heard Rose's sarcastic laughter as she walked away. Patsy smiled a little nervously. "Don't mind her, Tilly. She don' mean no harm. I'm so glad ya're here because . . . " Patsy proceeded to talk for thirty minutes without seeming to take a breath. Tilly welcomed her nonstop chatter because it prevented her from having to say anything.

At last, the dinner bell rang, and Patsy escorted her into the dining room. Nine girls filed in and stood behind their chairs until Miss Dawson took her seat. Three additional girls served the food. After grace was said, the only sound to be heard were the utensils scraping the empty plates as the food quickly vanished.

"You are excused," announced Miss Dawson at the end of dinner. "Tilly, please meet me in the library. It's the last door at the end of the hall."

Tilly made her way down the hardwood corridor until she came to a room richly lined with scores of books. A simple but interestingly designed round clock on a wooden base occupied the middle of Miss Dawson's large maple desk, and its ticking reverberated from one end of the room to the other. A picture of Miss Dawson and a man in a stately pose directly behind her rested next to the clock. Both were young and neither was smiling, yet they appeared quite content to be together.

Tilly took quick notice of the desk accessories, but her attention was soon focused on the library itself. It had been a long time since Tilly had seen a book. She gently ran her fingers across the backs of several editions as she slowly read their titles. Some she recognized immediately, others she could not read at all. As Tilly examined the books, her mind reviewed a scene that had taken place the day the wagon had stopped in front of Ben's place. After he'd finally put her down, Tilly had hugged Auntie Ruth as hard as she could and had given her a letter to take back to Meri.

Then Tilly had walked over to where Ruby and Adam were seated among the other runaway slaves in the wagon. She had noticed that although Ruby was smiling her face was sad. Ruby had told her earlier that their kinfolks lived about five hours away and she wasn't sure when they'd all see each other again. Just as Tilly had expected, Ruby had recited her favorite saying, "God is always by ya side" as she had done so many times during their trip. Adam had stretched his hand toward Tilly and said, "Friend, f-r-i-e-n-d." Tilly had smiled at her pupil. She had taught Adam to read. He had been a good student, hungry to learn and never able to satisfy his need for more knowledge.

Tilly had glanced Ben's way in time to see him put a piece of paper in Auntie Ruth's hand. The two had hugged each other warmly, then he had waved for Tilly to join him.

All at once a voice interrupted Tilly's thoughts. Miss Dawson was asking, "Can you read?"

Tilly spun around and felt her heart pounding.

"Yeah . . . yes I can," Tilly stammered.

"Good! You can help some of the other girls learn too. Please have a seat."

Tilly sat in the straight-backed chair with the red cushion across from Miss Dawson, who was studying her carefully. It made Tilly uncomfortable.

"You're here, Tilly, because you have nowhere else to go. Am I correct?"

Tilly nodded her head.

"Speak up child, I can't hear a nod!"

Clearing her throat, Tilly responded, "Yes, ma'am."

"Since you have no place to go, I expect you to serve me with gratitude. Tomorrow you will go with Patsy to clean the home of Mr. and Mrs. Grant. Do everything Patsy tells you to do. Work hard and you'll do just fine. Understand?"

"Yes, ma'am."

"You may come to the library after dinner, but no books are to be removed from the room. One of my patrons left these to me, and I plan to account for every one of them. Keep your room neat and do all of your assigned household chores. Are there any questions?"

"No, ma'am."

"Then you're excused."

Tilly was leaving the room when her eyes fell upon a picture hanging next to the bay window. It was the same picture that had always hung in the hallway over the picture vase just outside Meri's bedroom. For a moment Tilly could smell the magnolias and see the soft glow of lighted candles that had greeted her on so many past Sunday mornings. She looked over her shoulder almost imagining she'd see Meri asleep in her bed. Miss Dawson saw Tilly's eyes light up, then quickly extinguish. Tilly lowered her head then quietly left the room.

When Tilly returned, Miss Dawson's girls were in the living room and Rose was playing the piano. The melody was unfamiliar but pretty. When Rose saw Tilly coming down the hallway, she began to play a military march as she chanted, "Workin' hard is all ya do. Don' git paid, now whut a fool!"

"Leave her alone, Rose!" shouted Patsy.

Tilly turned the corner and proceeded up the stairs toward her room.

"Jes' 'cause ya rich don' mean ya bettah dan us," hissed Rose.

Tilly kept climbing the staircase, wondering why Rose thought she was rich. All at once Tilly's eyes widened. She rushed into her room, pulled out her drawer, and felt toward the back. It was gone—the red purse was gone! Tilly raced down the stairs two at a time. She rushed toward the piano and leaped onto Rose, knocking her off the stool.

"Give it back!" yelled Tilly as she pounded on Rose over and over again. Although Rose was much larger than Tilly, she was so startled by her attack she didn't try to defend herself at first. When she finally came to her senses, she grabbed Tilly by her hair and pinned her to the floor. The other girls were yelling, and from out of nowhere Miss Dawson appeared. She yanked Rose up by her shirt collar as if she were a rag doll.

"What is the meaning of this?"

Huffing and puffing wildly, Rose whined, "Dis crazy gal jes' jumped on me for nothin'!"

"Is that true, Tilly?" asked Miss Dawson.

Tilly panted hard and glared at Rose but did not respond.

Miss Dawson studied Tilly and Rose for a moment. "Come with me—both of you! Patsy, you come too."

The girls obediently followed Miss Dawson up the stairs to Rose's room.

"Rose get your things and move into Patsy's room. Patsy you move into the room across the hall. Rose and Tilly, the two of you will learn to get along or you'll kill each other trying!" With that, Miss Dawson marched out of the room.

Rose and Tilly stepped around each other for the rest of the night. The next morning, Tilly was assigned to work with Rose instead of Patsy at a customer's home. Tilly groaned inwardly as the wagon made its way back to Miss Dawson's after a long hard day. *"I've lost everything dear to me,"* she lamented inwardly, *"and I'm stuck in a home filled with complete strangers, an uncaring, overbearing new master, and a thief. Where is Na-Na's God now?"*

Miss Dawson went out of her way to make sure Rose and Tilly were always together. Three weeks passed with no conversation between them, except for the orders Rose barked out whenever she wanted Tilly to do some specific task as they cleaned one of the many Chicago mansions. As for Tilly, she never complained. This puzzled Rose, but she didn't mention it.

Returning home exhausted one night, Tilly fell into a deep sleep. That luxury eluded Rose as she tossed and turned on her bed. Just as she was beginning to drift off, she heard Tilly calling out in her sleep, "Momma, momma, please . . . don't die, don't die."

Rose felt her heart strings being pulled as she thought about her own mother, who had been captured during their escape. She could only guess that the slave master had taken her mother back to the plantation. Rose was haunted continuously with wondering if death would not have been better for her momma.

During that incident, Rose had hidden herself behind some thick bushes, trembling as she heard her mother being chained to some of the other captured slaves. Rose had not thought of her own momma for months and months. The painful memories of life on that plantation, the constant abuse, the shameful and appalling mistreatment—all these had left her angry and empty inside.

Again Tilly called out louder, "Momma, Momma!"

When Tilly awoke drenched in sweat, her chest heaving, someone was sitting on her bed. A hand touched her shoulder and a voice said softly, "It's O.K., Tilly."

Tilly didn't recognize the voice—not because it was unfamiliar, but because it was kind. The next morning Tilly opened her eyes and quickly shut them. She thought her eyesight was playing tricks on her, but when she looked again she saw the red purse next to her pillow. Sitting up in bed, she counted the gold coins and checked the black stone. It was all there.

Rose was busy making her bed and had her back turned.

"Thank you," said Tilly.

Rose shrugged her shoulders. "Ya can put it back in the drawer. No one would dare come in my room."

Tilly said with a lilt in her voice, "You mean *my* room!"

Rose glared at Tilly and then laughed, and that laughter began a friendship that grew with every passing day.

One Saturday evening, Tilly was sitting on the piano bench with Rose as she played an old tune. As she played faster and faster, Tilly started to laugh. Together their laughter overflowed and filled the hallway. Miss Dawson stopped reading her book and smiled while the girls in the other part of the living room stared at each other. To the amazement of everyone in the home, especially those who had been victims of Rose's hot temper and mean pranks, Rose had begun treating Tilly like her little sister. Only Miss Dawson seemed unsurprised.

8

*J*ack followed the three ladies dutifully to the dress shops for the rest of the day and was much relieved when they reached the last store. The couturiere was French, and Jack barely understood a word she spoke. Agatha, exasperated with her own inability to speak French, was quickly losing control of her temper. Finally Diane stopped rummaging through the bolts of material with Meredith and came to the rescue of the foreign dressmaker. Jack leaned his head against the soft, lavender-cushioned chair and appeared to be asleep. Diane spoke softly to the flustered designer. Jack didn't move his head but he opened one eye and wondered how a common schoolteacher could speak such elegant French.

Meanwhile, Agatha stood in front of a mirror holding a piece of fabric next to her face while watching Diane's reflection. She, too, was stunned by Meredith's teacher. Diane asked Agatha some specific questions concerning the design of her dress and interpreted the answers for the seamstress. When they were finished, she casually returned to help Meredith, who beamed with pride and winked at her father.

Jack tried to ignore the not-too-subtle gesture of his precocious daughter. He quickly closed his eyes, tried desperately to calm his pounding heart, and made a mental note to contact his longtime friend Edward Franks.

When Edward had heard that Jack was frantically looking for a replacement for Martha Grant, he'd written a letter recommending Diane. Franks had been Jack's best man when he'd married Becky and, even though they lived too far apart to see each other often, their friendship had endured through the years. Now the time had come for Jack to learn as much as he could about the person who was teaching his daughter. His logic was so reasonable he almost convinced himself that Meredith's education was the primary reason for his curiosity.

As for Meredith, she could hardly contain herself. This was the first time she had actually caught her father looking with interest at Diane. Her plan was working!

On the return trip, Agatha talked at length about her engagement party. She planned to stay upstairs until all the guests arrived. Then she wanted her fiancé to direct everyone into the foyer where she would be poised at the top of the stairs. Jack was to stand at the bottom, proclaim his undying love, and ask for her hand in marriage. She would then descend into his waiting arms. Agatha released a deep sigh of excitement when she had completed her dramatic disclosure and looked at the others for approval.

Diane smiled and Jack lightly applauded, leaving Meredith to give the final critique of Agatha's performance. Meredith began to cough. She suddenly felt sick but knew the symptoms would quickly pass as soon as Agatha departed the carriage.

Bertha was delighted to see Meredith when they returned home. Meredith rushed up the stairs and into her warm embrace. "Bertha, wait until you see what I brought you!" Meredith shouted over her shoulder as she ran back to the carriage, pulling out a square box and opening it.

Bertha took the pink hat with the white ribbon out of the box and held it as if it were a piece of fine china. "Oh no, Mis' Meredith. Dis heah is too pretty. Why I don' even have nowhere to go in dis lovely t'ing."

"Don't be silly, Bertha. You can wear it to church."

Bertha laughed, "Chile, if I wear dis heah hat to church de peoples gonna t'ink I'm a fallen woman!"

Meredith giggled even though she didn't know what a fallen woman was. She would ask Diane at their next lesson. As Meredith entered the foyer, she waved at Cory, who was polishing the stairs.

"Be careful, Mis' Meredith. Dis wax is very slippery 'til it be rubbed in. You bettah go up the othah side so ya don' fall."

When Meredith reached the top of the stairs she turned to look down at Cory. Then she smiled brightly and bounced off to her room, humming an old familiar tune.

Meredith didn't think she'd ever seen a more beautiful night as the guests began arriving for the engagement party. The stars were out, the moon was suspended like a golden orb on the horizon, and the air was fragrant with flowers. Her first impression of Agatha's family was that they did an awful lot of whispering among themselves. Every now and then they would glance her way and force a smile.

Bertha kept an eye on Meredith as she served hors d'oeuvres, musing that she seemed to be very relaxed in spite of the fact her father was marrying a woman she simply loathed. Her master looked nervous enough for both of them—not at all the way he had acted around Becky.

Bertha remembered the day Master Jack brought Becky home to meet his father. Up until then she hadn't thought his father liked anyone—not even himself. But to everyone's amazement the old man had adored Becky. The two of them would talk for hours. Bertha unintentionally shook her head from side to side as she thought about Master Jack's father meeting Agatha Stanton. She glanced over at his statue next to the fireplace and smiled in spite of herself—his expression said it all.

Jack knew Agatha was upstairs dressing, but his eyes kept wandering to the front door. He was sure Diane was coming. . . . *Where was she?* His friend Edward had not yet answered his request for more information concerning Meredith's teacher, and whenever he attempted to pose a question to Diane she gave vague replies. For the moment he had chosen to drop the matter rather than appear too interested.

Jack had rehearsed his engagement speech in front of his bedroom mirror over and over again, hoping it would sound sincere . . . refusing to consider why he had to practice it in the first place. Henry had moved toward the front door when he saw the next guest arrive. *It was Diane!* Jack caught his breath as she walked in. Her full, flowing rose-and-beige colored dress hugged her body as though it, too, were attracted to her. Jack had grown accustomed to seeing her in her governess' attire, and he knew this dress could not have been purchased on the salary he was paying her. Meredith was the first to greet her. She proudly walked Diane around the room, introducing her to everyone.

When Diane reached Jack, she smiled and said, "Why, Mr. Douglas, you do indeed look fitting to propose to Miss Agatha." She moved quickly to the next person, making light conversation, while Jack felt strangely disoriented. His head was arguing with his heart, and tonight he felt as if his heart was losing.

Jack checked his pocket watch and then announced, "My dear friends, I have asked you to come this evening to participate in a very important occasion in my life. If you would join me in the foyer, I would like to make my intentions known."

The guests filed into the entryway where Jack directed their attention to the top of the stairs. Agatha stood there in all her regal elegance, drawing the very breath out of her guests as they prepared for the surprising and intriguing way in which the announcement would be made. Jack continued, "It is my heart's desire that Agatha Stanton be my wedded wife. My goal is to love and cherish her forever. And when she takes my arm, I will accept that gesture as an acceptance of my proposal." Agatha beamed brightly and began to descend the stairs with all the grace of a queen. Even Meredith had to acknowledge she looked breathtakingly beautiful. Her father had given Agatha a single-strand pearl necklace with a diamond clasp that draped delicately on her neck.

Halfway down the stairs, however, Agatha's moment of glory ended without further ado. One last glamorous step and her feet flew up in the air, her white petticoats in full view as she began to bounce down the stairs, one after another. Grabbing for the stair railing, one side of her hair fell across her cheek, and her red tresses matched the flushed tone of her face. Nonetheless, embarrassment did not cloud her judgment regarding the proper thing to do. Surely a faint was necessary, so faint she did. Ever the gentleman, Jack rushed to her side and picked her up in his arms.

Bertha stood aghast, then looked at Meredith who was suppressing a full-blown outburst of inappropriate yet perfectly delicious laughter. All at once she remembered the opened wax bottle that had been left on the kitchen counter. *I thought it was unlike Cory to not put away his supplies!* Bertha covered her mouth, fled through the kitchen and out the back door. With one hand on her stomach, Bertha leaned against a tree and laughed harder than she had laughed in years.

Henry had seen Bertha's quick departure and motioned to three of the male servants to tend to Miss Stanton and Master Jack. Coming through the back door, Henry saw Bertha doubled over in what appeared to be a profound state of despair.

"Bertha? Is ya all rat?"

Bertha recognized Henry's voice. Before she could assure him that she was fine, Henry spoke to her with great concern, "I seen ya run from the room and I knowed ya was upset. I was worried 'bout ya."

Henry's statement sobered Bertha, and she slowly turned to face him. "Well, it seem to me, Henry, dat it's a little late to be worried 'bout me."

"Oh, for goodness sake, Bertha. How long is ya gonna be mad at me? I know I was wrong but I wasn' t'inking rat at de time. If ya could forgit de pas', maybe t'ings could change fo' us."

Just as Bertha was about to reply, a figure appeared in the doorway. "Henry, de massa is lookin' for ya."

Henry rushed into the house with Bertha following close behind him. Agatha was finally beginning to stir. When she opened her eyes, the first person she saw was Meredith, who was leaning over and calling her name with polite concern. Somehow Agatha suspected that Meredith had something to do with that slippery stair. She wanted to reach up and strangle the child. Instead, she chose to place the back of her hand across her eyes and softly call Jack's name.

"Take me to my carriage, dear."

Jack carried Agatha to her carriage with her family in tow. Bertha stood on the front porch with Meredith watching as the buggy rolled out through the front gates. Meredith whispered under her breath, "Good riddance."

Bertha sighed and said, "Don' be fooled, Mis' Meredith, 'cause 'every eye shut ain't sleep and every goodbye ain't gone.' "

Meredith had no idea what Bertha's saying meant. The only thing on her mind was rushing upstairs to write a letter and draw a picture of Agatha bouncing down the stairs for Tilly.

As Meredith headed for her bedroom, Diane escorted the last guest from the house. Returning, she saw Jack sitting on the sofa in the drawing room, his head in his hands. Diane approached quietly and sat next to him. Softly she said, "Mr. Douglas, I'd like to say how terribly sorry I am."

Jack dropped his hands slightly, barely exposing his eyes, and looked intently into Diane's face. Finally he asked inquisitively, "Miss Grant, do you believe in fate?"

Diane didn't know how to respond. The question was so unexpected that she found herself struggling to answer. Jack watched as she tried to compose herself. Finally she carefully explained, "If you mean the fate that determines what's going to happen in our lives whether we like it or not, then yes, I believe in fate. But fate is no friend of mine. This has been a trying night, Mr. Douglas. Now, if you'll excuse me. . . . "

"Please! I didn't mean to say anything to offend you," offered Jack.

"Be assured that you did not. Goodnight," was her quick reply.

Jack watched Diane exit hastily, trying to understand her reply. He walked to the window and saw her hurriedly enter her carriage. He whispered to himself, "Well, Miss Grant, fate can indeed be a friend. I'd like to introduce you two if you'd allow me."

The carriage door shut firmly, almost as if it were responding to his intentions.

The following day Jack rang the doorbell at Agatha's residence. He had come to pay his respects and to comfort her following the previous night's misfortune. He was led into the sitting room and found her seated on the tapestry-covered settee. She was facing the window, her gaze fixed on the backyard. She didn't hear him approach; she turned with a start as he touched her shoulder.

"Jack, dearest, I was so hoping you would come. Please do sit with me and let's not talk about last night. I am trying so desperately hard to forget."

Jack took a seat opposite Agatha and noticed her face looked drawn. They spoke of simple things—matters of no particular significance. Then, out of the blue, Agatha stated, "Well, Jack, I am sure you agree we should proceed with our plans. My suggestion is you complete your proposal in the presence of my father today, and we will have it printed in the social section of the newspaper this weekend. Then we can set the date for our wedding and all those laughing biddies in this town will be silenced. My honor will be restored—and it will be I who gets the last laugh."

Jack shifted nervously in his chair. Before he could reply, Agatha turned and called out, "Father, father? Please come. Jack would like to speak with you."

Mr. Stanton came in from the study and moved as if every step was a journey. The thin, sickly man with a bowed head and white hair took a seat next to Agatha. She placed her hand gently on his arm. Her father looked toward Jack Douglas with expectation in his face.

NIGHT COME SWIFTLY 107

Agatha prodded, "Well, go on, Jack. Don't be shy."

Jack cleared his throat and asked, "Mr. Stanton, with all due respect, may I speak with Agatha alone?"

Mr. Stanton looked at Agatha who, with a bewildered expression, nodded her head. As he made his way out of the room, his daughter turned with daggers in her eyes. "How dare you embarrass me like that in front of my father!"

"I'm sorry, Agatha, but what I have to say is personal. You called your father in here without inquiring of me first."

The truth of Jack's words seemed to calm her anger. Jack stood, holding both hands behind his back, and paced back and forth, causing Agatha's tensions to increase.

"Oh, for goodness' sake, Jack, do sit down. I don't know what has gotten into you today. A person would think it was you who had the most important night of your life crumble into a disaster right before your eyes."

Jack sat down next to her, studied her face, and took both of her hands in his. "Agatha, I'm having second thoughts. I'm sorry but I just can't propose right now. Perhaps in time . . . "

"You can't propose? Just because I fell down a couple of steps?"

"No, no, Agatha, that's not it. It's just that recently I've come to realize that I . . . I don't love you."

"You don't love me? What's not to love?"

Jack looked down at the floor and then up again and gently said, "You are indeed a wonderful person, Agatha, but I . . . "

"But you what? Go on, say it," she prodded.

"But I . . . love another."

Agatha looked as if all the life had drained from her body; Jack felt as if his soul had been cleansed. He had finally stated what he had been carrying in his heart for months. He had even surprised himself with how smoothly the words had flowed forth from his lips.

Agatha screamed, "Why, I'll be the laughingstock of the city! You can't do this to me, Jack Douglas! I'll smear your name in such a way you will never be able to hold your head up again—

you and your devilish child, Meredith. Oh, I know you think the sun rises and sets in her, but she's evil through and through!"

Jack pulled back as Agatha spewed her venom. Any respect he'd held for her vanished forever in that bitter moment.

"I think we've said enough, Agatha."

"Oh no, Jack, I've just begun."

"I'll be taking my leave, Agatha. Please say goodbye to your father for me."

Agatha jumped to her feet and glared at Jack. "This is not goodbye, Jack. This is only until."

"Until what, Agatha?"

"You'll see, Jack Douglas!"

The following morning, Jack waited for Diane to arrive for Meredith's lessons. He had asked his daughter to wait until she was called because he wanted to speak to her teacher before the lessons began. Her father tried to find a nonchalant voice, but Meredith had studied him all her life. She knew that something was different. The deep crease in the center of his forehead that seemed permanent had softened somewhat, and he seemed quite at ease. Meredith had calmly said yes but began wildly jumping up and down on the bed after he left the room.

Diane walked up the front stairs with an armful of books. She was surprised when Jack opened the door.

"Miss Bridges, it's so good to see you. Here, let me take those books."

Diane followed him into the wood-paneled study. She loved this room. The deep burgundy and green colors, blending with the wood tones, reminded her of home.

"Please let me take your wrap," Master Jack suggested. "And do have a seat, I'd like to speak with you."

Diane felt bad about leaving so abruptly the evening before. She had thought about it often throughout the night.

"Mr. Douglas, I want to . . ."

"Please call me Jack."

A puzzled look crossed Diane's face, but she managed to retain her composure. "All right . . . Jack . . . I want to apologize for the way I behaved last night. It's just that your question brought back bad memories."

Jack kindly acknowledged her apology with, "I understand." Clearing his throat, he said, "Miss Bridges, I went to see Agatha yesterday."

"Oh, how is she?" asked Diane with concern.

"She was fine physically, but in distress."

"And why was that?"

"She wanted me to propose in the presence of her father so they could print the announcement in the weekend newspaper."

"Did you do so?"

"No, I didn't."

Diane felt confused. "May I ask why not?"

Jack stood and walked to the back of his chair. He looked at Diane affectionately and said, "I told her I love another."

Diane gasped and covered her mouth with her hand. "Oh no! Who?" As she asked the question, the look on Jack's face gave her the answer. Diane jumped to her feet. "This must be some kind of terrible mistake!"

Walking quickly toward her, Jack said, "No, Diane, it's not a mistake. I have loved you for a long time. I tried desperately to convince myself it wasn't true, but I began to realize how you seem to be a part of my every waking thought. I love your smile, your laugh, your candor. I love the way you tilt your head when you talk and the way you move about a room with such elegance. It doesn't matter to me that you are not of high estate. It's you I love."

Diane walked to the window and stared outside for quite a while. She did not turn around when she spoke, "Let me first say, Mr. Douglas, how deeply honored and humbled I am that you have chosen me to love. I had no idea."

Diane turned and looked directly at Jack. "But I'm already married."

Jack was stunned. Seldom was he left speechless, but on this occasion he was at a complete loss for words. He simply murmured, "I beg your pardon, Miss Bridges. I didn't know."

"I know you didn't. Now if you'll excuse me, Mr. Douglas."

Diane picked up her books and began walking toward the door. "Miss Bridges, before you go may I ask you something?"

Diane nodded.

"Does your husband know how fortunate he is to have you?"

Diane forced a small smile and answered softly, "Yes, he knew that."

Jack sat in the chair behind his antique desk and pondered her strange answer as she left the room.

Two months later

Miss Dawson was weary from a long week. A wave of depression swept over her and, as miserable as she felt, she realized that most people would laugh at her condition. After all, how many colored women owned a large home and had a steady income? When her employer, Calvin Forsythe, left the house to her in his will, the courts had tried to overrule his decision. But he'd had no other family alive, and his lawyer had known how to fight the system so that Mr. Forsythe's caretaker would receive his generous endowment to her.

Still, the inheritance had brought her no happiness. All she wanted was David. Miss Dawson would have gladly lived in a one-room shack if she could have had him back. She picked up David's picture and stared at it until she felt he was once again in her arms. It was early evening, just after dinner, and Miss Dawson felt herself beginning to doze off when she remembered the mail delivery that morning. She forced herself to her feet and made her way to the library where she knew Tilly would be reading. She took note that the new girl was getting along well even without a teacher. A good book and a dictionary suited her just fine.

Tilly didn't look up when Miss Dawson entered. She had traveled to some distant land through the pages of the novel she was reading.

"Tilly," Miss Dawson said, "this came for you today, and I knew you would want to have it."

Miss Dawson extended the envelope to her. Tilly assumed it was a letter from Uncle Ben and was relieved. It had been several weeks since she had heard from him. One of the men in his battalion knew how to write and didn't mind writing letters for the men in his group. But when Tilly saw the handwriting on the letter her heart skipped a beat with excitement.

"Meri! How did she find me?" She asked the question to no one in particular as she tore open the envelope. Tilly continued, "I sent her Uncle Ben's address but after I left there so quickly, I figured I would never hear from her again."

Tilly ran her hand over the letter as if Meri was embodied in the written words.

Dear Tilly,

I have read your letter over and over again so that now I know it by heart. I am so happy you reached Chicago, but I was also sad to hear about your momma. Now when I think about my mother in heaven I see them standing together.

Tilly looked up at the ceiling and fought back tears. Miss Dawson had left her alone with Meri's voice speaking from the pages in her hand.

Ben gave Auntie Ruth your new address and she brought it with your letter. Tilly, I went past the barn after you left. I couldn't believe what I saw—how the slaves live on our land. Soon it will be getting cold and some of the small houses (they really aren't houses, they're shacks) don't even have glass in the windows. Most of the people don't even have shoes. I met Aunt Susie. She was on the porch in her rocking chair and is very old. I called her by her name, and she asked how I knew her. I told her you said she believed I wasn't your friend. She spit over the side of the porch and then told me she was wrong. She heard how I helped you run away. I have been back a lot of times. I sit with her and she tells me stories.

Tilly shook her head in unbelief. She couldn't imagine Meri down in the slave quarters talking to Aunt Susie.

I haven't said anything to my father because he'll stop me from going to see her. But when I get older, I'm going to do something about the way they live. I understand now, Tilly, why Ben left.

Meredith brought Tilly up-to-date on everyone in the house including Bertha. Then she began to describe what had happened to Agatha.

Miss Dawson sat up in bed with a start and hurried down the stairs to see what all the commotion was about. The girls were standing outside the library door staring in. When Miss Dawson made her way through, Tilly was rolling from side to side on the sofa, holding her stomach and screaming in laughter.

"Tilly, whatever is the matter with you?" demanded Miss Dawson.

Tilly held up a drawing that evidently had come with the letter. Miss Dawson saw a woman hanging onto a stair railing with her hair and dress in disarray. It meant nothing to her. Tilly sat up holding her stomach, "I'm sorry, Miss Dawson." Through bursts of laughter she continued, "You wouldn't understand."

"No, I wouldn't, Tilly. Now pull yourself together. You've disturbed the entire house!"

Tilly started to get to her feet, but her laughter had still not subsided. "Yes, ma'am, I didn't mean to bother anyone."

By now all the girls in the doorway were laughing and, in spite of herself, Miss Dawson even began to chuckle. She had never heard Tilly laugh like that, and the sound of it was really quite infectious. Miss Dawson didn't realize until later that her depression had rolled away with the sound of Tilly's laughter. Her heart felt a wave of gratitude spill over it.

Even after the other girls had dispersed, Rose continued to stand in the doorway and stare at Tilly. She knew the letter was from her white friend, and she couldn't understand how it could bring Tilly so much joy. In that moment, her friend's reaction to a letter did something that none of Tilly's lectures could accomplish. Tilly had tried time and time again to convince Rose of the importance of learning how to read. Tilly had even attempted to teach Rose but without success. Rose had simply said in frustration, "Why I gots to learn dis stuff? Ain't gonna make no difference. I jes' be a maid wid good talkin', but I still be a maid."

But now, as Rose saw the impact of the written word on Tilly, she wondered what it would be like if she were to receive a letter from her mother. She knew her mother couldn't read or write, but maybe someone could do for her what the man who wrote letters for Ben had done for him. That way Rose could speak to her mother, even though she might never see her again.

The next evening Rose came to the library with paper and pencil and, with Tilly's help, began to learn the alphabet.

9

One year later

*R*ose drove the rickety wagon through the Chicago streets on her way home. She loved this time of year. The October air was brisk but not cold, and the trees had exploded into vivid oranges, reds, and yellows.

Twelve-year-old Tilly sat next to Rose, who was contemplating about how different they were. Tilly was petite and beautiful; Rose felt plain and stocky like the horse that plodded along before them. Yet they were similar. Both carried holes in their hearts caused by loved ones lost, and both felt that life had already been too long. And that bond provided comfort to each of them.

Rose had become very protective of her little friend. Except for the one brief explosion of laughter when Meri's letter arrived, everyone at Miss Dawson's home thought Tilly's demeanor was a bit too serious. But Rose knew her friend had many sides, most of which had barely been revealed. When she was alone with Rose, Tilly seemed to become another person, vibrant and funny. Apart from Rose, however, Tilly kept pretty much to herself.

Rose pulled the horse to a stop alongside Bailey's Park. The two girls had finished cleaning early, and this was the way they rewarded themselves. A stolen moment on a park bench by a pond provided a much-needed break for the weary pair.

Tilly noticed that Rose was moving a little slower than usual and asked if she was feeling all right. Rose assured her she was fine, then plopped down on the seat near the water. Rose stared across to the other side for a long time. Then, without even looking at Tilly, Rose asked, "Tilly, did yo' massa ever mess wid ya?"

Tilly didn't understand. The question seemed to come from nowhere, and Tilly asked Rose what she meant. Rose reached down and picked up a stone, which she skipped across the water. Her time on the plantation was a subject that, thus far, Rose had kept buried deep within her. Now, however, she began to recount a day her master had approached her in the cotton field. He'd asked if it was her twelfth birthday. When Rose told him yes, he'd said he would be by later to bring her a present.

Rose remembered, "I couldn' wait to tell my daddy. He loved me so much. I'll nevah forget de look on my daddy's face when I tol' him."

Rose recounted how the master had come to see her that evening and had "messed wid her." A few months later her stomach had begun to grow. When she'd told her mother, her momma told her she had a baby living inside her, growing until it was strong enough to be born. When Rose asked how it got there, her mother said the master put it there. Nothing more was said.

"I got real sick one day an' my momma tol' me it was time to have de baby. I was hurtin' real bad," recounted Rose.

After a long torturous night, all Rose could remember was hearing a baby crying and seeing her mother place it in a blanket. Turning her head, Rose saw her father holding the bundle. Her mother was pleading with him, but he pulled away and left the house. Rose said everything went dark after that. When she finally woke up, her mother told her the baby had been born dead.

Tilly looked at Rose and wondered why she was telling her the story, but she didn't dare interrupt. Rose went on to tell her that when the master came the next day he was very upset when he found out the baby was dead.

"He walked ovah tuh me an' say he'd come an' see me ag'in soon."

Rose said she saw her father standing next to the pot-bellied stove, and he didn't look like himself. That night he ran away and she never saw him again. Rose looked at Tilly and murmured, "I was jes' wonderin' if yo' massa ever mess wid ya?" Tilly shook her head and Rose shrugged her shoulders as if it didn't matter.

When they arrived home, Rose stood up to get out of the wagon. As she was stepping down, she collapsed and fell to the ground.

"Rose!" Tilly shouted as she rushed to her side. "Somebody help me, please!" Tilly called out to several people passing by. Two men picked Rose up and Tilly led them into the house, up the stairs, and into their bedroom. Miss Dawson rushed in just as they were laying Rose on her bed. She quickly thanked the men for their help, then turned her attention to Rose who was still unconscious and lying perfectly still beneath the sheet.

"What's wrong?" asked Tilly.

"Don't know. She's burning up with fever. We've got to bring her temperature down."

Tilly sat at the edge of the bed and reached for a washcloth lying in a bowl of cold water that Miss Dawson had placed there. She squeezed it hard and made a flat compress to place across Rose's forehead. Rose stirred and opened her eyes slightly. She recognized Tilly and brought her hand out from underneath the blanket and reached for her friend. Tilly took her hand and held it gently in her grasp. Miss Dawson was right. Rose was hot, very hot.

Miss Dawson worked on Rose all evening. When it got late, Tilly volunteered, "Miss Dawson, I'll stay up with her." But despite Tilly's frequent applications of cool compresses, Rose got worse through the night. Her bed was wet with her sweat and, at one time, she started talking deliriously. When that happened, Tilly knocked on Miss Dawson's door to alert her to Rose's condition.

After a few short moments, Miss Dawson appeared fully clothed and headed for the front door.

"Tilly, I'm going to get Nurse Taylor. I'll be back as soon as I can."

Tilly walked back to Rose's bedside, trembling inside as she came to realize that her newfound friend could die. She shivered. *Maybe it was my doing,* she thought. She had heard of stories of people who were jinxes. *Everyone I've ever loved has been taken from me. Perhaps it is my fault!* Tilly shook her head hard, trying to force the ugly thoughts to leave before they consumed her soul. Instead, she picked up Rose's hand, forcing herself to think how they had grown to love each other like sisters. It was hard to believe that a year had already passed since they had rolled around on Miss Dawson's parlor floor trying to pull each other's hair out.

Master Jack was in his study when Henry entered. An early evening rain beat against the windowpane and the glow of the fireplace made the room feel as warm as an embrace. Henry waited until Master Jack looked up from his papers and then handed him the envelope that had just been delivered.

"Thank you, Henry," nodded Master Jack as he opened the letter.

Jack's heart skipped a beat when he realized the correspondence was from his old friend Edward Franks.

> Dear Jack,
>
> Please excuse my delay in responding to your request concerning Diane Bridges. I have just returned from the south of France. You must take Meredith there one day—it has to be seen to be believed. It was here, in fact, that I met Col. Thomas Hampton, his wife, and his daughter, Diane, ten years ago. She was attending school

and he had come to visit her. Her father was quite an admirable man and his wealth was enormous.

By the way, old chap, why have you waited so long to inquire and what is the purpose? Can I guess? Don't you just hate dear friends who can read your mind?

Jack paused and smiled as he thought about Edward. He could just see him sitting at his desk with pen in hand and a humorous smirk on his face as he wrote those lines.

Upon Diane's return home, she married a Lieut. William Bridges. She was quite in love with him. Unfortunately, both her father and husband were killed on July 11, 1861 when the Union army won the Battle of Rich Mountain in western Virginia. Their estate was ravished and, subsequently, Diane was left penniless. Her mother died several months later, some say of pneumonia, I say of a broken heart.

When I heard of your plight of looking for a governess, I thought it might be an opportunity for Diane to both help you and to heal from her tremendous losses. She requested that I not divulge her history unless you thought her unqualified for the position, thus the sparse information in my letter of referral.

I will be leaving for France again in six months. Please, do come and join me.

> Your friend sincerely,
> Edward

Jack laid the letter on top of the other papers on his desk and swung his chair around to look out the window. In the reflection of the glass, it was as if he could see Diane sitting in the chair behind him as she'd done on the day he'd made his intentions known. He had so boldly announced that he would marry her even though she was not of high estate. A grimace crossed his face as the weight of his careless statement sank in. In that moment, he loved her even more for having shown no sign of indignation at the very suggestion. No, she was too much of a lady for that. And now he understood her response when he asked if her husband knew how fortunate he was to have her. He could still hear her saying, "Yes, he knew that." She'd spoken in the past tense because her husband was deceased.

Now everything made sense. Jack also remembered having dinner with Meredith a few weeks prior when they had talked about her future. As they'd talked of her eventual marriage, he'd remarked that she'd have many loves before meeting the right man. She replied, "No, Daddy, I will be like Diane. She says that you only have one true love in your lifetime. Do you believe that?"

Her father had not responded.

Nurse Taylor arrived two hours later and quickly removed the navy blue cape which hung heavily on her tall, slim body. Tilly arose from the bed to give the nurse all the room she needed to tend to Rose. The nurse worked quickly, checking her patient's vital signs. She stayed with Rose throughout the rest of the night with Tilly by her side. As the morning light began to filter into the room, the nurse sat in the chair next to the bed.

By now, Rose was resting more comfortably. Nurse Taylor looked at Tilly and said, "Is Rose your friend?"

"Yes she is."

"She's blessed to have you. What's your name?"

"Tilly. Tilly Douglas."

"And what do you do, Tilly?"

"Right now I'm a maid. I thought one day I would like to go to school and be a teacher. But if you heal my friend, then I'm going to want to be a nurse—like you."

Nurse Taylor spoke in a hushed tone, "Only God can heal Rose. This girl is very sick and she needs to be taking medicine that costs a lot of money. I've known Miss Dawson for years, and she's not the kind of woman who would come up with that kind of money, no matter how much she cares."

Tilly looked at Rose lying helplessly in the bed. She got up, walked to the dresser, opened the drawer, and felt around in the back. Nurse Taylor saw her pull out a red purse with a gold pendant.

"Will this be enough to buy the medicine?"

Nurse Taylor counted out the gold pieces one by one. Then she questioned Tilly about how she happened to have them. As the sun continued to rise, Tilly shared the long, sad story. Finally the nurse asked, "But how will you go to school if you give me this money?"

"I don't know," replied Tilly softly. "I don't know."

"Bertha, where are you?"

"I be right heah, Mis' Meredith. Don' git yo'se'f in such a tizzy. Ya looks jes' fine."

Meredith stared in her full-length oval mirror turning right and then left. Bertha stood in the doorway admiring Meredith's young beauty. Although she would be a teenager on her next birthday, her body was maturing beyond her years. She looked very much like her mother, but she was also pretty in her own right. Today she was going to the Hunter Estate with her father and Diane to watch the horses run.

"Do you think I look too . . . too . . . ?"

"Too fancy?"

"Yes. But how did you know what I was thinking?"

" 'Cause I knows ya bettah dan de back o' my han'."

Meredith looked at Bertha's reflection in the mirror. "Yes, I guess you do," she replied smiling.

"No, Mis' Meredith. Ya don' look too fancy but when ya pretty as ya are, everythin' ya put on gonna look fancy."

Meredith walked up to Bertha, smiled, and announced, "You are the sweetest woman I know."

"Well, de good Lawd know dat I jes' be tellin' de truth."

Meredith's father was waiting at the bottom of the stairs when Meredith began her descent. "My aren't you the pretty one?" he commented. Diane looked on as Meredith thanked her father and kissed him on the cheek. Tears stung her eyes as memories of her own father floated back: the smell of his uniform, the way his beard had tickled her nose when she reached up to give him a kiss, the twinkle in his eye when he looked at her. Diane often admired Mr. Douglas for loving his daughter in such a warm and tender way.

It was a lengthy ride to the Hunter Estate, but Meredith's anticipation of what was waiting for them kept her alert. The horse races always thrilled her, and she loved watching the ladies attired in their elegant dresses with matching hats. The men looked ever so dignified, some in riding clothes, some in suits. And the horses were portraits of beauty and strength. Meredith had spent many hours learning how to ride horses, as well as having drawn countless sketches of them.

Jack, Diane, and Meredith made their way through the crowd. The races were about to begin. Jack pointed to a young man riding a horse named Startling Beauty. The horse's brown coat glistened in the sun. "That's Carter Hunter. Fine young man. Comes from a good family, and he knows how to race a horse," Jack said.

At that moment, as if he knew Jack was speaking about him, Carter looked into the crowd and caught the eye of Meredith's father. He tipped his hat, taking an extra moment to acknowledge Jack's beautiful daughter, to whom he also tipped his hat. Meredith looked away to hide the sudden blush that warmed her cheeks.

The race seemed to last only moments and then Carter was led to the winner's circle. Meredith's father asked her to come with him as he made his way toward the winner.

"Mr. Douglas, it's good to see you!" stated Carter.

Jack congratulated the young man and then introduced him to Meredith.

Carter bowed, kissed the back of her hand, and said, "Oh that my horse would race as fast as my heart is beating at this moment."

Chuckling Jack said, "Easy now, Carter! My daughter is only twelve years old." Carter smiled easily. He looked from Jack to Meredith and matter-of-factly announced, "Then I shall wait."

Meredith unsuccessfully tried to hide her pleasure and felt relieved when her father led her back to her seat. The next race was about to start, but Meredith's mind was not on the activities. As she stared into the clouds, her mind drifted back to the times when she and Tilly would chart their futures by the shape of clouds in the sky.

Meredith thought, *Well, Tilly, maybe that cloud I saw wasn't wearing a sword. Perhaps it was a riding stick!*

As Meredith attempted to look interested in the remaining races, she was mentally constructing a letter to Tilly. She wondered for a moment what would have happened if Ben had not given Auntie Ruth the address to Harriett Dawson's home. Or what if Diane had not given permission for Tilly to send letters for Meredith to her home? She would have lost track of her friend forever. Instead, God had honored their commitment. One way or another, they would always be together—even if all they had were words written on pieces of paper that somehow found their way across the miles.

Meredith seemed still to be glowing from their trip to the Hunter Estate when Diane arrived on Monday for her lesson.

"Guess what?" inquired Meredith.

"What?"

"I've decided what reward I want for completing my report. Remember? You said I could decide."

"That's true," Diane nodded.

"Well, I've decided to have a picnic at Sleepy Hollow today. We can do our lesson there."

Diane studied Meredith, still unsure why she seemed so happy. They'd had picnics there before. Just then Mr. Douglas appeared in the doorway.

Meredith explained, "Oh, by the way, I invited Daddy to come with us."

Diane hesitantly followed the two of them to Tilly and Meri's old playground. Jack listened attentively as Diane instructed Meredith. She saw him watching her, and it made her uncomfortable. She was grateful that he had never approached her again after the difficult day in his study. She was sure he'd have no problem finding another woman—he was indeed a very attractive man. Diane flinched briefly when she realized that she'd taken the time to notice.

Meredith broke into her reverie. "Diane, if you don't mind, I'd like to spend a little time sketching that rock formation next to those trees."

Diane followed Meredith's finger as she pointed to the left. It was short distance away—but nothing with which to be concerned. Diane looked at Mr. Douglas for his approval, and he nodded. Meredith picked up her sketching pad and pencils. If they had been able to see her face as she walked away, they would have known she had a far greater plan in mind than the sketching of rocks.

Meredith sat down next to a tree with the paper in her lap. She pretended to be very engrossed in her art. Jack and Diane both shifted nervously and tried not to look uncomfortable when they realized they were alone.

Jack began, "Miss Bridges, I haven't taken the time to thank you for the outstanding work you have done with Meredith. I really appreciate it."

"Thank you," replied Diane.

Jack cleared his throat and continued, "I received a letter from Edward Franks a few weeks ago."

Diane sat even more upright on the blanket and changed the position of her hands in her lap. She asked about Edward's well being, then tried to catch Meredith's eye—hoping that somehow she had already completed the picture.

"I must be honest with you, Miss Bridges. I inquired about you to him."

Jack tried in vain to read Diane's face but could not. He told her about the contents of the letter and offered his condolences for the loss of her family.

"Diane, I have something to say, and you never need be concerned that I will ever approach this subject again." He shifted to face Diane. "When I lost my first wife, I didn't think I could ever love again. Oh, I was going to marry Agatha because I felt Meredith needed a mother, but I didn't love her. I believed that caring for someone else would diminish my love for Becky. But what I have discovered is that my heart has not decreased for her, it has increased enough to accommodate my love for you."

Diane started to get up but Jack put his hand gently on her arm.

"Please, Miss Bridges, I'm almost finished." Diane sat back down on the blanket and Jack continued, "I recognize that you may never share the feelings I have for you, but I just want you to know that I will never love anyone else but you."

Diane looked into his warm gray eyes and felt the sincerity of his words. Tears began to fill her eyes and she replied, "Please excuse me, Mr. Douglas."

Diane walked quickly back to the house. When she felt herself completely out of Jack's sight, a floodgate of tears opened up. She stopped to lean against a tree and wept profusely. She had not allowed herself to do so since William died. Up until this moment, she had even refused to believe that he was gone. Now, for the first time, the weight of her loss came crashing down upon her, and she hurried to her carriage in order to make her escape.

Meredith, seeing Diane leave hastily, ran over to her father asking, "What happened, Daddy?"

Staring off in the direction of Diane's sudden departure, he hesitantly responded, "I'm not sure."

≈ ≈ ≈

Three months later

Nurse Taylor sat in Harriet Dawson's study waiting for her return. Looking around the office, her eyes fell on the picture of Harriet and David that was sitting on the desk. She had attended the wedding. When he'd left Harriet for another woman, his betrayed young wife had consumed herself in her work and now seemed to be married to money. Miss Dawson arrived shortly and Nurse Taylor did not take long to make her intentions known.

"Harriet, I have come to ask you to release Tilly Douglas into my care. I can use the extra help, but more importantly, I can begin her education in nursing—a profession for which she has expressed an interest."

"Why Tilly?" asked Miss Dawson.

Nurse Taylor went on to explain how their relationship had developed while nursing Rose back to health and how Tilly had sacrificed her money for school to provide medicine for Rose. Miss Dawson raised one eyebrow. It was the first she had heard of Tilly's secret treasure.

Tapping her pen against the desk several times, Miss Dawson responded, "Of course you know this is a difficult decision, Clare. I take these girls in out of the kindness of my heart."

Nurse Taylor's mouth twitched. She decided to stifle a comment concerning the sincerity of Miss Dawson's statement.

Miss Dawson continued, "The girls, of course, get a home. I, in turn, earn money from their housecleaning services. So actually I would be taking a loss, not only emotionally but financially."

Trying her best not to sound agitated, Nurse Taylor responded, "Harriet, do you remember when David left? All you wanted to do was die. I came to see you every week for months, encouraging and comforting you. One day you said if I ever needed anything, just ask. Well, now I'm asking."

A stunned Miss Dawson struggled to compose herself. "Well, all right, Clare, since you put it like that."

Nurse Taylor had come prepared for a long, drawn-out conversation, and she was taken aback when Miss Dawson acquiesced. She would not have been as impressed with Miss Dawson's surrender, however, had she known that the woman sitting before her had been struggling to figure out where to put a new girl who was scheduled to arrive at the house the next day. All the beds were full. Besides, Tilly was petite and this new girl was larger and older and could do more work.

Miss Dawson rang a bell and one of her girls appeared.

"Eve, get Tilly."

When Tilly arrived at the study, she was surprised to see Nurse Taylor. She smiled warmly at the woman whom she credited with saving her friend's life. Rose was feeling good as new, and they had gone back to working together.

"Tilly, sit down please," instructed Miss Dawson.

Without formalities Tilly was informed about the decision. She sat perfectly still, not reacting visibly. When she was asked if she had any questions Tilly replied, "What about Rose?"

Miss Dawson replied, "Rose can't go, Tilly."

"Then I won't go either."

Miss Dawson stood with an air of dismissal. "That's not your choice. Get your things together, Tilly. You'll be leaving with Nurse Taylor."

When Rose came home that evening and went to her bedroom, she was greeted by the sight of Tilly's stripped-down bed. Miss Dawson informed her of the decision about Tilly.

That evening, Rose did not come down for dinner.

10

Four years later

As her maid, Patience, slipped the ball gown over her head and began the arduous, painstaking task of buttoning her up properly, Meredith thought about the red purse with the golden pendant. The coins in the pouch probably would have not paid for one of the buttons on her dress. Edward, her father's friend, had sent the gown from Paris. She was sure to be the envy of every eligible young lady at her ball.

Patience asked Meredith to sit at the vanity table so she could make the final touches on her hair, which had been swept elegantly to the top of her head. As Patience adjusted the curls, Meredith reached over and pinched herself on the arm.

"Ow!" she exclaimed.

"My goodness, Mis' Meredith, whatevah are ya doin'?" asked Patience.

Meredith smiled radiantly, "I'm pinching myself, Patience, to make sure this isn't a dream!"

"Oh, it fo' real and I'm sure ya momma is watchin' ya right now."

Patience saw Meredith's countenance change and hastened to say, "I'm sorry, Mis' Meredith, I shouldn' a said dat."

"No, no, Patience, you're right. She is watching."

Meredith stared at her reflection in the mirror and thought of how her well-ordered life had been so brutally interrupted two years earlier. She could still hear the banging on the door and feel the cold fear that had gripped her heart.

Her father had been out of town on business when they'd heard that the Union Army was advancing in their direction. Bertha had been careful to hide the silver and as many valuables as possible. Soldiers had broken the door down while Meredith, Henry, and Bertha hid in a closet. When the three of them were discovered, one of the soldiers remarked, "Well, well, well, what do we have here?"

Meredith bolted out of the closet, pushing against him as hard as she could, causing him to lose his balance. Fortunately, there were only two other soldiers with him, and they were busy rummaging around through the rest of the house. Meredith ran into the dining room and up the stairs, with the blue-uniformed soldier fast on her heels. She dashed toward her bedroom but he caught her by the wrist and swung her around just before she reached the door. He pushed her back against it as she struggled to get away. Leaning his bayonet against the wall, he slurred, "Now where you going, pretty lady? I came all the way here to see you."

The man with the foul breath was still trying to kiss Meredith when she heard a loud crash. The soldier released her and swung around, picking up his bayonet. He looked at the floor, dazed, taking note of the broken pieces of the picture vase Bertha had smashed against his head. Before Meredith could grab his arm, he struck Bertha hard in the face with the butt of his gun. Then, as if the impact of the blow from the vase had just been felt, he collapsed on the floor. Meredith fell to her knees and threw her arms around Bertha.

She could hear the other soldiers coming up the stairs. One of them shouted, "We gotta get out of here. The general gave us orders not to stop!"

Another voice questioned, "But what are we gonna do about Sam?"

"Help him up. We'll strap him to his horse," was the reply.

Meredith kept calling Bertha's name. By then, Henry had made it up the stairs and stopped short when he glimpsed the unconscious figure of Bertha lying on the floor. He left quickly to get help. As he ran, his mind raced back to the conversation he had had just the night before with Bertha.

It had been a warm evening, and Bertha had been sitting on the back porch when Henry came out. He'd asked if she minded him sitting with her. Instead of her usual sharp response, she'd said it was all right. Since he had last spoken to her at Master Jack's engagement party, Henry had noticed a softening in her attitude. They'd sat for a while looking at the sunset and finally Bertha said she had been thinking a lot lately about her life and how many things she wished she had done differently.

There had been a long silence before she'd continued, "Ya know, Henry, when ya didn' show up fo' our wedding, I was sure I'd jes' die right there."

Henry had started to comment, but she'd raised her hand to silence him. She went on to say that she understood now. He was probably scared of marrying a woman with a little child whose daddy said it wasn't his baby. And it didn't help that he had lost his first wife just the year before.

Henry nodded his head. Bertha said she'd been too angry to see clear, and then when Henry tried to make it right she was too scared to let him try again.

"I was wrong," Bertha admitted.

Henry didn't understand what had come over Bertha. Years before, when he came to his senses and realized what he had done, he'd tried to get Bertha to understand that he was just afraid for a moment and that he had quickly gotten over it. But it was too late. She'd locked the door of her heart and hidden the key. For forty years he had searched for it. Now, tonight, she was about to give it to him.

Henry had reached over and placed his hand on Bertha's hand just as the sun said its customary goodnight and dropped below the horizon.

Henry took courage and asked, "Bertha, will ya marry me?"

Bertha had smiled and replied, "Only if ya git down on ya knee and ask."

"But if I do dat dees old bones might not let me git back up!"

"I'll he'p you, Henry. I'll he'p ya."

Now Henry snapped out of his remembrance and followed the men carrying Bertha to Meredith's bed. Bertha opened her eyes and reached for Meredith. "Oh t'ank de Lawd! You's all right," whispered Bertha.

Henry stood by Meredith and took Bertha's hand in his. He bent down and whispered something in her ear.

"Me, too," was her reply. And then suddenly she was gone.

Meredith was stunned. In her horror she collapsed. After being revived, she just couldn't believe Bertha was dead. Next to her own mother, Bertha was the only momma she had ever really known.

Meredith heard her name being called, and with a start looked up to see Patience standing beside her with a puzzled expression.

"Mis' Meredith, is ya all right?"

"Yes, Patience, I was just thinking that Bertha is watching too."

"Oh, fo' sho', Mis' Meredith, an' she's mighty proud of ya tonight. She would probably be fussin' about ya dress though."

Meredith looked surprised until Patience pointed to her slightly exposed bosom and they laughed.

"You're absolutely right, Patience. She would be fussing!"

Tilly trudged up another flight of stairs behind Nurse Taylor. In all her life, she had never known the days to be this humid, this stifling, and this overbearing. The heavy summer heat seemed to be sitting there watching them suffer as they climbed to the next landing. The expectant mother they were visiting was clinging tightly to her friend when the two of them arrived. Her husband was sweating profusely and gave a sigh of relief when they walked in. Four other children sat frightened on the couch across the room. A boy about seven years old was struggling to console his toddler sister who was crying.

"Nurse Taylor, I think somethin' is awful wrong with my wife. This never happened with the othah four children," said her husband.

Nurse Taylor kept her eyes on the expectant mother and instructed, "Hank, I want you to take your children for a walk. We'll come and get you when the baby comes." She could see Hank struggling with her directions so she spoke firmly, "Do it now, Hank!"

Hank snapped out of his mental paralysis and herded his children out the door and down the stairs. Without further instructions, Tilly knew what to do. She got a pan, filled it with water, and placed it on the stove. Nurse Taylor instructed the woman next to the bed to get plenty of towels. The baby arrived six hours later. For a moment or two, Tilly thought the mother wouldn't make it. But once again she watched what appeared to be the miracle-working power of Nurse Taylor.

As they had worked together over the years, Tilly had often heard her praying under her breath as she helped the sick. Time and time again people would return back to health. Some of her remedies couldn't be found in the books she'd given Tilly to study. When Tilly inquired, Nurse Taylor just smiled and explained, "Some of these medicines come from our ancestors, and I honestly don't know why they work. They just do!"

As they walked toward home, exhausted as usual, Nurse Taylor said, "Tilly, I've enrolled you in school to get your certificate as a nurse's assistant. You'll be starting in two weeks."

Although Tilly's heart skipped a beat, she protested, "But who will help you? There's too much work for one person."

"The same person who helped me before you came: God."

Tilly continued, "But I have no money. How can I go to school?"

They had reached the front door of their apartment. Nurse Taylor put her hand on the doorknob and smiled at Tilly. "You've worked for me for almost four years, Tilly, I've barely paid you anything. I've been saving to send you to school."

Tilly felt like she had as a child when Bertha had put fresh-baked apple pies on the window sill to cool: full of excited anticipation. For six years Tilly had suffered through tremendous losses and long, hard work. She had accepted this as her lot in life. Now, with one sentence, Nurse Taylor had turned the light back on in her dreams. She repeated it over and over again in her mind, "Tilly, I've enrolled you in school."

In the hours that followed, Nurse Taylor began to regret telling her the news, because it started Tilly on a marathon chatter session that went on endlessly into the night.

Meredith walked out of her bedroom and up the hallway. The sound of music from the chamber orchestra drifted up the stairs. Her appearance captured the attention of everyone in the foyer. One woman noticed how Meredith turned her head toward the other stairwell and smiled broadly as if she were looking at someone.

Meredith could still feel the book on her head and could hear Tilly's laughter as she floated down the staircase, top to bottom. Her beauty held the crowd in awe as she descended in the light-blue flowing gown.

Taking his sixteen-year-old daughter's arm and leading her to the center of the room, Jack and Meredith began the first dance. Every eye was on them, while one by one, other couples joined them on the dance floor. Jack felt happy, but his happiness was tinged with loss. He began to recollect that it had been a mere two years ago when he had returned home to find his plantation in disarray. . . .

A white sheet had been draped over a body being carried down the front stairs, and Meredith was walking alongside sobbing. When Meredith saw her father, she cried out, "She died protecting me!" He knew from all the talk at the burnings along the road that Union soldiers had been responsible for this tragedy.

With one arm around Meredith, he took his other hand and slowly lifted the sheet, seeing Bertha, the woman who had helped raise him. She had been his buffer against his stern and critical father and his ever-distant mother. She'd brought laughter to his soul and had imparted to him age-old wisdom. Bertha had been waiting at the door when he'd brought Becky home to meet his parents. It was her comforting squeeze on his arm that had given him courage. How was he to know he wouldn't need it: Becky had gotten along famously with them. He wondered when the last time was he had told Bertha thank you. Sadly, he realized he never had. With a trembling hand, he raised the sheet once more, bent down and kissed Bertha's cheek, then ushered Meredith back into the house. Shortly thereafter he raced to Diane's house to check on her safety.

He knew immediately that Diane was frightened when she'd opened the door looking relieved to see him. As he entered her home and closed the door, she'd leaned against his chest crying softly. He gently put his arms around her and led her to a chair in the parlor. Dabbing at her eyes, Diane thanked him, explaining that she had been unbearably frightened when she'd heard the soldiers were on the way. All the memories of the loss of her family had come back to her. Then she apologized for the way she'd acted when he first arrived.

"I accept your apology, Miss Bridges, but be assured the pleasure was all mine."

Diane stopped wiping her eyes, smiled nervously, then told him how grateful she was for his concern.

Jack continued to comfort Diane, giving her an opportunity to share her fears. She hadn't known whether the soldiers would come to her home; she had been fortunate that they had passed her by. As Jack prepared to leave, Diane placed her hand on his arm and suddenly said, "When you talked of how your heart had not decreased but increased that day at Sleepy Hollow, I didn't think it was possible . . . "

Jack waited for Diane to finish the sentence, but she seemed distracted by her thoughts.

"Miss Bridges?" There was no answer. He spoke her name again. She had a distant look in her eyes when she finally looked up at him.

"Miss Bridges, you have had a most traumatic day. May I call on you tomorrow and we'll finish our conversation?"

Diane seemed to snap out of a trance as she walked Jack to the door. "Please don't think terribly of me, Mr. Douglas. You're right, this has been a most trying day."

"And for me also, Miss Bridges. The Union soldiers ransacked our home, and I'm sorry to say, we lost Bertha."

"Bertha! Oh no, not Bertha! Jack, I'm so sorry, I know she meant a lot to you."

"Yes, she did. And it wasn't until today that I realized I had never told her—not once."

Diane took Jack's hand and said, "She knew. You could tell by the way she talked to you that there was a special bond between you."

"You're very kind."

"No, I'm very confused." Diane paused and then seemingly out of nowhere stated, "The heart is a funny thing, and I don't quite understand it."

"It's not meant to be understood. We should simply allow it to lead us," Jack said.

"But how do I know it won't lead me to disappointment and pain?" Diane questioned.

Putting his hand on Diane's cheek, Jack spoke softly, "You will never truly know, but I can promise you the risk will be worth the reward." As he rode off that day, he kept hearing her call him Jack. It was a bittersweet day—losing Bertha and possibly gaining Diane.

That was the beginning of a warm and wonderful relationship between Jack and Diane. It was not unusual for them to talk for hours after Meredith's lessons or to go for long walks. The first time he took her in his arms he thought the heavens had opened. He felt as if his heart would explode from such overwhelming joy.

The dance with Meredith was almost over, and Jack remembered two other occasions that had brought him such wondrous delight. His marriage to Becky was the first. And happiness had touched him again when Diane became his wife. It had been just a year before.

An hour had passed when the band stopped playing, and Meredith lightly applauded and bowed slightly toward her current dance partner. As she turned, Carter Hunter was standing directly in front of her. Meredith caught her breath. The music started again and Carter said, "I've been waiting to dance with you for a very long time."

Meredith looked apologetic and replied, "I'm ever so sorry. I didn't see you come in. How long have you been waiting?"

Carter put one hand on her waist and took her other hand in his and whispered, "Four years."

As they twirled around the room, people stopped to watch the most handsome couple in the room. Meredith marveled at the perfection of that moment, wondering how it was possible to feel the way she did and still remain awake and rational. This was just as she had imagined it.

Carter's dark hair and eyes seemed even darker against his white suit. His smile was just for her. His gaze never left her face and, as the dance concluded, he walked her through the open terrace doors onto the patio. Magnolia and rose blossoms perfumed the air as they walked toward the garden. Carter reached over and picked one of the flowers.

"You remind me of this rose, Meredith."

Meredith smiled and asked, "How so?"

"The fragrance is soft and sweet, like my thoughts of you. Its petals are delicate like your skin."

Carter turned to face Meredith and traced her face with the rose. "And I have to be careful to inhale its fragrance ever so gently or it might overtake me."

Carter lightly laid his cheek next to hers and inhaled the scent of her skin. His lips softly brushed against her lips. "But I will not allow myself to enjoy your blossom until you are my wife."

"Your wife?" Meredith repeated almost incredulously.

Carter repeated, "Yes, Meredith. I knew I wanted you the moment I first saw you."

"But I was a child."

"No, you were a bud. But I saw you in your fullness. Just as you look tonight."

When Carter and Meredith returned to the ball, Jack and Diane smiled at one another. They knew.

After that evening, Carter made the eight-hour trip from his home to see Meredith once a month. When eight months passed, he invited her to his estate for a ball and to formally meet his family. Diane agreed to accompany her on that warm May day.

The Hunter plantation was three times the size of Meredith's home. The house, shutters, and pillars were all white and surrounded by lush, green gardenia bushes. Carter's father was known far and wide as a raiser of champion racehorses. Diane and Meredith arrived on a Wednesday so that they would have plenty of time to relax and meet with Carter's family before a big party that was planned for Saturday.

Solomon and Dorothy Hunter were delighted with Meredith and thought she was the ideal mate for Carter. On Friday evening after dinner, everyone met in the parlor. Mrs. Hunter seemed to be captivated as she listened to Diane playing the piano. She had been quite ill, so one of the servants was by her side at all times. As she talked to her, Meredith noticed that her memory seemed to come and go.

Carter's brother, Jerris, sat near the fireplace reading. Jerris was twenty-six years old—four years Carter's senior. The two brothers appeared to be unrelated. Carter had inherited the sharp, dark, rugged features of his father, and Jerris the soft, delicate lines of his mother. Both were attractive in their own way but very, very different. And the difference didn't stop with outward appearances. While Carter was outspoken and entertaining, Jerris was withdrawn and quiet. Their relationship with their father also seemed dissimilar. Carter seemed to hang on every word Solomon spoke; Jerris appeared disinterested.

Meredith sat next to the fireplace across from Jerris. He had spoken only five words to her since they met: "Pleased to make your acquaintance."

Meredith interrupted his reading with, "Are you enjoying that book?"

Jerris looked up smugly and said, "Yes, I was."

She felt uncomfortable for a moment but decided to try again. She asked what he was reading. He informed her it was a book of poetry from a little-known poet.

"Would you read me one of the selections?" asked Meredith.

Jerris looked reluctant but flipped through the book and found a poem that seemed to strike his fancy. He was halfway through when Meredith began to recite the remainder of the piece. Jerris closed the book on his lap and looked at her in amazement. Finally he spoke. "Why, Meredith, I'm quite impressed. Few people even know of this poet's work. How did you ever happen to memorize one of his poems?

Meredith motioned toward Diane, who was still playing the piano. "I had a teacher who was well traveled and loved to read."

Jerris began to talk of his favorite authors, and half an hour had passed by the time Carter had reappeared at Meredith's side and announced, "I do say, Jerris, I don't believe I've ever seen you talk to another person for this long."

Jerris chuckled and answered, "That's because everyone else, excluding you of course, happens to be a complete bore. But you, my brother, appear to have happened upon an unusual treasure. I will be proud to have her in the family."

Meredith beamed. She had won the approval of all the other family members, and now even Jerris was in agreement with Carter's decision. Carter took Meredith by the hand and eased her out of the chair. As he began to lead her away, he jokingly suggested that perhaps Jerris would find a jewel as rare as Meredith at the ball.

"My dear Carter," Jerris responded, "Surely you know that I do not, nor will I ever have a desire to wed. I find my pleasure between the covers of an enjoyable book. For a novel will never tell you what to do and makes no demands."

Carter laughed and replied, "Nor will it keep your bed warm."

Meredith blushed and Carter looked amused, "I'm sorry, darling, I have embarrassed you. I must take leave of my brother. We have a long day ahead of us tomorrow as we prepare for the ball."

Jerris sighed and said, "Well, you know where to find me. I'll be sitting in the far corner waiting for the blasted event to be over."

Tilly pushed the schoolbook away from her and leaned back in her chair as she took a long stretch.

"How are things going?" asked Nurse Taylor.

Tilly gave a tired smile and answered, "Well. Very well. But there is so much I don't know. I thought I knew it all after having spent four years working with you, but I have a lot to learn."

Nurse Taylor responded, "Well, if anyone can do it, Tilly, you can."

Tilly smiled fondly at the woman who had changed her life with unexpected acts of kindness. She had been just a shell of a person before Nurse Taylor came and cracked open her casing with love.

The nurse's compassion was certainly not focused solely on Tilly. It was also directed toward a hurting, diseased, and illiterate community. So many ex-slaves had flocked into Chicago after the Emancipation Proclamation, hoping to find freedom and fortune. Both those dreams were difficult to fulfill because jobs were scarce, and those that were available paid very little. Physical enslavement had been transformed into a mental and emotional prison of hopelessness. Poverty fostered unnecessary illnesses due to the lack of proper sanitation. It was into these gloomy conditions that Nurse Taylor brought her particular ray of sunshine.

The nurse's love for God was infectious to most of those who knew her, but Tilly had been inoculated with too much pain and too many disappointments to respond. Even though she had been through severe traumas and had obviously received much-needed divine intervention from time to time, Tilly couldn't bring herself to believe in a God who would take her mother and rob her of her best friend. No, she would put her faith in Nurse Taylor—her benefactor was someone she could see and, therefore, trust.

The Hunters' ballroom was very beautiful. It had a high ceiling with glistening chandeliers suspended from the center. As a full orchestra played melodic waltzes in the background, Meredith was overwhelmed by the splendor. She had never seen such luxurious gowns and jewelry. She and Carter danced continuously throughout the night. Meredith laughed and nudged Carter when she saw Jerris sitting in a far corner looking as if he'd like to snap every individual before him into a closed book and store it on a shelf.

When the music stopped, Carter said, "Meredith, I have someone I want you to meet. Her family moved here a few years ago, and she immediately became an active part of several community charities. My father loves her dearly. Our cousin, Albert, lost his wife last year and he's been seeing this lady, whom I think you'll find charming."

Carter led Meredith to a small group of people. Her attention was still turned toward the dance floor, and it wasn't until he said, "Excuse me," that she looked at the family friend Carter wanted her to meet.

When the woman turned around, Meredith caught her breath.

"Meredith, I'd like you to meet Agatha Stanton. Agatha, this is my fiancée."

"But of course she is, dear. And a prettier one you could not find," Agatha's eyes glittered strangely.

Meredith felt lightheaded and was suddenly at a loss for words, "Carter, Agatha and I have known each other for many years."

Agatha interjected, "Yes, Carter, I guess you could say that one day I fell for her."

Agatha laughed at what Carter understood to be an inside joke, but he was puzzled at Meredith's troubled expression.

Meredith couldn't remember anything else that was said. She quickly suggested she and Carter get some punch. As they made their way to the refreshments, Meredith looked back and saw Agatha dancing with Carter's father. She thought it strange that Agatha still wore the engagement necklace given by her father. All of a sudden she didn't feel well.

Agatha was, of course, delighted to see Meredith squirm. She thought she deserved it. Carter's father made small talk with her as they danced.

"So how have you been enjoying the ball, Agatha?"

"Solomon, how can you ask such a question? It's simply delightful. The best I have ever attended—and you can imagine how many that has been!"

The music continued and Solomon's eye was drawn to his wife, Dorothy, who seemed comfortable in her chair next to the fireplace. Her servant stood nearby in case she had to be ushered out quickly. Dorothy waved at Solomon when she noticed him looking at her. He smiled and nodded his head.

Agatha interrupted his thoughts with, "I hope you have been pleased with my handling of your foundation for the orphans."

"Pleased? I am thrilled. For years I was unhappy with the distribution of the funds, but one of the best things that ever happened to this town was when you moved here and became involved in community service. You have done wonders for this town and I am indebted to you."

Agatha was ecstatic with his high praise, filing his words away for future reference.

Solomon changed the subject and noted, "I see you've met my son's fiancée."

"Oh, I've known her since she was a little girl. She is simply exquisite but . . . "

"But what, Agatha?" inquired Solomon.

Agatha laughed nervously. "Please do excuse me, Solomon. I'm not the type of person to gossip."

Solomon nodded and said, "I appreciate that about you, Agatha. I have never heard you say an unkind word about anyone. But what do you mean?"

Agatha looked dejected, "I guess it would be unfair for you not to know. She does live quite a distance. Well . . . it seems to be a well-known fact that she is not of the purest nature."

Solomon stepped on Agatha's toe. "You don't mean . . . ?"

"I'm afraid I do. But you didn't hear it from me."

When the dance ended, Solomon excused himself quickly and left the room. Later on, while Meredith was sleeping, Carter and his father met in his study. Their conversation carried on long into the night.

11

*M*eredith and Carter had made plans to go riding the morning after the ball. At first she'd been afraid it would rain, but she was greeted by a beautiful morning when she threw open her bedroom shutters. As they walked to the stables, Meredith noticed that Carter seemed distracted. When she asked him if he was feeling well he abruptly replied, "I'm fine."

Charlie, the stablehand, was talking to Jerris when they arrived. Jerris was sitting on the fence and Meredith heard him burst into laughter. He seemed very relaxed. As Carter and Meredith reached him, he slid his tall frame down and introduced Charlie to Meredith. Charlie smiled warmly and said he'd be right back with their horses.

Carter asked, "Will you be joining us today, my dear brother?"

Jerris smiled and said, "And be embarrassed by a master horseman? Oh no. Surely you two need to be alone so I'll be striking out on my own. I have a lot of work to do." He lifted up a book and chuckled.

As Jerris rode off and Carter left to mount his horse, Charlie commented, "Don' let Mr. Jerris fool ya, Mis' Meredith, he's de best ridah anywhere."

Carter rode quickly across the pasture. Meredith's black Arabian kept his pace. He had planned to give her the horse as a wedding present. Just the thought caused Carter to grow angrier as he spurred his horse on. Meredith was relieved when they finally stopped. The horses were hot and sweaty. She climbed down and sat on the grass under a tall oak tree.

When Carter sat beside her, she asked, "Do you always run your horses so hard?"

Carter shrugged his shoulders and looked off into the distance. His turbulent emotions were festering inside. When his father had told him of Miss Stanton's comments the night before, Carter had been adamant that Agatha was lying. He wouldn't allow himself to believe that he had been fooled into loving someone with a tainted reputation. His father reminded him of Agatha's excellent background and the fact that she had nothing to gain from her revelation. It wasn't like she had a daughter waiting in line for Carter to marry.

One moment Carter had been sure Meredith was pure and nothing or no one could change his mind. The next moment he would remember how uncomfortable Meredith had seemed when she saw Agatha. Was she hiding something? Was he being betrayed and deceived? If so, he would be thought a fool in the community—and the thought of such a thing stiffened his resolve.

"Carter? Carter?" Meredith called his name softly.

As Carter turned he couldn't help but admire her beauty. She was indeed lovely. Meredith placed her hand on his cheek and he kissed it. He leaned forward and kissed her lips, then pulled away quickly as negative thoughts pierced his mind and altered his heart.

"Carter, something is bothering you. Won't you discuss it with me it?" she asked.

Meredith saw his cheeks flush. He sighed, "Unfortunately truth is like an elusive butterfly. Just when you think you've caught it, it seems to fly away."

Now Meredith was becoming agitated. "You're talking in circles and acting very peculiar. I'm afraid if you don't stop, I'll have to ask you to take me back to the house."

Carter stared intently into Meredith's face and asked, "Are honor and dignity important to you?"

"Of course they are. Honor and dignity are everything. Why do you ask?"

Carter looked puzzled, then seemed to come to a resolution. Perhaps there was only one way to find out. He leaned over and kissed Meredith again. At first he was gentle, but quickly became more passionate. Meredith kissed him back, thinking her response was appropriate, since he was her intended. Carter thought her warm response was the proof he was looking for. He placed his hand on her shoulder and then began to slowly move it down. When it slid across her bosom, Meredith attempted to pull away.

"Carter, stop. This is not right!"

"Don't you like it, my love?" Carter whispered.

Meredith frowned as she tried to push him away. "Please stop, Carter. I don't want this!"

But Carter didn't stop. Instead, he continued with more force. "Why are you playing this cat-and-mouse game, my dear? You know it's what you want."

Meredith tried to push him away with all her might, but he was too strong. She screamed but no one heard her calls of desperation. Meredith sobbed as he tore at her clothing. He was like a madman. When it was over, Carter stood up to readjust his clothing. As he did so, he saw the blood of her purity staining her white petticoat. He covered his mouth in shame.

"Oh no!" he cried out.

Meredith lay on her side sobbing into the grass. Carter continued to back up until he was beside his horse. He hoisted himself up and thundered up the grassy knoll. Meredith pulled her clothes together, mounted her horse, and began riding back to the stables. She couldn't see through the tears that were pouring from her eyes. Charlie saw her coming at a distance. He could tell she was in trouble. He ran out to meet her, and she fell off the horse into his arms.

Meredith looked up at Charlie with pain-filled eyes and pleaded, "Please, Charlie, don't let anyone see me like this."

Charlie's heart sank as he realized what had happened, "Oh, sweet Jesus, have mercy," he murmured under his breath. He led Meredith to the barn and got her settled in the hay. She asked him to send for Diane. As she entered the stable, Diane saw Meredith sobbing in the hay with her clothing torn. She pulled down an old horse blanket from the fence and covered her. Meredith could hardly talk as she gasped for air. It didn't take long for Diane to figure out what had taken place. She looked at the stablehand and directed, "Get our driver and have our carriage brought now. We're leaving."

Meanwhile, as he rested in the shade, Jerris saw Carter riding across a ridge in the distance. He knew something was wrong when he didn't see Meredith with him. He quickly mounted his horse and began to pursue Carter. He called to him as he got closer, yelling at him to stop. Carter saw Jerris behind him but kicked his horse to go faster. Jerris could see they were approaching a patch of trees. As Carter turned again to look over his shoulder, a low-hanging limb struck him on the head and knocked him from his horse.

Jerris dropped from his mount and ran to where his brother lay. He gently lifted his head and whispered his name. Carter opened his eyes slightly and struggled to speak. Jerris put his ear next to his brother's mouth in time to hear him say, "She is innocent."

Carter closed his eyes, and Jerris struggled to lift him to his horse. He knew his injuries were serious and that he urgently had to get him back to the house. Jerris saw Meredith's carriage pull off as he came into a clearing near the stables, but he was too stunned to try to figure out what had happened.

Jack mounted Fury and raced down the road while Diane stood on their porch, feeling as if the world had come to an end. She had tried to stop her husband from going to the Hunter Estate until he'd had time to calm down. He had told her that he was going to kill Carter, and she knew his life would also be in danger.

"Why did this terrible thing happen?" Diane whispered, knowing there would be no reply to her question.

Jack stopped only once to rest his horse before he pressed on to the Hunter Plantation. When he reined the animal to a halt in front of the mansion, dismounted, and ran up the stairs, the butler opened the door as if he had been expecting him. He didn't say anything, just extended his hand in the direction of the parlor. Jack brushed past him and saw Solomon Hunter seated, staring at the cold, unlit fireplace. He didn't attempt to get up.

Jack demanded, "Where is Carter?"

"He's not here."

"Where is he?"

Solomon lifted his weary eyes and exhaled. "He's dead. He fell from his horse."

Jack sat in the chair across from the grieving father. He stared at the floor in disbelief. "I . . . I don't know what to say."

Solomon thought to himself, *Jack rode all this way to inquire as to why Carter broke the engagement with Meredith. But there is no reason to bring up his daughter's spotted reputation—it won't change anything now. My son is gone.*

The silence between the two men became deafening. Solomon finally said, "You've come a long way, please let me get you something to drink."

Jack had brought his own assumptions and thought, *Solomon knows his son violated my daughter, but I can't bring myself to rail against Carter at a time like this. In any case, justice has been served.*

Solomon raised his hand to motion for the butler but Jack interrupted, "No, no, that's quite all right. I'm fine."

Jack's anger had been appeased. Politely excusing himself, he said, "I want to return home as soon as possible, so I'll take my leave now."

Solomon nodded mutely as Jack left the room.

Later that day Jerris tried to get his father to talk about what had precipitated Carter's wild, fatal ride on his horse.

His father stared at the wall, not appearing to direct his comments to anyone in particular. "Carter decided the night before his death to break off his engagement to Meredith."

"But whatever for, Father?"

"I don't want to talk about it."

Jerris raised his voice, "You must tell me! I have a right to know!"

His father did not reply, and Jerris was bewildered. *Why would Carter end his relationship with Meredith? Carter had always had a way with women, and there had been many of them in his life. But Meredith was different. He had really seemed to love her....* After much reflection, Jerris concluded that Carter had gotten cold feet over the thought of marriage. It hadn't been Meredith's fault and that is why he had said "she is innocent."

Since Solomon hadn't been willing to discuss the situation with his remaining son, Jerris did not relay Carter's final words to his father.

One month later

When Tilly received Meredith's letter, she couldn't wait to devour its contents. She read it through the first time, then reread it over and over again, hoping her eyes were playing tricks on her. When the reality of what had taken place sank in, she wept as if the tragedy had happened to her. Months earlier, she'd felt as if she'd been at the ball with her friend when Meredith had sketched a picture of her and Carter dancing. Tilly had propped it up on her dresser so she could see it first thing when she woke up in the morning. Meredith ended her letter with,

There were no clouds in the sky today and I understand why. The dream I had was just a vapor and is forever gone.

Four weeks had passed since Jack returned home from his encounter with Solomon. The house, which had once been filled with laughter, was solemn and still. Joy had died and now sorrow mourned its passing. The first morning after her return home, Meredith had awakened with a desperate plea that everything she had just experienced was simply a cruel trick of a nightmarish imagination.

But as soon as her mind was clear, she tasted a bitterness which only reality could concoct. Every day Meredith remained secluded in her bedroom, refusing to see anyone. Patience grew terribly alarmed because Meredith was barely touching her food. Anyone could see that her beautiful mistress was gradually wasting away.

"Mis' Meredith," she would beg, "if ya don' git up outta dis room, ya gonna jes' fade away. Den whut would Bertha say?"

But nothing seemed to matter. Meredith's only company was the canvas, paint, and brushes that she kept with her. Not even Diane could penetrate her pain.

It was the beginning of summer, and the estate was in full bloom. The family had just returned from church one Sunday when they found Jerris Hunter waiting in the parlor. Jack felt his anger rising when he saw him.

"Why are you here?" he demanded.

Meredith spoke up for the first time in weeks. "Father, please. He's come a long way and suffers as we all do. Please, Jerris, have a seat and I'll have Henry bring us some tea."

After a few moments of informal conversation, Jerris asked, "Meredith, I wonder if I might speak to you alone."

Her father leaned forward, ready to refuse, but Diane stood and extended her hand to him. The look in her eyes calmed him, and they left the room. Jerris put his teacup down and turned toward Meredith. He could hardly believe this was the same young lady. When he last saw her, she'd looked like a ray of sunshine. Now her radiant glow had been extinguished. Her eyes were shadowed from too many sleepless nights, and she looked considerably thinner.

Jerris spoke gently, "Meredith, I came to express my sorrow for what you have been through. I would have come sooner but grief over my brother's death prevented it."

Wringing her hands nervously, Meredith nodded slowly.

"I'm sorry for my brother's decision. I came here because I want you to know how much I respect and honor you."

Meredith looked at Jerris forlornly and asked, "And will you honor the child I carry in my womb?"

Jerris sat frozen. He heard the words but they didn't make sense. He questioned, "What are you saying?"

Looking confused, Meredith stated, "I am pregnant with your brother's child. A child was conceived when he violated me—the same day he had the accident."

There was only silence as Jerris stood and stared at Meredith. A dumbfounded look settled on his flushed face.

Meredith questioned, "You didn't know?"

Jerris shook his head.

"I'm so sorry," was all Meredith could say as she cast her eyes out the window, fixing them on the distant horizon.

Jerris inquired, "Does your father know what my brother did to you?"

Meredith did not respond.

"Does your father know about the child?" he repeated.

"What?" she said. His voice had finally penetrated her maze of bewilderment. Shaking her head, Meredith responded, "It was only recently that I became sure."

Jerris was overwhelmed by this shocking revelation. He apologized for leaving so quickly, but Meredith's news had caught him off guard and he needed time to think. He left in a hurry.

≈ ≈ ≈

Tilly made her way down the busy Chicago street, not looking to the right or left. Any remaining energy she had would be used to get home. Every muscle in her body ached from her long hours of study and from working on the weekends with Nurse Taylor.

Directly in front of her Tilly noticed that a large gathering had formed on a street corner. As she came closer, she heard a man's voice speaking loudly and emphatically above the murmur of the crowd. The rhythm in which he spoke and the response of the gathering told Tilly that he was a street preacher. Such men seemed to appear from time to time all over the city—but especially in the colored community. She could barely see the top of his head. A woman turned to her with excitement and said, "Dat man's a silver-tongued devil, yes he is!"

Tilly briefly wondered why folks used that expression when referring to a minister who spoke well. The woman's comment, however, made Tilly's ears perk up. What was immediately evident was the preacher's eloquence. This was a learned man. She continued making her way through the throng. Tilly was almost out of earshot when she heard the minister say, "I'm telling you God will never leave you or forsake you. Or as my mother used to say, "God is always by ya side!" The crowd laughed as he used the slave colloquialism.

Tilly stopped and slowly turned around, walking toward the preacher's voice. She was much too short to see him. By then, he had come to the end of his sermon and was asking people to come forward if they wanted to experience a personal relationship with God. Shortly thereafter the crowd began to disperse. The preacher's back was to Tilly as he shook a number of hands.

"God bless you, brother," she heard him say.

Tilly said it softly at first and then spoke more boldly. "Adam?"

Adam turned around and looked down at the small woman who had placed herself in front of him.

"Tilly?" he said almost inaudibly. Then with a loud shout he said, "Tilly Douglas!"

Adam picked Tilly up and kissed her on the cheek. Tilly started laughing, aware that people were watching the sophisticated preacher hoisting a small lady into the air. When he put her down, he marveled that she was more beautiful than he had remembered. Two dimples punctuated her irresistible smile, and her large, penetrating, brown eyes reflected the joy of seeing him. Tilly's navy blue dress with a white collar accentuated her slender form.

Tilly thought Adam looked as if a thousand candles had been lit around his face. She wondered if it was possible for anyone to look happier. He began rambling so fast Tilly could hardly understand what he was saying. All she knew was that he was leading her in a direction away from her apartment. Soon they found themselves at a tiny diner not far from where Adam had preached. He pulled out a chair for her and asked for two sodas. Tilly piled her books on the table and removed her coat. Adam started talking, and she couldn't get a word in edgewise.

"My word!" Tilly finally announced. "Are you the same person I saw leave in the wagon? The one who had trouble putting two words together at one time?"

Adam laughed and replied, "No, I'm not the same person. Thanks to you, Tilly. It was you who taught me how to read and gave me a love for words. When you read out loud a whole new world opened up before my eyes. I promised myself that one day I'd be just like you, and now here I am."

Now it was Tilly's turn to chuckle. "Well, you're not just like me because I wouldn't be caught dead standing on a street corner yelling that Bible-talk at people."

Adam smiled and said it was called preaching.

"Tilly, you're a part of every sermon I give. You cross my mind each time I prepare to speak because it was you who gave me my thirst for knowledge."

Time flew by as Tilly and Adam caught up on old times. She thought about how he was like the brother she'd never had and how precious his friendship was to her. When Tilly looked up at the clock on the wall, she realized that two hours had passed.

There was much more to talk about, but she hurriedly put her things together and stood to leave. She knew Nurse Taylor would be worried.

Adam walked her to the corner and explained that he'd have to leave to meet his ride. He was traveling to a city six hours away. In the days to come, he would be running a revival in four cities and wouldn't be returning for three months. He asked Tilly if he could visit her when he came back to town. Tilly nodded and Adam began to cross the street. Then it appeared he'd forgotten something because he dashed back to her side. "I've been wondering all these years," he smiled, "did you keep the sun in your heart?"

Tilly's face broke into a wide grin. "On many, many nights it was the only thing that kept me warm."

Adam replied, "Well, one day I might want it back."

Tilly waved until he was out of sight and then headed for home. She thought about his parting statement; she had no idea what he meant.

Mr. Hunter was sitting in the garden when Jerris found him.

"Father," he announced, "I've just returned from seeing Meredith."

Jerris' father set his glass of lemonade firmly on the table and shouted, "Whatever for?"

"I went to pay my respects for the grief she must be suffering over the loss of Carter."

His father was visibly upset. He derided Jerris for going without talking to him first. Jerris pointed out that he had been trying to hold conversations with him for weeks, but his father had been closed and withdrawn. As Solomon continued with his criticism of his son's actions, Jerris interrupted. "She is with child."

Not appearing shocked Solomon replied, "I'm sorry to hear that. Who is the father?"

"Surely you jest, father. Why would you ask that question?"

When Solomon went on to explain the comments made by Agatha Stanton, Jerris was noticeably confused. He had been there the night Carter had alluded to the bedroom in Meredith's presence, and he still recalled that she had blushed as deeply as a fully ripened cherry.

"Father, I didn't tell you this because it didn't make sense at the time, but Carter said something when he fell from his horse."

"What was that?"

"He said, 'She is innocent.'"

Jerris' father waved his hand and said, "Oh, for goodness sake, Jerris, are you going to believe your brother, who was almost unconscious at the time? He refused to believe what Agatha said the night I told him. He was convinced Meredith was pure. Are you going to believe your brother, who was blindly in love, or are you going to believe a respected woman in the community?"

Jerris sat in his chair and tapped his foot rapidly on the floor. His father continued asking questions that Jerris could not answer. "Why didn't Meredith come to the house after it happened? Why did she dash away in her carriage?"

Solomon began supplying the answers to his questions. "She left in a tizzy because she was upset after Carter broke off the engagement."

Then Jerris suddenly exclaimed, "Charlie!"

"What about Charlie?"

Jerris went on to explain that before Meredith left in the carriage she would have had to bring her horse back. The stable man would have been the last to see her.

Solomon had his butler summon Charlie, who nervously came in with his hat in his hand. He smiled at Jerris and looked startled when Solomon called his name.

"Charlie, did you see Miss Douglas the day Carter died—when she had returned to the barn?"

Charlie recounted how he had run out to meet her and how she had collapsed in his arms.

"Was she hurt?" Mr. Hunter asked.

"I'm not sure, suh. She seemed mo' scared and shamed."

Solomon asked what he meant, and Charlie told him that Meredith had asked him not to let anyone see her in the condition she was in.

Sighing, Solomon stated, "The shame of breaking off the engagement was too great for her. That will be all, Charlie."

Charlie was leaving, but then turned back around.

"Mr. Hunter, suh."

"Yes?"

"There was blood on her dress."

Charlie left and Solomon's face drained of its color. He said to Jerris, "Oh no! What have I done?"

Jerris responded, "I can't speak for what you've done, Father. But I know what I must do."

"No, I will not!" shouted Meredith. "And you can't make me!"

Meredith's father left his chair and knelt down in front of her as she sobbed into her hands. He looked up at Jerris and then back down to his broken daughter.

"Meredith, listen to me. We can't make this go away. I know you are crushed, but we have to consider the baby. It will be born out of wedlock and branded illegitimate and an outcast. The baby will be disgraced unless you accept Jerris' proposal of marriage."

Meredith jumped to her feet and faced Jerris, who was standing next to the bookcase.

"But I don't love you!" she exclaimed.

Jerris responded softly and in earnest, "Nor I you, Meredith. But out of respect to my brother's memory, and for the baby's namesake, I promise to provide for you and the child. I offer you my friendship."

Meredith dropped into the chair shaking her head from side to side in vehement objection.

Jerris looked at her father, "I will be staying in town and will call tomorrow for an answer. He looked tenderly toward Meredith and said, "I'm so very sorry."

Tilly tossed a piece of bread to a pigeon as she and Adam walked through the park. It had rained during the night, and the air was fresh and sweet. Tilly breathed in deeply and exhaled the air as if expelling a great burden. She caught herself and then began to giggle.

"What?" asked Adam

"I know it's been years, but sometimes I still think about how wonderful it is to walk without being worried that someone is going to capture us. I guess I'll never forget the feeling of being chased at gunpoint."

Adam nodded. He removed his handkerchief and wiped the bench clear of the accumulated water from the night before. Tilly sat forward on the end of her seat with both hands at her side and rocked back and forth.

"Sit back, Tilly, you're making me nervous." Adam smiled.

Tilly noted in passing that this was the same bench she and Rose had sat on the day Rose had become ill. Because of their work schedules and inadequate transportation, she had seen Rose only a couple of times after her bout with fever. And now Rose had gotten married and moved to Cleveland. She reckoned she'd never see her again.

Tilly rested her back against the bench and looked at Adam, who had grown much taller but still had the same sweet face. His almond-shaped eyes were almost black, but with the sun shining directly on them Tilly could see small specks of brown. His skin was a smooth, dark brown and his nose was gentle yet strong. His countenance was one of confidence; his smile was absolutely captivating. Tilly thought he would make someone a wonderful husband.

"What are you thinking?" Adam questioned.

Tilly looked thoughtful and replied, "How you grew up to be quite a handsome young man, and you'll probably make some woman a great husband. Did I tell you about Catherine? She's in my nursing-school class. When you get back, I'd like you to meet her."

A slight frown creased Adam's brow and he chuckled nervously. He cleared his throat and said, "I see."

Tilly began chattering and the two of them had covered a myriad of subjects before they returned home. When she was with Adam, Tilly always felt her old self coming back to life. She was free to laugh and cry, joke and cajole. She read Meri's letters to Adam, except for the most recent one, and they sometimes reminisced about their journey to freedom. It saddened Tilly when she discovered that Adam's mother, Ruby, had passed away the year before. Adam said her heart just seemed to give out one day. As they walked back toward her apartment, Adam told Tilly he would be leaving again for several months but would like to see her when he returned.

"Come anytime, Adam. My schooling is almost over, and once I'm done I will probably become utterly consumed with helping Nurse Taylor. But you know I'll always try to make room for you."

Adam stopped walking and looked at Tilly. "Maybe one day I'll come back and never leave."

Tilly grinned and said, "Well, that would be wonderful Adam. You travel considerably too much, and it would be good for you to stay in one place."

Adam threw his head back and looked at the sky. He sighed. Then he touched Tilly on the cheek and left.

Pastor Duncan's voice rose and lowered monotonously as he performed the marriage ceremony in the study. Jack and Diane looked on while Meredith stared out the window into the garden and Jerris stood perfectly erect like a soldier reporting for duty. Shortly afterward, Meredith entered her carriage for the ride to the Hunter estate. She wished they were on the way to her funeral, for it seemed the only thing alive inside her was the child she carried in her womb.

Her father stood nervously beside the transport with a book in his hand.

"Meredith," he haltingly said, "I'm not sure I should give this to you . . . but it was your mother's request that I do so. She wanted me to present it to you on your wedding day."

Meredith reached out and took the white book. A glance at the front cover told her it was a Bible. The inscription on the first page said,

> Dear Meredith,
>
> Everything you need to know about life is contained in this book.
>
> Love forever, Mom

Meredith held the small Bible close to her chest as the driver slapped the reins on the back of the horses and they began their journey to her new home.

Solomon waited for the door to open then entered quickly. The maid ushered him into the parlor where Agatha was seated. From the look on his face she sensed that something was very wrong. Nonetheless, Agatha was ever so gracious, stating how honored she was to have Mr. Hunter stop by for a visit. Her nervousness was well disguised, except for the slight shakiness of her hands as she poured two cups of tea.

Not bothering to pick up his teacup, Solomon immediately stated, "Miss Stanton, because of some unusual circumstances it has become clear to me that the statement you made concerning Meredith Douglas at the ball was false. I wonder if you might tell me where such a rumor began?"

"My dear Mr. Hunter, does anyone ever know where rumors begin? One credible person tells another and it finally gets to you. Tell me, just how do you know it was untrue?"

"That is neither here nor there. However, it has come to my understanding that you were once engaged to Jack Douglas and that he broke the engagement."

His comment caused Agatha's seething anger to turn her face a fiery red. With great effort, she calmly tried to explain that it was she who had ended the engagement, not Jack. Then she asked Solomon if he would mind getting to the point of why he came.

"I've been doing some checking, Miss Stanton, and it appears to me that you purposely and maliciously lied about Meredith's reputation in a vengeful attempt to get back at her father. Your lie cost me a great deal. If it wouldn't disgrace my family and I had my way, I'd probably kill you. But the very least I can do is make sure you die a poor and lonely woman. I have spoken to my cousin, who was considering proposing to you at Christmas. Your chance of marrying that very well-to-do gentleman is hereby destroyed. I will also see that your name is removed from every social calendar this side of the Mississippi."

Agatha sipped her tea and calmly replied, "Is that all, Mr. Hunter?"

Solomon stood and looked at her in disgust. As he walked toward the door, Agatha asked, "By the way, when Meredith has her baby you will name it Carter, won't you?"

Agatha wasn't sure her assumption was right. But the look on Solomon's face when he spun around confirmed her suspicions: *Why else would Jerris marry Meredith only six weeks after Carter's death? And why else would Meredith marry such a boring man?*

Solomon stormed out of Agatha's house and settled into his carriage. Agatha's maid heard her mistress begin to laugh a little, and then more and more until it sounded as if she was hysterical. At last Agatha shouted, "It was worth it, Jack Douglas!"

The maid pretended not to notice Agatha's anguish and went about her work in another room.

12

With the Emancipation Proclamation in effect and the Civil War over, many of the slaves fled the plantation. But Patience chose to stay on with the Douglases. When she had been assigned to Meredith years before after Tilly's departure, Patience had seemed scared of her own shadow, always afraid she'd say something wrong. But gradually, Meredith's kind ways had put her at ease, and she now delighted in serving her.

Patience remembered the day Cory left. Master Jack had pleaded with him to stay and had even given him a piece of paper deeding him five acres of land. Cory had briefly looked at the paper, which of course he couldn't read, and had let it slip from his hand to the floor. Afterward Cory had glared at Master Jack with deep hatred and stalked out the door. Patience recalled Master Jack looking at Meredith and saying, "Your mother was right—I should have done this long ago."

At first it seemed the Douglases would lose their home, but Edward Franks came to the rescue and bailed the plantation out. His investments in Europe had paid off enormously. Over the years, things had gradually stabilized until Jack was able to get back on his feet.

But now Meredith was leaving her father's home for good, and Patience was going with her. Meredith looked sadly out the coach's window as she approached Jerris' home. It was just a ten-minute ride from the huge Hunter estate. The mansion could be seen over the tops of the trees through Meredith's second-story bedroom window. One look at it, and she decided to keep the shutters closed.

Jerris' servants were waiting in a line when Meredith's carriage arrived. Selina, his head housekeeper, and her staff flanked Clyde, the butler. Clyde opened the door and assisted Meredith out of the coach. "Good day, Mrs. Hunter. We are honored to serve you."

They all greeted Meredith very warmly but looked at each other nervously as she walked up the stairs. Their master had never so much as mentioned a lady's name in all their years of working for him. Now suddenly he was married. They dared not ask any questions but they had some ideas of their own. No one down at the stable could get Charlie to talk. He was a private man, very faithful to Jerris, who had always been his favorite. The others knew that Meredith had once been engaged to Carter and now she was Jerris' wife. Anything else was sheer conjecture.

The staff worried at first how the new lady of the house would treat them. They had heard a few horror stories but soon discovered that their concerns were unfounded. First of all, they seldom saw her. She ate most of her meals in her own bedroom, which was across the hall from Jerris'. They saw her go for long walks every day, always with sketch pad and pen in hand. Months passed, and the only one who heard her speak was Patience. Meredith declined every invitation from the Hunter estate. Meanwhile, Solomon was too ashamed to face her, so he never darkened Jerris' door.

Seven months later

There were eight other girls graduating with Tilly on that cold winter day. It had snowed all night, and the city was blanketed with a rich, white covering. Refreshments were set up in the back of the room, and Tilly's instructor gave a speech before she handed out the certificates. When Tilly's name was called, she went up to receive her certificate. As she was returning to her seat, she saw Adam standing in the doorway. He flashed his heart-warming smile and gave a salute. The girls in Tilly's class began to giggle, but from the look in their eyes Adam met with their full approval.

After the ceremony Tilly motioned for Adam to come forward. "Catherine, this is Adam Jensen. Adam, this is Catherine, the smartest girl in the class—and the most beautiful, I might add."

Catherine was clearly embarrassed. Adam shifted nervously, but Tilly didn't seem to notice. She continued introducing him to all her classmates. Tilly had told Catherine she knew someone who would make a perfect husband, and it didn't take long for Catherine to agree. As the group feasted on the graduation snacks, Adam ushered Tilly to a desk in the corner.

"Tilly, I'm so proud of you. You'll make a tremendous nurse one day. Getting your certificate as a nurse's assistant puts you one step closer. Your compassionate heart will bring comfort to many."

"Oh, Adam, I can hardly believe I've graduated. It is a dream come true!"

"I understand. I've recently had a dream come true myself. But, if you don't mind waiting for me to tell you about it, I'll wait and share it over dinner," Adam said.

Soon they were trudging through the snow to a fancy place where well-to-do colored people socialized. As they waited for their meals to arrive, Adam reached over and placed his hand on top of Tilly's.

"Tilly, I'm going away again, and it will be a long time before I return."

Tilly pulled her hand away and asked, "Where are you going?"

"I'm going to Africa—"

"Africa!" Tilly said the word so loudly that several people in the restaurant turned to look at them.

Adam grinned. "Yes, Tilly. Africa. And I want you to come with me. Our group is going back to Africa to serve as missionaries in

Liberia. A nurse would be a big plus on our team. I understand there are many medical needs."

It took Tilly a long time to respond. She waited until the news fully sank in and then reminded Adam, "Well, you know there is also a great demand for medical attention in Chicago."

I know that, Tilly. But wouldn't you like to return to your homeland? It was you who gave me my first interest in the African continent with your tales about Na-Na."

Tilly didn't want to admit it, but her heart pounded at the thought of actually going to Africa. She quickly dismissed the idea when she thought of how much Nurse Taylor was counting on her to use her training to help her.

"Tilly, I know this is a shock, but I'll be leaving in six weeks and I wanted to give you time to think about it. Don't worry about the money for your passage. It will be taken care of."

"How can that be? Who would do that? It must cost a fortune!"

As Adam flashed his contagious smile, Tilly shook her head emphatically. "Adam, I would not allow you to use your money to pay for the trip. There is no way to know what the future holds, and you might need the money to start a church or get married."

Adam insisted that had it not been for Tilly, he would be working in the steel mill for little or nothing, and then only if he'd been able to find a job. He went on to say, "I owe you a great debt, and this is just a small way to return your kindness."

When Adam took Tilly home that evening, she was adamant that going to Africa was out of the question. But she was careful to let Adam know how much she appreciated his invitation and his gesture to pay her way there.

"Six weeks, Tilly. Don't make up your mind now. Pray about it." These were Adam's parting words.

Tilly thought, *Pray about it? Who would I pray to? and why would anyone listen? If prayer worked, my mother wouldn't be dead, and I wouldn't be miles away from Meri and Rose.* But as she closed the door, her mind started to race in what seemed to be a hundred different directions. She tried to quiet her thoughts, but it seemed she was no longer in control of them. Before she fell asleep, she decided to talk with Nurse Taylor about Adam's offer. Nurse Taylor would give her all the appropriate reasons not to go, thus providing the support Tilly so desperately needed to silence her anxious heart.

Jerris saw Meredith sitting on the enclosed verandah overlooking the stream that ran past the house. Even the cold weather outside could not obscure the beauty of the countryside. By this time she was heavy with child, and it was clear that within a matter of weeks they would be holding a baby.

He had seen very little of Meredith. If it hadn't been for the sight of Patience walking through the house, it would have seemed as if she had never come to live there. So it was an unexpected pleasure to see her sunning herself on the porch.

As Jerris took a seat across from Meredith, Clyde brought them tea on a silver oriental platter. After it was poured and they had taken a few sips, Meredith sighed and looked as if she was hoping some words would escape her lips and rescue her from her ambivalence.

Finally she looked up at Jerris and said, "Thank you, Jerris. I know I've seemed totally ungrateful, but I'm not. What you did was a very noble thing. It's just that I was hurting so badly at first that I couldn't appreciate the sacrifice you made."

Jerris didn't know what to say. He just nodded his head and looked out at the bubbling stream.

"On the day you proposed marriage," Meredith went on, "you said your desire was to give the child a name, and you have done that. But you also said you would be my friend. I hope that offer still stands."

Jerris assured her it did. And on that cold winter's morning, Jerris and Meredith began to talk, not about anything in particular, but about many things in general. Jerris reawakened her mind to her love for reading and poetry. Before he left the house, he brought her a book he had recently finished, and Meredith spent the rest of day enjoying it.

Three weeks later, on February 1, 1869, Jackson Solomon Hunter made his entrance into the world. Meredith was in labor for twenty-four hours, and there were times she didn't think she'd make it. Patience refused to leave Meredith's side even for a moment. Her constant encouraging words helped usher in little Jackson. It was hard for Meredith to imagine that she could go through such pain and still live. Yet, at the sight of her newborn son, all the agony was forgotten.

Jackson was named after both of his grandfathers, but everyone said he looked just like Mr. Hunter. The dark-brown hair and eyes were evident at his birth. Jerris stood next to the bed as Meredith looked down at the baby. Her face was still flushed from the trauma of birth. Jerris thought she had never looked more beautiful.

Jerris' father and mother had finally made an appearance, commenting upon, among other things, how long the baby's fingers were. Solomon tried to maintain his composure as joy and pain mingled in his heart. He marveled at the baby, thinking it was as if God was giving him a second chance. His wife's illness had continued to worsen, so she'd had no idea what had happened nine months before. For the first time Solomon was grateful for her memory loss. When Meredith didn't visit the estate, he had continued to make excuses for her. Both the excuses and the absences were quickly and mercifully forgotten.

Meredith smiled and looked at her father, who was seated on the bed facing her. Diane stood behind him with her hand on his shoulder. Both of them prayed that this would be the beginning of Meredith's healing and that her life would still be full of many happy years.

Fortunately that had already begun when she and Jerris began taking their long walks. It was during that time that he filled Meredith in on the details of what had happened on that unfortunate day, and how Agatha Stanton had been the culprit. When Meredith wrote Tilly that evening she concluded by saying,

I thought I had gotten away with stealing Agatha's dream, but she in turn stole mine. I was reading a Scripture that says when you "sow the wind, you reap a whirlwind." I'm beginning to be grateful that I was not utterly destroyed. When I felt the baby move inside me, I realized that Carter would always be with me. She wasn't able to take that away.

The next day, as Meredith and Jerris enjoyed some quiet time by the fire in the parlor, Meredith said, "I've been thinking, Jerris. I believe it's important that the baby not know that Carter was his father. It would cause unnecessary pain and, after all, the only people who know the truth wouldn't have any reason to mention it.

Tilly planned to tell Nurse Taylor about Adam's offer the next day, but she couldn't bring herself to do so. Finally the wise nurse asked her young assistant what was wrong.

"What do you mean?" Tilly innocently answered.

Nurse Taylor responded, "You've been as nervous as a June bug on a hot summer day."

Tilly could no longer hide her agitation. She asked her friend to sit down so they could talk. Nurse Taylor sat in her favorite chair, which was worn in several places but had been covered with a white sheet tucked in around the edges. Tilly sat in her favorite position on the floor, her legs crossed.

Taking a deep breath Tilly started. "Adam is going to Africa, and he has asked me to go along to assist with medical needs." She quickly added, "I told him I couldn't go because there were too many needy people here, but . . . "

Tilly looked in Nurse Taylor's eyes for a reaction. She didn't get one. Tilly talked until she couldn't think of anything else to say. Nurse Taylor got up from her chair and headed toward her bedroom.

Tilly called out, "Where are you going? Aren't you going to say anything?"

Responding without turning around, Nurse Taylor answered, "I'm going to pray about it. Then we'll talk."

A whole week passed and Nurse Taylor didn't utter a word about Tilly's concern. It didn't matter, however, because Tilly had decided she wasn't going anyway. Nurse Taylor had done too much for her; she wasn't about to leave her alone to care for the elderly, sick, and dying colored people in Chicago.

Tilly had just gotten in bed one night when Nurse Taylor entered her room. It was dark, but Tilly could see her silhouette in the doorway.

"Tilly, I talked to the Lord. I tried my best not to tell Him what I thought. It's a good thing, too, because He wants you to go."

Without waiting for a response, Nurse Taylor closed Tilly's bedroom door. Tilly could hear the old house slippers shuffling across the floor as Nurse Taylor made her way to her room. Tilly lay on her back and stared at the pitch-black darkness. Stories her mother told her of Africa began to overwhelm her. An African melody she'd often heard her mother humming was caught up in her heart. But just as if someone had slammed a cabinet shut, the pictures and music stopped when she remembered her decision not to go. She'd talk to Nurse Taylor in the morning.

Their day started before the sun came up. The list of people Nurse Taylor and Tilly were to see was long, but beating the sun up made it seem like twice as much would get done. Their first stop was quite a distance away, and riding their bicycles helped them arrive faster. When Nurse Taylor and Tilly stopped to eat their lunch, Tilly took the opportunity to broach the subject.

"Nurse Taylor, I want you to know that my desire is not to go to Africa but to stay with you."

Nurse Taylor put the remains of her lunch back in the sack and looked at Tilly. "God told me to send you to nursing school and I did. I thought I knew why He wanted you to go—that He was sending me some help. But I was wrong. He wants you in Africa."

"How can you be so sure it is God telling you that?" Tilly asked.

Wiping her mouth with a napkin, Nurse Taylor replied, "Since I don't want you to go, Tilly, there must be someone else speaking inside of me. Now I know the devil can imitate God's voice. But I've discovered, if you give Him time, the Lord will confirm if He's the one speaking. And that is how I know it is God."

When Tilly continued to resist, Nurse Taylor stated, "Even when you don't understand, Tilly, you can expect to be blessed when you obey God's will for your life. I haven't spoken to you much about God because I know you're mad at Him for taking your momma. But believe me, He's real. I just pray that one day you'll come to know Him for yourself."

Tilly huffed, "Well, I don't know why He just doesn't tell me Himself!"

"Oh, I'm sure He's tried. But the deaf can't hear even when they want to. You're just gonna have to trust me, Tilly."

When Nurse Taylor made that last statement, Tilly remembered that she had long ago decided to put her faith in Nurse Taylor. And so, against her will, she reluctantly decided she would go with Adam to Africa.

Meredith was sketching the baby as he slept. Winter was easing its hold on the land as they entered the month of March, but it wasn't going without a fight. A fierce rain driven by the wind was pounding against the window in the study. The flames from the fireplace cast a soft light across Jackson's face, like the brush of an angel's wings. The thought inspired her to draw an angel behind the bassinet keeping a gentle but watchful eye over her precious baby.

Jerris stood unnoticed in the doorway, not wanting to disturb the scene. Meredith was humming a tune. He tried to hum along, and when she saw him standing there she started to chuckle.

"I've never heard that tune before."

Meredith smiled at him affectionately. "I made it up with a friend."

"Tilly?" he asked.

Meredith stopped sketching and smiled. "Yes, Tilly." At first, she wondered how he had heard of her long-lost friend, but then assumed he'd had a conversation with Diane.

"Do you think about her often?" Jerris asked.

"Every day."

That evening after dinner Jerris asked Meredith to tell him about her relationship with Tilly. When the clock chimed nine times she realized how long she had talked. Jerris had encouraged her to continue by asking questions, seeming to hang on to every word. At one point, Meredith excused herself and returned with a box of letters. Jerris was amazed by what Tilly wrote, and he acknowledged her exceptional poetry skills. He found the entire story fascinating.

"You have stimulated something in me, Meredith. I look forward to the next time I'm with Charlie. I wonder if he would tell me about his past."

Charlie had been with the Hunter family before Jerris was born and had taught him how to ride horses. Jerris had thought, on occasion, that if the stableman had not been colored, he would have been considered a master horseman. And if the truth were told, there were very few people he enjoyed talking to as much as Charlie—the character of the man was so great.

When Jerris turned in for the night, he was grateful that Meredith had challenged him to see deeper than color. And when Meredith retired for the night, there was an unusual peace in her soul. She had accepted the fact that she would never again experience the excitement of romance. But somehow she was becoming content with the genuine friendship she had begun to share with Jerris. For some reason, it even lifted her spirits.

13

Four months later

The harsh Chicago winter had delayed Tilly's departure, and she was grateful for the extra time. One moment she was totally excited about her journey to Africa. The next, she was overcome with doubt and fear. But finally the day had come.

As Nurse Taylor drove the wagon through the bustling streets to the pier, she kept fighting back the tears that were welling up in her eyes. She looked away from Tilly often to hide her obvious distress. She had thought at times how Tilly was like the daughter that she'd never been able to have. Her original intentions had simply been to equip Tilly to become a nurse. At the time the two of them met at Miss Dawson's home, she'd never imagined how deeply she would come to love her.

Tilly caught her breath as they rounded the corner of the pier. Their ship, *Sea Hawk,* was enormous even without its sails unfurled. This was the first time Tilly had been this close to a seagoing vessel. Adam had boasted that the ship was 247 feet from figurehead to stern galley, and 85 feet wide. Her eyes were wide in amazement as she tried to contain her excitement.

Adam stood at the ship's landing looking anxiously to his right then left. It was apparent he was watching for someone. Even though Tilly had assured him the night before that she would be there, he still had his reservations. Nurse Taylor was once again struck by how handsome Adam was, although he seemed quite unaware of it. His focus seemed to be entirely on other people and how he might help them. But Nurse Taylor smiled. Whatever else mattered to him, she knew that, next to God, his main focus was Tilly.

When Adam finally caught sight of their wagon, he began making his way through the crowd. As they came to a stop, he helped Nurse Taylor down, then ran to the other side to assist Tilly.

"You made it!" Adam exclaimed.

"Of course I did! I said I would, didn't I?" Tilly smiled.

Turning to Nurse Taylor, Adam said with enthusiasm, "Isn't the weather beautiful? It's a perfect day to set sail for Africa!"

Nurse Taylor put her hand on top of her hat and tilted her head back to blink into the bright noonday sun. She smiled and nodded in agreement. Two men had already begun taking Tilly's trunk up the plank to the ship. This was not the only ship leaving that day, so the dock was full of arriving and departing passengers and cargo. The *Sea Hawk* was an old but sturdy vessel whose bow wore the scars of having made countless journeys across the Atlantic.

Adam walked over to Tilly and took her hand.

"So how are you doing?" he asked.

"I'm doing fine, I think."

Adam grinned and said they would shortly be underway so it was time they boarded the ship. Tilly looked around to find Nurse Taylor, who was now standing at the back of the wagon. As Tilly approached, Nurse Taylor extended both hands and pulled her close. She wrapped her strong arms around Tilly's tiny frame and began to pray out loud, "Lord, take care of this precious child. Keep her safe and use her to Your glory!"

Then pushing her back and holding Tilly by her shoulders, Nurse Taylor forced a smile and said, "Now, Tilly, I'm not big on goodbyes. I'll watch you walk to the top of that plank, and when you turn around and wave, I'll be leaving. That is how I want to remember you."

Tilly nodded her head and tried to speak, but the words caught in her throat. A stream of tears trickled down her face. She hugged Nurse Taylor again, then walked toward the ship. Adam was standing at the top of the plank encouraging Tilly to hurry. After making her way to where he was, she turned to say one last goodbye. She smiled brightly and, with a broad sweep of both her arms, waved to Nurse Taylor, who returned the wave one last time.

A voice interrupted Tilly's goodbye and said, "We'come 'board, Tilly."

Tilly looked over her shoulder and saw Gus standing in the ship, his hand stretched out to help her down. Panic swept over her, and she looked quickly back toward Nurse Taylor with fear in her eyes. It was too late. Tilly watched the familiar wagon disappearing down the street.

Adam noticed Tilly's reaction and took her arm, asking "Tilly, what's wrong?"

Tilly didn't answer; she just shook her head and stepped down into the ship.

Meredith was sitting in the parlor after dinner when Jerris entered. He walked to the fireplace and put his arm on the mantle. Noticing his demeanor out of the corner of her eye, Meredith put her book down and inquired, "Is something troubling you?"

"Yes, very much so!" Jerris responded and then continued, "My parents have asked for the third time if you and I would join them at their ball next Saturday."

"But this is the first time I've heard anything at all about a ball, Mr. Hunter," Meredith chided.

Jerris admitted that in times past he had simply neglected to mention their invitations because he knew she wouldn't be interested in attending. However, since the baby had arrived, and there seemed to be reconciliation in the relationship between Meredith and his father, they were becoming quite insistent that they come.

Meredith chuckled, and Jerris questioned, "Now what could be so funny about what I just said?"

"It seems to me, my dear Jerris, that I have been a very convenient excuse for you."

At first Jerris looked surprised, but he really couldn't help laughing at himself. "You're right. I hate the thought of going to such boring affairs with all those stuffy people."

"Jerris, I find that to be a contradiction in your nature."

"How so?"

Meredith reminded Jerris of his utter fascination with books and asked him who wrote them. When Jerris looked puzzled, she gave him the simple answer, "People."

Jerris continued to look confused so Meredith went on, "Treat everyone you meet like a chapter in a book and you will never be bored again. Each person has a history, a story of what shaped and molded him or her. On leaving every ball, you should have completed a book."

Jerris looked thoroughly entertained by this new train of thought, but his demeanor quickly changed as he reminded Meredith of his inability to dance.

"That's nonsense, Jerris. Of course you can dance!"

"Obviously you've never seen me make a complete fool of myself trying to dance."

"But you know how to ride a horse, Jerris," Meredith responded.

Now Jerris looked thoroughly amused. "That is a very strange statement."

Without another word, Meredith stood up and moved over to where he was standing. She took him by the hand and led him to an open space in the parlor.

"When you ride a horse," Meredith explained, "it's important to follow its rhythm up and down. Dancing is no different. Now just imagine I'm a horse . . . "

Jerris laughed loudly. "I'm sorry, but my imagination couldn't possibly stretch that far."

But Meredith was insistent. She began moving to a hummed tune. Jerris had spent countless hours with dance instructors and was convinced that he had two left feet. But somehow, when he equated dancing to horseback riding, his dance steps began to click. He found himself moving effortlessly around the floor with Meredith.

They twirled past the large beveled glass window overlooking the side garden, past the walnut armoire which stood guard over the sofa, and past Clyde, who had entered the room to find out if there was anything else they needed. Clyde left hurriedly, but not without taking note of the thrill he saw in his employer's face.

As they turned, Meredith increased the rhythm until they were both out of breath. When they stopped, she looked at Jerris with admiration and panted, "Now you are not only a master horseman, you are also a master dancer."

Jerris continued to hold Meredith. One arm was around her waist, and the other hand held her hand firmly. Before he could catch himself, his lips were on hers. Meredith paused for only a moment then quickly took a step back.

"What are you doing?" Meredith asked.

Jerris blushed and began to apologize. He said, "I don't know what came over me." Then he stopped abruptly and looked intently at Meredith. He announced, "No, that was a lie. I did know what I was doing. You see, Meredith, it appears I have fallen hopelessly in love with you."

Meredith began backing up slowly, shaking her head. "No Jerris . . . "

Jerris walked quickly to Meredith, took her hands, and pleaded, "Please, Meredith, I think I would die if we were no longer friends. I'm sorry. I shouldn't have told you. I want you to be assured that I would never force myself on you. Let's pretend we never had this conversation and just return to the way we were."

Meredith nodded, lowered her head, and turned to leave the room. She stopped momentarily when he called her name. She didn't turn around as he made one more comment. "I will never approach you in this manner again. However, if you find your feelings toward me become more than those of friendship, please leave your bedroom door open, and I will know."

Meredith left the room numb, feeling the effects of a full-scale assault on her senses.

Adam showed Tilly to her quarters. They were very small, with hardly enough room for her to turn around. Attached to the wall with chains, a wood plank would serve as her bed. A small closet to her left would hold her few possessions until they reached their African destination.

Adam noticed that Tilly had become withdrawn, so he attempted to cheer her up. "Dinner will be at five o'clock ma'am, and then with your permission I would like to take you on a grand tour of the ship." He bowed dramatically at the waist, then looked up to see that a slight smile had crossed Tilly's face.

Tilly unpacked some of her clothing and went back to the main deck. The ship was just pulling away from the dock, and people were still waving to their loved ones. Tilly could hardly believe she was leaving Chicago. Yes, she had seen many hard days there, but she had also made some wonderful friends. Nurse Taylor, who had, in a way, taken the place of her mother, was already on her way to work in one of the tenement buildings. Tilly sighed as she watched the people on the pier growing smaller and smaller. Out of the corner of her eye she saw Gus leaning against the boat's railing. She didn't turn her head, but she could feel his eyes burning into her.

Adam's cheerful voice interrupted her thoughts. "You're off on an exciting adventure, Tilly. Your life will never be the same."

Adam came and stood beside her as she looked at the shrinking shoreline of Chicago. He placed his arm around her shoulder, and Tilly leaned her head against his chest.

"Reverend Jensen?" called a short, stocky man standing at the stern.

"Yes, Samuel," shouted Adam over the sound of the waves slapping against the sides of the ship.

"We did it!" declared Samuel with both hands in the air.

Adam chuckled and looked down at Tilly, whose eyes questioned him about the man. Adam explained, "Samuel has been with me since the beginning of my ministry. He is a true and valuable friend. You have never met him because he has been living in the small town where I stayed when I was not travelling. Samuel was born in the north and knows nothing of the cruel hardships we endured on the plantations in the south. But he has a good heart, and he has faced his share of adversity. His lifelong dream has been to return to Africa."

Adam walked with Tilly to one of the ship's masts, with its large ropes holding one of the sails firmly in place. She sat down nearby, and they talked until it was almost time for dinner. Tilly's fears and worries began to subside as she conversed with Adam. There was so much peace in his eyes. Talking to him was like traveling to a beautiful deserted island where only love lived. He told her that she would never be the same, but Tilly knew Africa would never be the same once Adam had blessed it with his presence.

As the ship continued to pick up speed, Tilly thought about Meredith and wondered what she was doing at that moment.

Meredith spent extra time getting ready for the ball, and Patience was delighted to see her eighteen-year-old mistress preparing to have a good time. She had watched Meredith's relationship with Tilly from a distance. She knew of Meredith's early years of happiness and had been there when it was ripped from her. Patience had also seen the unfolding of Diane's relationship with Meredith, and the pain that had resulted from Carter's wrongdoing. Then Jackson had been born, and the light had begun to come back into Meredith's eyes. Now, as her friendship grew with Jerris, Patience watched Meredith begin to blossom once again.

Tonight Meredith was sure to be the belle of the ball. Her teal-colored dress accented her aqua-blue eyes. The cream lace, which covered the gown, was pulled up at either side with a beautiful bow. Tiny cream roses were interwoven into her gleaming auburn hair. Patience thought she was the picture of perfection.

Meredith was the talk of the ball, not only because of her beauty but also because of her disappearance after Carter's death and her subsequent marriage to Jerris. And for each person who was impressed with Meredith, there were an equal number of people who were astonished at Jerris. Not the least of these was his father, who noticed that Jerris didn't miss a dance and seemed to be utterly fascinated by each dance partner.

The evening was nearly half spent when Jerris asked Meredith to dance. As he took her into his arms, he smiled and said, "And now for my favorite chapter."

Meredith seemed pleased as they began to dance. The music was beautiful, and Jerris talked continuously about his previous dance partners. He wondered if she knew that the broach worn by Mrs. Bennett had been passed down through her family for four generations. In fact, her great-great-grandfather had been a czar in Russia, and when he'd fled the country after a war, the only valuable possession he took with him was the broach.

Meredith was amused by Jerris' newfound enthusiasm and also noticed that he was so enthralled by his inquisitions that he had taken little notice of his purported lack of dancing abilities. In fact, he was quite good. As he continued to tell her all he had learned, Meredith found herself at one point quite overtaken with laughter. A group of elderly women lifted their eyeglasses and peered onto the dance floor.

One of the old dowagers remarked, "I say, isn't that Meredith Douglas?"

"Meredith Hunter," corrected one of her friends.

"Well, Meredith Hunter or Meredith Douglas, she appears to be completely happy. Don't you think so?"

The women standing in their circle all agreed, and when they joined Agatha Stanton a week later for tea, they gave her a full description of the ball's events. As they began to describe the change in Jerris and the joy in Meredith, Agatha reached over and rang a bell.

Shortly thereafter a tall butler in a black suit responded, "Yes, Miss Stanton."

"Harry, please get these women's cloaks. They're leaving."

"Leaving?" asked one woman. "Why we just got here. We have so much more to tell you."

"No you don't . . . I mean, I suddenly feel ill," replied Agatha.

The confused women were quickly ushered to their carriage and left to talk about the incident all the way home.

Upon their departure, Agatha sat stirring her tea furiously and staring into the distance. "Anyhow," she thought, "they are very simple minded. Who needs them?"

Her plan for Jack and Meredith's misery had failed. However, just then an idea crossed her mind that caused her to chuckle as she raised the cup to her mouth.

The constant lapping of the ocean against the ship awakened Tilly. She struggled against the urge to cry, which had accompanied her every day since she'd left Chicago ten weeks earlier. The only thing that seemed to keep her from losing her mind was remembering that her mother had traveled to America on a ship much like this one. Although Tilly's living quarters were tight, she could imagine her mother being stacked in the bottom of the ship with layers of slaves lying next to each other above and below her. Tilly kept telling herself, *If Momma made it, I'm going to make it, too.*

Adam proved to be a neverending source of encouragement. Each evening after dinner he would preach from the Bible to the ship's crew and passengers. His messages were so inspirational that Tilly wished she could believe. One night, as Adam watched her leave the meeting, he lifted his eyes and cried out to God in his heart. Adam saw how miserable Tilly was and wondered if his invitation for her to come hadn't been the result of his own personal desires rather than God's direction. Regretfully, he repented of his decision to take Tilly to Africa.

After spending several days secluded in her cabin, Tilly forced herself to get ready for breakfast and made her way to the top deck. A fine mist of ocean spray greeted her, and she had to admit it was a beautiful morning. The overcast skies from the day before were gone, replaced by a blue expanse that reflected the richness of the waters below.

When Adam saw Tilly emerge, he rushed to greet her. He thought she spent far too much time in her cabin. What he didn't know was that for her the sleeping quarters were a hideaway from Gus' lustful stares. The sparkle Adam once saw in her eyes at home was gone. He felt responsible.

"Good morning, Tilly. How was your rest?"

"Fine, thank you."

"I thought we could read from this book after breakfast. It's such a glorious day!"

Tilly nodded and looked at the title of the book. It was one she had wanted to read but hadn't found the time to in Chicago. After they'd finished eating, Adam led Tilly to a chair at the front of the ship and leaned against the railing. Together, they read for almost two hours then agreed to continue that afternoon. Adam closed the book and sat next to Tilly.

"Tilly, I've been wondering about something," Adam said as he looked out over the ship's bow. "Why is it you never speak of marriage?"

Tilly sighed, unfolding her hands in her lap. She looked up at Adam who by now had fixed his dark eyes upon her. "In order for me to get married, I would have to fall in love. And so far everyone I have ever loved has been taken from me. So I've decided to make sure that doesn't happen again."

"By refusing to fall in love?" Adam questioned.

Tilly nodded then asked, "What about you, Adam, why haven't you married yet? I went out of my way to introduce you to a wonderful woman at my school, but you showed no interest."

At a loss for words, Adam squirmed. Before he could speak, Tilly continued, "Well, perhaps you will find a wife in Africa."

Adam looked into Tilly's innocent face and stated, "I'm sure the woman I want to marry will be in Africa."

From the other end of the ship, Gus watched their conversation out of the corner of his eye. He focused his attention on Tilly. He was glad that Auntie Ruth had stopped him at the river when Tilly was younger because now she looked ripe for the picking. He was looking forward to the harvest. He'd have to wait until they reached Africa though, because his nephew Adam seemed to always be just a step behind her.

Jerris twitched his nose and tried not to sneeze. His back ached and Meredith acted as if she was just getting started. The easel holding the canvas caught the morning light coming through the window of her attic studio. She sat perched on a stool with brush in hand. Her hair was swept to the top of her head, with rebellious strands making their way over her face and along her neck.

Jerris wondered why it had taken him so long to suggest that she convert the upper room into her art workroom. The idea had crossed his mind a month earlier while he was dancing with Meri at the ball. When it was completed, she had insisted that he be her first subject. Jerris would have refused because he hated the process, but he couldn't deny Meredith.

Meredith knew it was time she began working on subjects other than Jackson. He was six months old, and she had probably sketched close to a hundred different poses of him. Three of her favorites she had sent to Tilly, who had kept them safe with her other letters from her best friend.

Meredith smiled as she thought of her baby. He was the spitting image of Carter, and even at his young age was showing signs of possessing his father's ways. A note of concern accompanied that thought. Still Jackson seemed never to meet a person he didn't like. A smile was ever present on his lips, and he was the life of any social gathering in which they participated.

Meredith studied Jerris' nose carefully as she continued to dip the brush into the paint, then back to the canvas. She had just completed his eyes and was amazed that she had never noticed how intriguing they were. They were deep blue with specks of gold, and his long, dark-brown eyelashes seemed to brush his cheeks every time he blinked. His nose looked carefully sculpted, and his lips were softly shaped. The only thing rugged about his appearance was the cleft in his chin.

As the paintbrush continued to move across the canvas, Meredith began to remember the many conversations she and Jerris had shared since she had arrived at his home. He had a humorous side that very few people saw, and many evenings after dinner they spent hours laughing and talking late into the night. She wondered what would have happened if Jerris had not come to rescue her and Jackson. Surely she would have been an outcast, and her father would have been disgraced.

Meredith continued to paint but found herself trying to control feelings she hadn't felt since being with Carter. She shook her head firmly as if trying to release the sensations. The abrupt movement startled Jerris causing him to ask, "Are you all right, Meredith?"

"Yes, yes. But we should probably take a break."

Jerris gave a sigh of relief, stood, and arched his back. He walked over to Meredith and looked at his portrait. Putting one arm around her shoulder he said, "It's amazing how good you are without ever having had any formal training."

"Surely you jest. I learned from one of the best! Diane studied in France, and she spent years teaching me her skills."

"Well, you were a great student because, of all the paintings I have in the house, I believe I will enjoy this one the most."

Wiping one of her brushes clean, Meredith stopped to look at Jerris.

"What's wrong, Meredith?"

"I was just wondering if you know how much I appreciate your continuous encouragement. You make me feel as if I could accomplish anything."

Jerris appeared embarrassed by her expression of gratitude.

After dinner that evening, Meredith shared with Jerris a letter she had received from Tilly. She waited until they were together to read it because he seemed to be as excited as she was when Tilly's letters arrived. The letter had been mailed the day before Tilly had left for Africa and expressed her concern about how long it would be until Meredith heard from her again. She wasn't sure when they would arrive in Africa, but she would send a letter as soon as she got there.

Tilly's correspondence stimulated a conversation between Meredith and Jerris about distant lands and traveling together, with Jackson, to some faraway places. The candles were very low when they decided to turn in for the night. Jerris stayed behind to complete the last chapter of a book he was reading. When he finished, he leaned over and blew out the candle on his desk. He slowly began climbing the stairs. As he reached the top and looked to his right, he stopped. Meredith's door was slightly open. Had she made a mistake?

Jerris hesitantly approached, and through the opening he saw Meredith sitting at her vanity table brushing her long auburn hair. A soft, ivory-colored nightgown graced her body. As she looked in the mirror, her eyes drifted toward the door. She saw Jerris standing outside. Putting her brush down, she turned slightly in her chair. Jerris came in and closed the door. He walked slowly to Meredith and knelt beside her, running his fingers through her hair.

Meredith put her arms around his neck and pulled him to herself. Jerris was trembling. As they pulled away, she realized they were both crying.

"How can this be?" Jerris asked in wonder. "How can I love you so much? It wasn't my goal. It wasn't my plan. But here I am, enraptured by your every move."

Meredith shook her head and whispered, "And how can it be that you would even want me? I'm not worthy of your love. I can't even offer you my purity."

Jerris wiped the tears away from her cheeks. "But my love, in my eyes you are pure. What is given and what is taken away are two totally different things. This is the first time you will give of yourself freely." Laying her head on Jerris' shoulder, Meredith wept softly. Then she pushed herself back and said, "There is something I must do."

Meredith stood, pulled Jerris gently up and took his hands in hers. Looking deeply into his eyes, she began reciting the marriage vow. "I, Meredith, do solemnly swear to take Jerris as my lawfully wedded husband. I promise to love . . . "

Jerris put his finger to her lips and asked, "Why are you doing this?"

"Because when I said it the first time, I didn't mean it. Now every part of me wants to say it to you."

Meredith and Jerris repeated their vows to one another in the romantic glow of the bedroom candles. The night was full of beautiful discoveries, and just before they fell asleep Jerris asked, "And will you tell Tilly about our night together?"

Meredith lay her head on his chest and said, "Uh-hum."

"And what will you say?"

"I will tell her that the sky was full of billowy white clouds, and the one to the left was you."

Jerris looked puzzled but only for a moment, as Meredith ended their night with a lingering kiss.

Part 3

14

October 1869

Tilly never forgot the day she first saw the African shoreline. Her heart began to pound, and she felt a strange new happiness unlike anything she'd ever experienced. Clutching the railing of the ship, Tilly saw Adam making his way toward her.

"Adam, look!" she shouted as she pointed to the green lush vegetation, which seemed to call out to her. "I declare Adam, if I weren't a grown woman, I'd be jumping up and down!"

Thoughts of Na-Na came drifting back, and she couldn't wait to plant her feet on the African soil. The dock was full of people in brightly colored clothing, many of them waving joyfully at the incoming ship.

Adam had spent a considerable amount of time preparing Tilly and Samuel for Liberia. She remembered the day he'd explained that a boatload of freed slaves from the United States had founded Liberia in 1822. The U.S. Government and the American Colonization Society had supported them, and the capital, Monrovia, was named after President James Monroe. The official language of Liberia was English, but Adam also told of sixteen different tribal groups and their customs and ways. Tilly found the history fascinating, flooding him with questions. She couldn't help but marvel that this time he was the teacher and she was the student.

The boat docked and Tilly made her way down the gangplank. At that moment something came over her, which later she was never able to explain. She found herself dropping to her knees and kissing the warm African earth. Many of the Africans around her smiled brightly, nodding as if they fully understood her action.

When Tilly stood up, she felt lightheaded. She looked around for Adam, who was just an arms-length away. Adam put his hand under Tilly's elbow and led her through the crowd. Just then a hefty, middle-aged gentleman in a straw hat approached them. "Adam, bless de Lawd, ya made it safely!"

After a warm embrace, Adam introduced Tilly to Pastor Miller. "Tilly, this is the pastor who invited me to come to Liberia. He, like us, was a runaway slave who thirsted to return to his homeland as a missionary."

"It was my countless letters," Pastor Miller interjected, "urging him to join me in Africa that brought him here."

Chuckling, Adam said, " I was told repeatedly that there were tremendous needs and opportunities awaiting me."

Pastor Miller slapped Adam on the back and smiled. "Indeed der are my son, indeed der are. Come, let us make our way to de church. Der are people waitin' to meet ya and we've prepared food for ya and yo' friends."

Tilly found Pastor Miller to be delightful. Even when he wasn't smiling there seemed to be laughter in his eyes.

Samuel administrated the loading of their luggage onto the wagon. Once he had finished, they began making their way down the street toward the parsonage where they would temporarily be living. Tilly didn't know where to look first as they rode through the marketplace. Off to her right was a woman walking with a large basket of eggs on her head, her arms relaxed at her sides. A baby was strapped to her back with a large piece of red material. The child appeared to be up in a cloud as it rode along in complete peace.

On her left, fruits and vegetables were displayed in wooden stalls or laid out on blankets that were spread across the ground. Tilly could smell roasting peanuts and sensed an air of perpetual excitement created by the constant chatter, laughter, and the incessant bargaining going on between the merchants and customers. It was with a nurse's eye, however, that she noticed some of the medical challenges facing the people.

"Adam," Tilly said, looking up with a twinkle in her eyes, "thank you for bringing me to Africa."

Tilly didn't understand why, but Adam looked toward the heavens, breathing a huge sigh of relief. Gus, on the other hand, rode in the back with the baggage, wondering with a scowl on his face why he'd let Adam talk him into coming to such a weird, foreign place.

The wagon came to a stop in front of a church. Pastor Miller looked at his passengers and announced, "Welcome to Providence Baptist Church. This was the first church to be built in Liberia. It was constructed by freed slaves."

Tidy wooden huts surrounded the church. Tilly looked on with amusement at a woman bent over, carefully sweeping in front of her home. She thought it was funny that the woman was sweeping the dirt, yet at the same time she admired her desire for cleanliness.

Pastor Miller jumped down and ushered Adam, Tilly, Samuel, and Gus through the opening in the low-built wall that enclosed the church. A grass-covered area under a large, full tree to the left was scattered with chairs. The pastor led them through the simply furnished sanctuary, then down a corridor to a room where some members of the church were waiting to greet them.

Based on what Tilly had seen in the marketplace, she knew the people present were dressed in their best attire. Several of the women had beautiful fabrics wrapped around their bodies with matching headdresses.

Adam and the group from Chicago proceeded down the receiving line and were greeted with handshakes and hugs. Tilly was drawn to a tall, dark-skinned woman at the end of the line.

The woman leaned forward, looked intently into Tilly's eyes, and said, "Hello, my name is Naomi; I have been praying especially for you."

There was kindness in her expression accompanied by an unexplainable peace, which seemed to radiate from this unusual woman. Naomi pulled Tilly close and whispered, "Welcome home!"

Charlie smiled as he saw Jerris and Meredith riding over the hill toward the stables. He hadn't seen Meredith up close since that tragic day when she'd returned in humiliation from her ill-fated ride with Carter. Earlier that morning, before she and Jerris had left, Charlie could sense Meredith's hesitation when she first took her mount. It had clearly been a long time since she had ridden a horse. A look of concern and excitement seemed to cross her face all at the same time, but with sudden determination she turned the horse, kicked its side, and dared Jerris to catch her.

Jerris and Meredith were gone for hours before they returned. Meredith's cheeks were flushed, and she looked happier than she had long ago when she'd ridden off with Carter.

Charlie continued to be astounded at how Jerris had changed. It was hard to believe that one woman could have that much effect on a man. Like the rest of the servants, he'd heard the story about Meredith and Tilly, and his eyes sparkled when he thought about the day Jerris came to the stables and started asking him questions about his life. At first he'd been uncomfortable, but once he saw the sincere interest, he began to share some of his experiences. Jerris had seemed captivated.

Meredith was the first to return from the ride. As she and Jerris approached the stable, their laughter grew louder. "I beat you!" she shouted over her shoulder.

Meredith dismounted handing the reins to Charlie. Jerris followed suit, then they began walking toward the house. Meredith suddenly stopped and came back to where the stableman was standing.

"Charlie . . . " Meredith struggled to find the right words. "I . . . never thanked you for the way you . . . "

Charlie remembered well the day she had collapsed in his arms. Her torn, bloodied dress and tear-streaked face were forever etched in his memory. He could see she was stumbling, so he interrupted, saying, "Anythin' fo' a lady, Mis' Meredith."

His kind words felt like a healing balm. Meredith hugged him, which left Charlie in total shock. He heard Jerris say, "Don't mind her, Charlie, she does that to me all the time."

Meredith laughed and made her way back to Jerris, who took her hand as they strolled up the path. They were almost at her in-law's house when Meredith suddenly turned toward Jerris, started to say something—then collapsed. Jerris picked her up in his arms and carried her quickly into the parlor. He laid her down on the tapestry sofa. Never taking his eyes off her face, Jerris began calling out for someone to help him.

Doctor Harper was summoned and arrived within the hour. After being with Meredith for quite some time, the doctor walked out of the bedroom in deep thought. Jerris and his parents were waiting outside the door. Jerris rushed over asking, "What's wrong, doctor? Is she all right? Can I go in? Will . . . "

"Slow down, Jerris," Dr. Harper said chuckling, "your wife is going to be fine. I was here the day you were born and it looks like I'll also be here the day your child makes its way into the world."

At first the news didn't sink in. Then Jerris looked anxiously from his father to his mother and then back to Dr. Harper. "You mean . . . ?"

Dr. Harper nodded his head and said, "Yes, I mean."

Jerris let out a hoot and rushed into the bedroom, where Meredith was propped up against several pillows. He sat on the bed gingerly as if he were afraid it would topple over. Meredith giggled while taking his hand. She held it to her face whispering,

"Oh, Jerris, imagine God loving us so much that He would give us a child. I am so happy."

Then, as if something had suddenly come to her remembrance, she exclaimed, "We must get word to my father and Diane immediately!"

Jerris smiled and replied, "Yes, darling, I will."

Solomon Hunter stood in the doorway of the bedroom with tears in his eyes, marveling at the sight before him.

Tilly sat rocking Kimani, the three-year old boy who lay dozing in her arms. Kimani was from the Kru tribe. His father and most of the men in the village were fishermen and were part of one of the largest of the twelve tribal groups spread across Liberia.

Tilly had adjusted quickly to her surroundings, working as a nurse almost immediately after her arrival. Fortunately, she had been able to bring medicine with her from the states and began using it on the Liberians. Although there was much joy in the tribal way of life, few people lived on more than a subsistence diet. Many were afflicted with malaria, yaws, leprosy, or tuberculosis.

Kimani moaned with pain while Tilly listened to the witch doctor outside the hut chanting in a wild monotone. Although she kept hoping he would go away, he had been there throughout the night. Many of the village people also stood outside the hut trying to see in. Tilly could hear some of them arguing with the child's father. They were telling him that the witch doctor had always been the one to cure the people of their tribe. Bringing in a strange woman would surely mean the death of his son.

Tilly laid Kimani on a mat, where she began sponging him down once again with a rag dipped in cool water. The medicine she had administered still had not taken effect, and she was beginning to fear she'd lose him. Naomi was there to assist her; she began humming a spiritual tune. Tilly had heard her praying under her breath during the night as she lay her hands on the boy. She felt the pang of loss, thinking about how Nurse Taylor would be doing the same thing right now if she were there.

"Naomi, I don't know what more I can do," Tilly anguished.

"Have you prayed?"

Tilly looked into Naomi's eyes, shaking her head.

"Then you haven't done all you can do. Now is the time, child. Now is the time."

Tilly struggled in her heart. *Would God hear me?* she wondered. *After all, He isn't a friend of mine so why would He even care?* But Tilly was desperate. She couldn't stand the thought of losing Kimani. Because of his fever, he was too weak to speak, but his eyes continued to plead with Tilly to save his life.

Naomi took Tilly's hand and laid it on the boy's chest. "Why don't I pray and you believe with me, O.K.?"

Tilly nodded and Naomi began calling out to God. At first it was a quiet prayer, but as she continued her words grew louder. Even the witch doctor paused in his chanting when she lifted her voice to the heavens. She asked God to heal Kimani, not only for his sake, but so it would be a testimony of His divine power to the people of the village.

At first Tilly thought it was her imagination, but even before the prayer ended, she felt Kimani's temperature begin to drop. She noticed the same peaceful sensation she'd experienced the first time she'd met Naomi. She figured that sometimes you can want something so badly you just convince yourself it is happening. But over the next two hours, the boy definitely began to improve. By that evening, he was able to sit up and start taking liquid into his body. Naomi was no longer in the hut. She had gone out among the people, telling them about the love of God.

As Naomi and Tilly started the long journey back to town, Tilly asked, "How did God do that?"

"Do what?"

"Heal Kimani."

Naomi laughed then put her arm around Tilly's shoulder. "My child, God made us. Don't you think He would know how to fix us?"

Adam arrived shortly after her return, and Tilly couldn't stop talking about the events that had taken place. He listened attentively and then used the opportunity to explain God's saving grace to her. It was on that night that Tilly finally stopped fighting with Jesus and asked Him to be her friend.

Tilly carefully unfolded the letter from Meredith. It had taken almost six months for it to arrive; now she savored every word. Her friend was happy, which made Tilly rejoice. It had been a long day; Tilly could see the sun going down outside the window of her small cottage. She had never seen anything like the African sunset. An earlier rain seemed to cause the deep red dirt surrounding her abode to sigh with relief, releasing an exhilarating aroma.

Tilly opened the correspondence again, reading the section that had most caught her attention.

> During our night of love, I saw a blue sky full of billowy white clouds and, to my surprise, the one on the left was Jerris.

> Tilly, I know we have had our share of heartaches but promise me you'll keep your heart open to love. Yes, there is still a chance it may cause us to one day suffer again. However, I believe the joy we experience in loving will buffer the pain of any potential loss.

> Jerris sends his regards and hopes that one day he will be able to meet you.

There was a knock at Tilly's door, and she sat up with a start. Adam was standing in the doorway, but his usual smile was not lighting up his face.

Adam stated, "I heard about the problems the Kru tribe at the coast are facing."

After inviting him in, Tilly leaned down and, from under the bed, pulled out a box of Meri's letters. She placed the latest correspondence inside, replaced the box, then turned to face Adam. She had just returned from another of her weekly journeys into the bush and along the coast, caring for the sick. This time, to say the least, she was overwhelmed.

"Adam, it's terrible. There is an outbreak of dysentery. And because of their ancient beliefs, they don't want to initiate any of the sanitation instructions we are trying to teach them. It seems hopeless."

"Nothing is hopeless, Tilly, as long as we serve a God of hope," Adam replied. Then he continued, "Let's pray about it. Since we've been here, we have witnessed one miracle after another. I know God is with us."

Tilly sat at her small table with Adam across from her. As he reached out and took her hand, something happened inside her. She couldn't explain it. Adam prayed aloud and together they said, "Amen."

Adam began to tell her of events happening at the church. In passing, he mentioned that Pastor Miller needed to return to the States to tend to his elderly mother.

"But Adam, who will be the pastor?" Tilly asked.

Adam grinned and said, "Guess?"

"No! I mean, yes! That's wonderful, Adam. We couldn't ask for a better clergyman."

"I hope the local people share your confidence."

Tilly put her hand on Adam's arm and told him that if she had anything to say about it, he would be the pastor tomorrow. Adam covered her hand with his and told her how much he had appreciated her support over the years. He went on to say, "It seems like God has destined us to be together for that very reason."

For some reason, Tilly suddenly remembered how much his hand resting on her back had meant to her when her mother had died. There was that feeling again. Tilly pulled her hand back.

"What's the matter, Tilly?"

"I'm not sure."

Adam had noticed a look in Tilly's eyes that he had not seen before. It was slight, but he knew her so well that he couldn't help but see the change. Just the thought that the response indicated a slight interest on her part caused his heart to flutter. He tried desperately to control himself, but after all the years of containing his feelings he felt impelled to test the waters.

"Tilly . . . do you remember back in Chicago when I said one day I may want the sun back?"

Tilly nodded.

"What did you think I meant when I said it?

Tilly moved uncomfortably, then replied, "I thought that one day when you were feeling discouraged . . . well . . . maybe . . . I thought . . . well, I don't know because I guess I have never pondered the question."

Adam was momentarily quiet. Speaking softly, he simply said, "Well, if you don't mind, I'd like you to think about it." Then he stood up, leaned over, and kissed Tilly gently on the cheek.

Tilly watched Adam as he strolled up the path to the church. He turned toward Tilly's cottage when he reached the gate, almost as if he knew she was watching him. Adam lifted his hand; Tilly waved back. She didn't know that when the sanctuary door closed, Adam fell to his knees, lifted his hands to the unseen heavens, and shouted, "Thank you, Jesus!"

Jerris Richard Hunter was born March 17, 1871. It was clear upon birth that his eyes were blue and his hair blond. Although it was uncommon for that day, Jerris refused to leave Meredith's side and had insisted on watching the birth. Now he sat next to her in the bed holding his son.

"I'm going to write a book," announced Jerris. "It's going to be about the miracle of childbirth."

Meredith's father smiled brightly, and Diane beamed as they sat nearby. They had talked at length during their long trip to the Hunter Estate about the events that had led to this glorious occasion. Both continued to be amazed at the transformation in the relationship between Meredith and Jerris. Diane firmly doubted that Meredith could ever love anyone more than she loved Jerris.

Two-year-old Jackson sat at the end of the bed cross-legged. He looked around the room, noting the smiles of admiration for the baby on every face. Suddenly he blurted out, "Hey, what 'bout me!"

All eyes focused on the two-year-old, who seemed perilously close to tears. They laughed, then Meredith extended her hand and Jackson crawled quickly into her arms.

"What about you?" Meredith asked as she cradled him close to her heart. "You will always be my special baby boy. Nothing can change that!"

Jackson looked comforted, and Meredith fondly kissed the top of his head.

15

July 1877

Meredith wondered if there had ever been a more humid day in Kensington. She had decided to take the children into town for the day and now realized it had been a bad decision. Eight-year-old Jackson was sweltering in the backseat of the carriage. He complained constantly, while his brother, "Jerry," seemed oblivious as he observed the people walking along the street.

The driver of the carriage slowed in front of City Park. Jerris Jr. and Jackson dashed from the transport even before it had come to a stop. Meredith looked down at her nine-month-old daughter, Priscilla, whom she was holding in her arms. The baby's light brown ringlets lay flat against her perspiring face. Neither the heat nor the jerking of the carriage had caused her to wake up.

"Children, be careful!" exhorted Meredith as Jackson and Jerry played tag with one another. The first park bench suited Meredith just fine. She had been sitting there just a short while when Mrs. Young, the mayor's wife, walked by with her governess and five-year-old daughter. When they recognized Meredith, a conversation ensued. They had been talking a while when Meredith began searching the park for signs of little Jerris and Jackson. Jerry was a short distance away chasing a squirrel, and Jackson was standing off in the distance. A woman was bent over talking to him as he smiled up at her.

Meredith was about to direct her attention back to Mrs. Young when the color of the woman's hair, peeking out from underneath her large hat, caught her attention. It took a moment before a break in the conversation allowed Meredith to excuse herself. As she headed toward Jackson, the red-haired woman began walking in the opposite direction.

Jackson got a good look at his mother's face as she approached and asked, "What's wrong, Mommy?"

"Nothing, darling," she replied. Meredith leaned down so she was even with her son's eyes and calmly asked, "Who was that lady speaking to you, Jackson?"

Jackson shrugged his shoulders.

"What did she say?"

Jackson looked exasperated. The heat and his mother's persistent questioning were irritating to him. He shouted, "I don't know!"

"Jackson Hunter, you lower your voice this instant!"

Jackson looked as if he was going to cry, then dug the toe of his shoe into the dirt. Finally he said, "She said she knew my daddy."

Meredith's heart was pounding. "Did she say anything else?"

"Come on, Mommy, I want to go. I'm hungry!"

"Not until you tell me what else she said," replied Meredith.

Jackson scratched his head as if he were searching his memory. "She said . . . she . . . uh . . . had a present for me and would give it to me one day."

Meredith took Jackson's hand, called to Jerry, and walked hurriedly up the street to where their carriage was waiting. Jackson never forgot that day, because they headed for home without getting ice-cream cones.

≈ ≈ ≈

"What are we going to do?" asked Meredith frantically as she paced back and forth.

Jerris stood up from his chair and walked over to Meredith, putting his hands on her shoulders, trying to calm her. "Don't worry about it, Meredith. She doesn't know anything, and she just wanted to upset you. I must say, she did a splendid job."

"Oh, Jerris," Meredith exclaimed as she laid her head against his chest. "I'm so afraid."

"Don't be, darling. Haven't you been trying to teach me that God has everything under control?"

Jerris' words snapped Meredith out of her panicked state. For years she had been trying to explain to Jerris what it meant to know God's love through His Son, but Jerris' intellect kept getting in the way. This would be an ideal opportunity to demonstrate her belief and commitment to God to her skeptical husband.

Meredith remembered that when she had arrived at Jerris' house after their marriage, she had placed her mother's Bible in a drawer and hadn't taken it out until she was eight months pregnant. To her surprise, her mother had written words of inspiration and encouragement on almost every page. Meredith thought it was almost as if she'd known her daughter would need the emotional support in the future. It had worked because Meredith had begun to feel a change in her heart.

Now she dried her eyes and said, "Yes, Jerris, I did tell you God has everything under control. And I'm grateful that you reminded me of that fact. I'm O.K. now."

Jerris walked Meredith to the sofa and sat next to her.

"Since you're upset, you won't want to read this," Jerris said holding a letter.

"Is it from Tilly?" Meredith asked.

Jerris smiled and held it out beyond her reach. Meredith grabbed for it and began to giggle as Jerris continued to move it around.

"Jerris Hunter, you give me that letter!"

Jerris laughed and watched Meredith gleefully tear it open. He chuckled at the remembrance of Meredith receiving a letter in late autumn six years earlier. She had torn into the letter with great excitement. Remembering back to that day, Jerris had to finally ask her what it said, because a frown had quickly creased her forehead.

Looking up with concern in her eyes, she had explained, "It only has three lines." Jerris asked her to read it and Meredith recited,

> Dear Meri,   July 23, 1871
>
> I know it has been a while since I last wrote but do you remember when I told you Adam had given me the sun? Well, I gave it back.
>
> Love,
> Tilly

Meredith had kept reading the lines over and over again. Jerris broke into her thoughts and said, "I'm sorry, dear. I know you had hoped Adam and Tilly would get together one day. It sounds like it's not going to happen."

Meredith stared at the correspondence and then blurted, "Don't you see, Jerris?"

"See what?"

"Don't you see what Tilly is doing?" Meredith released a cascade of laughter.

Jerris sat in confused silence as he waited for Meredith to explain. By then tears were streaming down his wife's face and he couldn't tell if she was laughing or crying.

"Please, Meredith. Whatever are you talking about?"

"Jerris, Tilly's back. She's back!"

Meredith went on to explain, "When we were together, Tilly was always playing pranks. She was such a riddler. This is Tilly's way of telling us she and Adam are together. Can't you see?"

Jerris remained puzzled, but two weeks later another letter had arrived from Tilly, and Meredith's predictions proved to be true. Jerris listened intently as she read the correspondence.

> Dear Meri,
>
> Did you receive my short note? I mailed this letter on the next boat leaving Liberia, hoping it would arrive shortly thereafter and end the suspense. However, I'm sure you already figured it out because you know me so well. When I received your letter describing your billowy white cloud . . .

Meredith looked up at a blushing Jerris and smiled. She continued,

> . . . I started thinking about my life. You're aware of the pain I have suffered since we left one another and I was determined to protect myself from it happening again. I have lost or been separated from everyone I have ever loved, and so I concluded the safest thing to do was to never love again. I guess my life was like living in a house with no windows or doors and the only thing inside were memories of my loved ones.
>
> I'm ashamed to say I tucked your letter away for a month or so, and then I happened upon it one day as I was reading through your correspondence. It was as if I were seeing it for the first time.
>
> When I read your letter again, I realized the only reason I had those precious memories is because I had allowed myself to love.
>
> Shortly after I finished your correspondence, Adam came to see me. It's funny but somehow he

looked different. He asked me to think about what he meant when he said he wanted his sun back. It took me a little while to figure it out. At first I thought he wanted it back so he could give it to someone he loved. My other conclusions were just as foolish. Then I began remembering some of my conversations with him and seeing them in a different light.

One day after church, Artina, a young woman from the congregation, confided in me that she was in love with Adam and she was hoping he would notice her. Meri, something came over me that I couldn't explain. She wanted my Adam! I didn't know what to do. How could I tell him? How would he know?

As Meredith continued to read she could literally envision Tilly writing the letter. She remembered how her friend used to tap her left foot as she constructed her thoughts on paper—maybe it was the rhythm of her poetry that caused her to do so. And Meredith was right. As Tilly had sat in her candlelit cottage composing that piece of correspondence, her left foot had moved up and down relentlessly.

The letter continued by explaining that not long after Artina had confessed her undying love for Adam, Tilly had seen him sitting in the open grass area next to the church. The large, leafy tree provided welcome shade and he looked like he needed the rest. Tilly watched him from a distance and then decided to take courage. As she approached, he seemed too tired to stand but forced himself to get up in order to receive her properly. Sitting in the chair opposite him, Tilly tried to make small talk but Adam appeared distracted.

Finally she said, "Adam, I have been thinking..." Tilly's voice trailed off, but the look in his eyes encouraged her to continue.

Almost as if someone had squeezed the question out of her, Tilly asked quickly, "If I give you the sun back, what will keep me warm?"

Adam, awestruck, sat up in his chair and stared at Tilly. At first she didn't think he was going to say anything, but then he smiled and answered, "Let me think about that for a minute."

Tilly had excused herself very soon after that. She wanted to kick herself a thousand times for having revealed her true feelings. Surely he had noticed the beautiful Artina. It seemed every man in the church wanted her—and why shouldn't they? Many people in Monrovia said that God had kissed her face.

Two months passed and, to Tilly's chagrin, Adam did not say a word. Then one rainy Saturday afternoon there was a knock on Tilly's cottage door. Adam came in carrying something wrapped in burlap. After greeting one another, Tilly offered Adam something to drink. He refused and told her he had come to answer her question. Tilly felt a lump form in her throat and tried to fight back the tears she felt would spill over when Adam rejected her.

"Tilly, please sit down," Adam instructed as he laid his package carefully on the table. "You asked what would keep you warm if you gave me back the sun."

Adam walked over to the window and looked out. When he turned around, Tilly thought he had a strange look on his face. As he continued, she understood why. He began telling her of the day his slave master had whipped the skin from his back for picking cotton too slowly. In all their years together, he had never mentioned it.

Adam said, "I became very ill afterward as infection set in. I spent weeks lying on my stomach waiting for my back to heal. The only thing I could do was look out the window next to my bed. I would ask God to hurry up and make the sun go down so the day would be over and I could sleep away the pain. Each evening when the sun was about to set, I would rest my hand just below the bright orange ball. I decided God had made it just for me and that if I kept it in my heart I would always be warm.

Adam looked at Tilly and remarked, "It was the only thing I owned, and it meant everything to me. When we met, I was a frightened boy who admired a bright, beautiful girl. I was afraid to talk, but after your mother died I had to do something. The only thing I could think of that might bring you any joy was my sun. Do you remember the day I gave it to you?"

Tilly nodded.

"You smiled. I'll always remember that smile."

Adam paused and then said, "When I saw you in Chicago, it was a dream come true. Sure, I thought about you because you opened up the world of reading to me. But more than that, I was happy to see you because I was in love with you."

Tilly caught her breath and her eyes grew wide. She was overwhelmed by the thought that Adam had loved her even then. He went on to tell her how he had repented on the ship when he'd begun to doubt that it was God's will for her go to Africa. He couldn't stand the thought of not seeing her again, so he had conveniently used her nursing education as an excuse for her to come.

"And so, Tilly, I have come to answer your question of what will keep you warm when you give back the sun."

Adam untied the string around the burlap and folded it back. He unfurled an exquisitely stitched quilt; in the center was a burnt orange sun. Tilly responded in gleeful admiration. Adam laid the quilt across the table and said, "There have been some faithful women in the church working on this quilt ever since the day you asked me the question about what would keep you warm. Naomi supervised them."

"She knew?"

Adam smiled and took Tilly's hand. "Yes, Tilly. For some reason you're the only one who has been blind to the incredible love I have for you. And now if you don't mind, I'd like to answer your question."

Bending on one knee, Adam recited, "Tilly Douglas, if you would be my lawfully wedded wife, it will be me, under this sun, who will keep you warm."

Tilly threw her arms around Adam's neck and began to cry. Adam asked her if the hug meant yes. She nodded her head. Tilly would always remember their first kiss—their first gentle and then passionate kiss.

On November 20, 1871, Tilly married Pastor Adam Jensen. Their early evening ceremony allowed Adam and Tilly to leave the church as the sun was setting. The wedding guests didn't understand why Tilly extended her hand toward the sun, placed Adam's hand on top of hers, and then watched as Adam put his hand on his heart.

Jerris drew his attention back to Meredith and said, "I was just thinking about the letter you received from Tilly six years ago."

"I know, but this letter has more than three lines. I'll read it to you after dinner, but I'll tell you one thing now. Andrew James Jensen was born May 22, 1877, weighing in at 7 lbs. 8 oz."

16

*T*he years passed quickly as Meredith and Tilly both enjoyed their marriages and their children. Far apart though they remained, their letters to one another were a constant source of encouragement and hope. Tilly sometimes included her poetry, and Meredith occasionally sent drawings. Both art forms were skillful and beautifully composed and spoke volumes to their hearts.

On an autumn day, Jerris and Meredith sat in the stands waiting for the horseraces to start. Although dark clouds could be seen in the distance, it appeared they would be able to make it through the last race before the heavens opened up. Ten-year-old Priscilla fidgeted in her seat. The loves of her life were about to race, and she could hardly contain herself. She came very close to worshiping her brothers. They, of course, adored her too.

Jerris picked up four-year-old Becky and put her on his lap. She had come as quite a surprise because Meredith had thought her childbearing days were over. She smiled as she thought, *God finally gave us a child who looks like me!* Becky's long auburn hair hung down her back, and she had her mother's aqua-blue eyes.

The sound of the trumpet signaled the beginning of the race. The riders were led to their starting positions. Meredith thought her heart would burst with pride as she watched Jackson and Jerry on their mounts.

Jackson and Jerry were as different as night and day and, although they were fiercely competitive, they clearly loved one another. Meredith thought it probably didn't matter how many riders were involved in the race because Jackson and Jerry would be racing against each other. They were known throughout the adjoining counties as excellent horsemen. And, naturally, they had been looking forward to this day for months.

The brothers removed their caps and waved them in the direction of their family. Although Jerry was smiling, Meredith thought he looked pale. Their parents and sisters waved back and then held their breaths as the shot was fired for the race to begin.

The horses thundered past the grandstand and around the track. Jackson was leading; Jerry was two heads back. The pack was tight, and it looked as if Jackson was assured of the victory. But when they came to the final stretch, Jerry's horse seemed to sprout wings and began to fly by its opponents. Jerry won the race by a nose, and Meredith saw Jackson shaking his hand as she and the family made their way to the winner's circle.

Meredith looked down at Priscilla and reflected that she had been just a little older than her daughter when she'd stood in that very place and had shaken Carter's hand. She smiled at the thought of returning to her seat and mentally drafting a letter to Tilly, describing the love of her life.

Jerry rode his horse to the center of the winner's circle and graciously accepted the flowers and praise. His brother came through the crowd of people to slap him on the back and openly proclaim his victory. Jackson smiled and asked the crowd, "Did anyone here see the nails my brother threw down in front of my horse?"

Everyone laughed and Jerry responded, "Those weren't nails, my brother. It was the smoke that got in your eyes as I blew past you!"

"Touché!" responded Jackson.

Charlie took the reins of the winning horse, winked at Meredith, and began leading the mount back to the stalls. Meredith was deeply proud as they walked back to their carriage. During her ride home she continued to formulate plans for Jackson's eighteenth birthday party. It would be an affair to remember.

Meredith began to think aloud, "You know, Jackson, I plan to invite your entire high-school senior class to your birthday party. You can recite that debate speech you won an award for last month. That valedictorian speech would be wonderful!"

Laughing, Jerris responded, "If you keep getting ideas like that my love, I'm going to have to take over the planning of the event myself."

Everyone in the carriage looked amused. However, Jerry was unusually quiet on the way home. Soon after the carriage arrived at their residence, he politely excused himself and went hurriedly to his room.

Meredith remembered thinking something had seemed different about Jerry at the horseraces. Maybe her mother's eye was playing tricks on her, but there was something dull about his eyes and his coloring was pallid. Two days later Jerry did not come down for breakfast, which was very uncharacteristic because it was his favorite meal of the day. Meredith went up to check on him. He lay motionless in his bed. With the whole house in an uproar, the doctor was summoned. By that night Jerris and Meredith were notified that Jerry had polio.

As the family gathered in the drawing room, four-year-old Becky asked, "Mommy, what is polo?"

Meredith smiled at her mispronunciation. She put Becky on her lap and held her close. Her tears fell upon her daughter's hair as she tried to speak. Her voice unsteady, Meredith answered, "Polio, Becky, is like the lightning that struck the tree in our yard one night not long ago. Do you remember? It broke off a big limb that crashed to the ground."

"Uh-huh. I was so scared and you came and got me and took me to your room."

"Well, polio is like lightning. It strikes very fast, but it happens inside a person's body. It hits a place in the back and keeps a person from walking, even though they are still able to talk and do things with their hands."

"Why did it hit Jerry?"

Meredith looked up at the ceiling as if there were an answer written on the rafters. Then she asked, "Why did the lightning strike that one tree when there were so many others around it?"

Shrugging her shoulders, Becky answered, "I don't know."

"Who do you think knows?"

At first Meredith's little girl looked puzzled. Then she smiled sweetly, as if a light had come on in her mind. "God?"

Nodding her head, Meredith said, "Yes, Becky. Only God knows why it happened to Jerry."

Becky looked up into her mother's face and brushed her hair out of her eye. "Does that mean Jerry will never be able to ride a horse again?"

Patience saw the pain in Meredith's eyes and rushed over quickly to take Becky out of her lap.

"Do ya know whut, Mis' Becky? I has somethin' special fo' ya in the kitchen. It's dat cookie ya been askin' fo' all day."

At first Becky looked upset, but the idea of getting a cookie seemed more important than any other issue facing her at the moment.

Meredith waited until Becky left the room before she broke down. Priscilla sat at her feet weeping, while Jackson and his father remained on the sofa motionless.

At first Meredith refused to believe that Jerry would never walk again. It seemed impossible that her young, vibrant son would be sentenced for life to a bed. She struggled during the countless days and nights when Jerry cried out in pain as the doctors worked with his body. She thought it would never stop, but one day it did. The physical suffering finally subsided, but it was replaced by no feeling at all in his legs. Jerris spent hours reading to Jerry, playing chess, and thinking of ways to keep him distracted from his condition.

One Saturday morning, Meredith reached for the curtains in Jerry's room to pull them back. He murmured, "Don't open them mother. I want it to stay dark."

Meredith sat down on her son's bed. "Whatever do you mean, Jerry?"

He turned his face away from her and lamented, "The light has gone out of my life. I'm nothing and never will be anything. Darkness is my friend. Darkness understands me."

Meredith put her hand on Jerry's cheek and silently asked God to give her the right words. She hesitated for a moment then said, "Jerry, even in this state you are more of a man than anyone in this county. A man is not judged by the strength in his legs but by the strength of his heart, and that is where you shine. No, my son, your friend should be the light because the light truly understands you."

Meredith walked to the window and pulled back the drapes. Jerry was quiet and didn't stop her. As she walked out of the room, Meredith determined in her heart to get Jerry out of that bed. Inquiry after inquiry led her to information concerning exercises he could do to strengthen his back so he would be able to sit up. Eventually she found a new therapy, which showed early indications that it could work. Meredith could hardly wait to share this good news with the family that evening after dinner.

The room was filled with joy and optimism when Clyde walked in and handed Jerris a sealed envelope. After reading the contents, he asked Meredith to join him in the study. Closing the door behind them, he said, "I just received word that there has been a fire. It was Agatha's home. She was asleep inside when the flames started. She's dead."

Meredith walked to the emerald-green striped chair and sat down. She honestly didn't know if she wanted to laugh or cry: Laughter seemed cruel, but tears would be deceitful because she felt a tremendous relief. Meredith looked at Jerris, and she knew he understood.

The Liberians sat in a semicircle on the benches Samuel had constructed. He had continued in his faithful service to Adam over the past thirteen years and was a very important part of the ministry—especially when their group went into the bush country.

Tilly watched as her nine-year-old son, Andrew, walked into the middle of the circle and began singing, "Amazing Grace." It seemed almost as if he had the voice of an angel. Tilly often told him it came from Na-Na.

The jungle was full of the rich fragrance that was experienced only after a rain. Tilly loved the smell. Her three-year-old twins, Lydia and Rachael, had chosen to sit on each knee rather than the open spaces next to her. Andrew finished his selection, and Adam stood to preach. His style was different in the jungle. Gone were the big words he used when teaching at the church. They were replaced by simple stories that would help the natives understand God's plan for their lives. Tilly thought it would be impossible for her to love another human being as much as she loved Adam. He had kept his promise to keep her warm. Looking at her twins, Tilly smiled and thought, *Very warm.*

The service was held in the early morning, so they could make their way back to Monrovia before sunset. Their guide sometimes had to cut new paths through the thick green jungle, and Tilly was relieved when they finally made it home. Naomi was waiting for them and had prepared a hot delicious meal. Her husband, Gus, had set the table and looked delighted as he watched the family devour his wife's cooking.

Tilly tore off a piece of bread and dipped it in the hot soup. Her eyes drifted to Gus and she remembered in amazement the day he had made his way to the front of the church with tears streaming down his face. Adam had preached a message on overcoming bitterness, and the words had pierced his heart. He had knelt at the altar and committed his life to God.

A few days later, Tilly had been sitting in the open area next to the church watching the twins chase each other from one end of the wall to the other. Gus came and sat down opposite her. Tilly remembered a time when she would have trembled if he'd come anywhere near her. Now, however, there was a softness that had touched the harsh creases etched in his face. He had become a very humble person.

As Gus turned his straw hat over and over again in his hands, he said with hesitation, "Tilly, der's somet'ing I need to tell ya. It seem God won' let me res' 'til I speaks to ya."

Tilly smiled encouragement, and Gus continued, "Dat day at de rivah—I could have he'ped ya when ya couldn' hold on to de rope."

Anger began to rise in her as the picture of her mother's face flashed before her eyes just before Sadie had been washed downstream.

"Tilly, I done some terrible t'ings in my life an' had some terrible t'ings done to me. I know sayin' I'm sorry won' bring yo' momma back, but I want ya to know dat I am awful sorry an' I hopes ya kin fo'give me."

Tilly couldn't explain it afterward, but something happened within her and she was overcome with peace. She reached over and put her hand on his and stated, "God has forgiven me of every wrong I have ever done, Gus, and now I forgive you."

The memory of that day stayed fresh in Tilly's mind.

After finishing their soup at the parsonage, the twins looked at Naomi and simultaneously said, "Mommy and Daddy going for a walk?"

Naomi smiled, and they knew the answer was yes.

Walking together up the dirt road outside the parsonage at sunset had become something of a ritual for Tilly and Adam. Time seemed to stand still as they talked a little about everything and much about nothing. The neighbors had grown accustomed to seeing them strolling hand in hand and waved as they went by.

After they had traveled a short distance, Adam took a seat on a big rock and pulled Tilly into his lap. "Mrs. Jensen," he smiled, "you are the most beautiful woman in the world."

Tilly cupped Adam's face and closed her eyes. Adam asked, "What are you doing?"

"Shhh, I'm trying to picture your face in my mind: every curve, every line, every detail."

"And why, might I ask, are you doing that?"

"Because if I wake up one morning and discover this was a dream, I will have your image stamped in my memory and I can be content just thinking about what could have been mine."

Adam said, "Oh, oh, I can feel a poem coming on."

Opening her eyes and laughing, Tilly said, "Pastor Jensen, you know me far too well."

Kissing Tilly's lips Adam whispered, "Let's go home. I want to know you better." Tilly pushed Adam and began running up the road with him in hot pursuit. They raced all the way home.

Before Adam and Tilly fell asleep that night, he mentioned the trip he would be making early the next morning. He would once again travel into the jungle to visit another tribe. Samuel was going with him, and he reminded her that he would see her in three days. Tilly knew she would be asleep when Adam left, so she gave him an extra hug.

As usual, three days later Tilly was helping Andrew with his studies. He was reading aloud and was trying to finish quickly because then his mother would tell him a story. It was his favorite part of the day. She could paint pictures with words that made him feel as if he were there. Sometimes she would tell him of her exploits with Meredith or she would share amusing stories Meri had written about her children in the letters she sent. Andrew would laugh then ask her to tell him more.

Andrew had just read the last word of his assignment when Naomi came running into the parsonage. She looked visibly shaken, trying to control herself in Andrew's presence. Naomi whispered, "Tilly, please come with me."

Then she looked at Andrew and said sweetly, "Why don't you go out and play until your mommy comes back?"

Disappointment was clearly visible on Andrew's face. He closed his book and trudged out the back door. Tilly followed Naomi outside and saw Adam's wagon. She saw some men carrying a body toward the parsonage.

"Who is this?" she questioned Naomi.

"It's Adam."

Tilly ran toward the men and began pushing them away so she could get close to Adam. When she touched him, he was drenched in sweat. Tilly looked up at Samuel. He said only one word: "Malaria."

The days turned into weeks as Adam kept fighting off the terrible illness that was ravaging his body. Tilly was by his side night and day, serving as both nurse and wife. She cried, she prayed, and she continued to stand against the waves of desperation that threatened to wash over her and carry away her hope.

Adam's condition seemed to stabilize one day, then plunge near death on the next. The sun was about to set one evening when she heard Adam faintly call her name. At first she thought she was dreaming because she had drifted off to sleep while sitting in her chair.

"Tilly," Adam called again. Tilly hurried to his side and sat on the bed. Holding his hand she anxiously answered, "Yes, Adam."

"Tilly, it's time for me to go. I saw the Lord and He's waiting for me."

Tilly shook her head and pleaded, "No, Adam, you can't go! You have to fight. We need you, Adam."

Tilly continued to petition Adam and then began to get angry. Finally she grabbed Adam by the shoulders, shook him, and shouted, "God can't do this to us, Adam. Didn't God promise in the Bible that we would live a long life? You're only in your thirties!"

Tilly released Adam and began to sob on his chest. He waited for her crying to subside, then whispered, "How old was Jesus when He died?"

There was no answer from Tilly so Adam continued, "He was thirty-three years old. Am I better than He was? No, Tilly, God has given me a rich and full life, but now I must go on. You have to hold every memory of my love in your heart. It will keep you warm."

Tilly continued to cry. She heard Adam ask for Andrew, and Gus hastened to bring him to Adam's bedside. Adam took his son's hand as he looked at him longingly. Speaking slowly, he said, "You're the man now, Andrew. Take care of your mother and your sisters. When you feel like you're getting weak, remember to pray and ask God to strengthen you. He will. I love you, son, and I'm proud of you."

Sensing the urgency of the moment, Naomi brought the twins. They had been told their father was sick, but they bolted for the bed when they caught sight of him, unaware of the severity of his condition. Lydia pulled on Adam's finger and stated, "Daddy, get up. I wanna ride on your back!"

Rachael interrupted, "No, it's my turn."

Masking his pain, Adam smiled. Stretching his hand toward the girls he whispered, "Let me touch you."

The twins moved closer. Adam placed his hand on Lydia's head and closed his eyes. Tilly knew he was praying. He did the same to Rachael. Then Adam looked at Tilly. Naomi would always remember the love that glowed in his eyes as he fastened his gaze on his wife.

Naomi walked to the head of the bed. She seemed to know exactly when Adam had breathed his last breath because she reached over and with the palm of her hand closed his eyes.

Jackson's eighteenth birthday party was everything Meredith wanted it to be. People had traveled from miles around to celebrate the auspicious occasion. The young ladies did their best to garner Jackson's attention, but it was clear that he was smitten by Candace Evans. Her father and mother lived one county away and had been in the banking business for years. Jerris and Meredith approved of his choice.

The ball hosted in Jackson's honor was grander than any ball ever given by Solomon and Dorothy. As Meredith and Jerris danced around the room, Meredith's eyes fell on Jerry, who was sitting in his wheelchair next to the parlor sofa. Young ladies, all of whom were enchanted by his wit and candor, surrounded him. He was a more avid reader than Jerris, a fact that Meredith would have, at one time, believed to be impossible. Priscilla was being led around the dance floor by grandfather Jack. Her young body was beginning to bud; in just few short years she would dance at her own coming-out ball. The evening was a grand success.

Jackson was at the door saying his last goodbyes. Everyone said he looked just like his grandfather, Solomon, but the truth was he was the spitting image of his father, Carter. Sometimes he caught Meredith off guard when he walked unexpectedly in a room. She had to remind herself that he was her son. Just as Jackson was closing the door, there was a knock. He opened it and an elderly gentleman, all dressed in black, was standing there with a small box in his hand.

"Are you Jackson Hunter?"

When Jackson answered yes, the man handed him the box and wished him a happy birthday. Jackson carried the box into the study and sat down in his father's chair behind the desk. He put both hands behind his head and smiled broadly as he thought of the evening's events—and especially of Candace's beauty.

Removing the bow from the box, Jackson reached inside and pulled out a single-strand pearl necklace with a diamond clasp. A frown crossed his brow, and he pushed the paper in the box to the side. A letter lay on the bottom. He opened it and leaned back in the chair as he read,

> Dear Jackson,
>
> We met years ago in a park. I was the nice lady with the red hair. I told you one day I would give

> you a present and here it is. It is very special to
> me. I left instructions for you to receive it on
> your eighteenth birthday whether I am alive or
> dead. You'll remember I said I knew your father.
> Carter was a wonderful man . . .

Jackson read the line over and over again. He concluded that she had made a mistake and continued with the letter,

> I wanted to make sure you had something of
> value because I wasn't sure if your Uncle Jerris
> would leave anything to you in his will. When
> your father died, his fiancée, Meredith, didn't
> spend any time working her way back into the
> family. It's a pity when money is more important
> than love. I simply detest greed and wanted you
> to know that I deeply care for you.
>
> Just in case you doubt what I'm saying, check
> your birthday next to the day your father died
> and when your Uncle Jerris and your mother got
> married. Never allow yourself to get discouraged,
> Jackson. Remember that I believe in you.
>
> Love always,
> Agatha Stanton

Jackson's head was reeling. Over and over again he asked himself, *Can this be true?* He stood so quickly the chair he was sitting in toppled over. He marched to the living room, where a life-size painting of his Uncle Carter hung. For the first time, he realized that looking at the picture was like looking at a reflection of himself. He walked over and read the inscription on the plate, which stated Carter's date of birth and death. Jackson began to count on his fingers. His birth had taken place almost nine months to the day of Carter's death.

Jackson began to pace the floor, trying to remember the date of his parents' anniversary. He froze when he recalled that they had married six weeks after Uncle Carter's death.

Jerris and Meredith were preparing for bed when Jackson flung their bedroom door open. Meredith exclaimed, "Jackson, whatever is the matter?"

Jackson strode over to his mother, who was seated at her vanity table, and lifted the pearl necklace out of the box. "This, mother, is the matter!"

Meredith gasped and stared at Jerris, who, for a moment, didn't understand the significance of the pearls.

"What are you talking about, Jackson?" His father's voice was puzzled.

Jackson turned slowly around, and Jerris thought he actually saw hatred in Jackson's eyes. Jackson announced, "These pearls, Uncle Jerris, were given to me by a woman who knew the lie you and my mother have been secretly carrying all these years. Carter Douglas was my father—not you!"

Jerris' face grew ashen. He slowly sat down on the bed, speechless. Finally he said, "Jackson, listen. You don't understand. Give us a chance to explain."

"Explain what?" Jackson shouted. "That you deceived me?"

Jerris looked at Meredith and said, "Tell him the truth."

Meredith got up and reached out to Jackson, who pulled away from her. As she recounted the story of Agatha's broken engagement, the strand of pearls, Carter's violation of her, and the subsequent marriage, Jackson's face flamed.

Once Meredith finished talking, Jackson replied, "There's only one problem, mother. The only person who knows the whole truth is dead. And until I hear it from Carter Hunter, I will always doubt that you have told me the truth."

Jackson stormed out of the room. Meredith collapsed into a heap on the floor, sobbing as if her heart would break. Jerris helped her to the bed and rocked her in his arms.

≈ ≈ ≈

Naomi sat on the bed as Tilly numbly paced back and forth, gathering clothes and putting them into a worn suitcase. Misery and grief hung on her face like a heavy drapery. Although several months had passed, it seemed as if Adam's funeral had just taken place. It had been attended by a great multitude. When the church filled up, hundreds more stood outside in solemn silence. Naomi had seen many dignitaries come and go in her country, but no one had ever been paid the honor and respect that Pastor Adam Jensen had received.

"Tilly," Naomi said, "Tilly—"

Tilly didn't seem to hear the calling of her name. She appeared to have traveled to an emotional place that allowed her to function but kept her safe from the depth of her pain. Naomi decided to try again. "Tilly, please don't go. We're your family now, and we will take care of you. Andrew, Lydia, and Rachael belong here. So do you."

The sound of her children's names caused Tilly to stop and look at Naomi. Tilly held in her hand the dress she had worn the day Adam had proposed to her. She pulled it to her bosom and then pressed her face against the fabric. A tear rolled slowly down her face as if it were following a deliberate course outlined by so many tears shed before it.

Finally Tilly spoke with a trembling voice, "No, Naomi, I must go. Soon another pastor will come, and he'll need this parsonage. Maybe I will return one day, but I can't continue to live among all these memories. I would die."

In that moment, Naomi knew Tilly wouldn't, and perhaps couldn't—change her mind. She had worked beside her for many years and had seen how unbending she could be once a decision had been made.

"Where will you go?"

Tilly explained that her mother's sister, Hannah Richardson, lived in Waynesboro. She would first try and find her. Aunt Hannah was her only known family member. She wasn't sure where she would go after that. Perhaps she would return to Chicago, where she could once again assist Nurse Taylor.

Naomi listened patiently and then asked, "Did you pray about it?"

Tilly answered honestly, "No."

Naomi began to pray aloud, as if Tilly wasn't even in the room. She pleaded with God for His grace, mercy, and direction. After she finished, Naomi walked over to Tilly and took her in her arms. Tilly sobbed brokenly.

The next morning, Gus helped carry Tilly's belongings to the ship. This time when he helped her into the ship there was no fear. Tilly knew she would miss this new Gus who had become so dear to her. Tilly's children boarded the boat with eyes wide in amazement. She was relieved—the trip would help distract their minds from the loss of their father. It would be a new adventure for them.

≈ ≈ ≈

Two months later

Meredith's father slumped in the parlor chair with a look of utter despair on his face. Straightening up he slapped his hand hard against his knee and stated, "That hard-headed boy of yours wouldn't listen to a word I had to say! Meredith, why can't he understand that it was not your fault?"

Jerris and Meredith sat opposite Jack. She sighed and said, "Because he feels deceived, and, in one sense, I guess he is right. We should have told him a long time ago in our own way and on our own terms. But there was no way for us to know the depth of Agatha's bitterness. No normal person could have imagined her vicious plan."

"And to think I almost married her!" Her father shivered at the thought.

Clyde interrupted their conversation, presenting a letter which had just been delivered. The correspondence was addressed to Jack Douglas. He seemed to read it several times before it made sense to him. Looking up at Meredith he said, "It's about your Aunt Beatrice. Apparently she is near death. I must go."

Without hesitation Meredith responded, "And I will go with you, Daddy."

Jerris joined in with, "All of us will go to see her."

Clyde was called and arrangements were made to prepare the family for the twelve-hour journey. They departed early the next morning, April 11, from the train station. Their train would make two stops, the last being in Ralston at 12:50 in the afternoon.

The journey back from Africa was far more difficult than Tilly's first trip across the Atlantic. The voyage took many months, but at last she and the children arrived in America. She purchased train tickets for Waynesboro, the last known location of her Aunt Hannah.

"You will have to make one stop in Ralston. You'll be there on April 11, at 12:20 in the afternoon," the ticket agent explained.

17

April 11, 1887

Watching the family carriage pull away from their house, Jerry hoped that his great-aunt Beatrice would be fine. It was during times like these that his inability to walk frustrated him the most. His parents had offered to take him along, but he knew the trip would be long and difficult and that looking after him would inconvenience them.

Jackson walked past the door of his bedroom, and Jerry called out to him. Jackson returned with a look of irritation on his face—a look Jerry hadn't seen since they were little boys fighting over some imaginary war zone. Jerry had noticed that both his parents and grandfathers had looked extremely upset, but hadn't felt inclined to ask why. He could only assume that it concerned Jackson.

Now Jerry said, "Come in, Jackson, I want to ask you a question."

Jackson stood just inside the doorway with his arms folded across his chest. Jerry questioned, "What is all the commotion about? Everyone seems so upset, and their upset appears to be centered around you."

"Well, my half-brother is quite observant."

"What do you mean, 'half-brother'?"

"Don't act like you didn't know. Everyone knew but me!"

"For goodness' sake, Jackson, what are you talking about?"

Jerry began rolling his wheelchair toward Jackson, who took one step back. Anger flashed from Jackson's eyes as he announced, "My father was Carter Hunter. He was engaged to my mother, and when he died she was already pregnant with me."

"That can't be!" replied Jerry.

"Oh, but it is true. She was so bent on becoming a Hunter, she married your father six weeks later. So much for love."

"How do you know all of this?"

Jackson left the room, returning with the pearls and the letter from Agatha Stanton. Jerry read the note and asked, "What did Mom and Dad say?"

"They denied it, of course. Mother said she was raped by my father, who had believed a lie told by Agatha Stanton concerning her reputation. Your father married her to protect my name and her reputation. They've been living a lie all these years!"

Jerry rolled closer to Jackson and said, "First of all, stop calling him my father. He's your father too! I don't know what happened, but this much I do know: Dad and Mom love each other deeply and have devoted as much time and attention to you as they have to the rest of us. Why would you believe some woman you don't know more than two people who adore you?"

Jackson looked as though Jerry had knocked the wind out of him. He shouted in disgust, "It's easy for you to say, Brother— you're the legal heir to your father's fortune. I'm an illegitimate nobody!"

"Jackson, listen to yourself! Our parents would never slight you in any way. Why are you doing this?"

"Because now I know who I am and who I am not."

Studying Jackson's face, Jerry's frustration turned to pity. He replied, "I see now that I have been wrong for many years. All this time I thought *I* was the cripple."

After hearing his brother's harsh words, Jackson stormed out of the room. Jerry wheeled his chair back over to the window.

Patience, who had overheard the conversation, went to her room and cried.

The conductor walked through the lumbering train announcing, "Next stop, Ralston!"

Reaching over, Tilly shook awake ten-year-old Andrew, who was sleeping against her arm. Lydia and Rachael were seated across from them playing with a rag doll. Tilly began gathering their belongings as the train whistle blew and the train slowed to a crawl.

Tilly and the children made their way down the steps as a burst of steam from the engine rose from beneath the wheels. Their next train would leave in forty-five minutes, so Tilly looked for a resting place. Spring had moved in but all traces of winter were not gone. She could smell the plants' new growth, and the sun seemed to be winning the battle against the chill in the air until she stepped into the shade.

Tilly found a bench in the sunlight and settled the children down. Not long afterward, a train coming from the opposite direction could be seen approaching in the distance. Andrew was completely fascinated by the "iron elephants," as he called them. He walked to the edge of the platform to watch the big engine's arrival.

Tilly had begun reading a book to the twins, so she didn't pay attention to the people disembarking. She overheard the conductor tell one of the passengers not to go far because the train would be leaving in ten minutes. After Tilly had finished reading, Lydia and Rachael wanted to play patty-cake. Out of the corner of her eye, Tilly saw a little girl picking a flower next to the platform. Her heart skipped a beat because the child looked like Meri.

Tilly shifted her attention back to the twins until she heard a booming, deep voice. Immediately she thought, *Master Jack! I'd know his voice out of a million voices.* Her back was to him and to the conductor. Both were standing by the entrance to the train, carrying on a conversation. Tilly felt as if her heart would never start beating again. She was grateful for the bonnet she wore that covered her face on both sides.

Tilly tried to calm down, to convince herself she should not be afraid. After all, slavery was over. The Emancipation Proclamation had been signed and she was free. But as she sat there trembling, she realized that none of that mattered. Her years of enslavement were not just physical but mental, and she discovered the prison that had been erected in her mind was greater than any bondage she might have felt on the plantation. Only Tilly's love for Meri and her desire one day to see her again shook her out of her panic. She tried to nonchalantly walk over to the little girl.

"Hello," said Tilly with a nervous smile.

The little girl with the long auburn braids continued to pull the petals off the flower. She finally looked up into Tilly's face and responded, "Hi."

"You're a pretty little girl. What's your name?"

"My name is Becky."

Tilly's mind began to whirl as she wondered whether it was a coincidence that she had the same name as Meredith's mother. She then asked another question. "What's your mother's name?"

Becky looked around to see if she could find any more flowers to pick. When she spotted one growing a foot away, she headed in that direction. As she began to skip ahead she replied, "Meredith."

Tilly followed Becky to the next flower and asked, "Is your Mommy with you?"

"Uh-huh," was the answer, "she's on the train."

Tilly glanced over her shoulder and saw Master Jack still talking with the conductor. Fortunately, he still wasn't facing her. Tilly felt helpless; just then she reached down and picked up a small black stone lying among the flowers.

"Becky, would you do something for me?"

"O.K.," Becky responded.

"I want you to take this stone and give it to your mother. Tell her a lady outside gave it to you and wants to see her."

Becky obediently took the stone from Tilly and headed toward the train. Tilly lowered her head and walked inside the train station where a big window looked out onto the platform. She began searching the train windows for a glimpse of Meredith. Becky had walked past her grandfather without taking notice and had climbed up the stairs.

Tilly saw the conductor shake Master Jack's hand. Then he announced, "All aboard!"

In that instant, Tilly saw a woman sitting beside the window on the train. Her head was resting against it as she stared straight ahead. Tilly thought she looked very sad, and she would have understood why if she had known what had recently happened with Jackson. Becky's little head could be seen passing each seat, and an older girl, who Tilly assumed to be Priscilla, reached out and tried to pick her up.

Once again the conducter called out, "Last call. All aboard!"

Tilly heard the engine start. Becky was patting Meredith on the arm but she seemed not to hear her. Finally she turned to look at Becky, who reached out with the little black rock displayed in her open palm. At first it didn't register with Meredith. Then it struck her. She looked quickly around the train station, in search of her dear friend.

Master Jack had boarded the train, so Tilly felt it was safe to return to the platform. The brake was released with a hiss, and the train began to slowly move forward. Meredith made a dash for the opening, and when she saw it had passed the platform, she ran through the next train car and then the next until she was standing at the back of the caboose. Tilly walked to the edge of the platform next to where Andrew and the twins were standing.

As the train continued down the track, Meredith shouted, "Tilly!"

Tilly lifted her hand and waved. Meredith raised the silver locket she wore around her neck, and Tilly held up the smooth, black stone that Adam had mounted and put on a gold chain as a present for her on last birthday. Just then, Jerris stepped from the train's door and stood next to Meredith. They both waved.

Andrew asked, "Momma, who was that?"

Tilly whispered, "Meri."

Andrew looked at Meri curiously as the train continued down the track. "You never told me she was white," he said.

Tilly spoke without taking her eyes off the train, "It was never important."

Tilly didn't notice when Andrew left her side, but was suddenly startled by a woman shouting, "And just what do you think you're doing, boy?"

Tilly spun around to see an elderly white woman holding Andrew by his shirt collar. She rushed over to Andrew, and the woman snarled, "Can't your son read?"

Tilly looked over at the wall and saw a water fountain. Above it were written the words, "White Only."

Tilly hastened to say, "I'm sorry, ma'am. He doesn't know any better. We've just come from Africa."

Just then a man who Tilly assumed to be the woman's husband drawled, "Well, unless you're gonna teach that boy right, it would be safer for him to be back in Africa." Then he looked down at Andrew and said, "And boy, if I ever see you looking at a white woman in the eye again, you'll be awfully sorry."

Tilly put her arms around Andrew and hastened him away from the couple. By now, Meredith's train was almost out of sight, but Andrew could still see the figures of Meredith and the man standing next to her. Andrew stared for a moment longer at his mother's lifelong friend and then glanced back at the couple he had just encountered. Clearly, he didn't understand.

When Meri could no longer see Tilly on the platform, she began to cry. Jerris drew her close. "Oh, Jerris," Meredith cried, "we were almost together again. Why didn't I get off the train? I could have seen her and the children. Weren't they just precious?"

"Yes, sweetheart, they were."

Meredith continued, "When I received her letter about Adam's death I should have hastened off a reply asking if and when she would return to the states. But what is she doing here?"

Before Jerris could answer, Meredith exclaimed, "We've got to go back, Jerris. We must catch the next train going to Ralston. I have to find Tilly!"

Returning to their seats, Meredith's father asked, "What was that all about?"

"Tilly was at the train station. I missed her, but I'm going back."

"You're what?" Her father said in a loud, irritated voice. "You're going back to see a colored girl when your aunt is at the brink of death? That's the most absurd thing I've ever heard!"

Meredith's face was set like flint. She responded, "I'm going to see my best friend, and I will be on the next train to Ralston!

With disgust, Jack sputtered, "Your best friend! You haven't seen her in over twenty-five years! How can she be your best friend?"

"We've stayed in touch with each other by letter." Then Meredith sarcastically stated, "You remember? Tilly could read and write."

Meredith's father shouted, "I won't stand for this! Jerris, talk to your wife."

Jerris reached over and took Meredith's hand, smiled at her father, and calmly said, "I've already talked to her. We're going back."

Tilly returned to their bench. She held all her children close to her until it was time for them to leave. Andrew hadn't noticed before, but now he could see that all the white people sat in the first three cars, which were beautiful and plush. The last car was reserved for coloreds, and it was old and run down. He hadn't paid attention on the first trip because in Africa he was almost totally surrounded by people of his own color, so it wasn't strange for him to be sitting among them on the train. But after the recent incident, he became aware of a distinct difference between white and colored people.

Tilly breathed a sigh of relief as their railway car began to move down the track. She settled back in her seat only to hear Andrew ask, "Momma, what did that man mean when he said I couldn't look a white woman in the eye?"

Tilly had hoped Andrew wouldn't bring the subject up. It was obvious that a bespectacled older man with salt-and-pepper hair had overheard the question because he looked up at Tilly and then back down at his book. His dark-blue suit gave him an air of sophistication, and Tilly thought he was probably an educator of some kind. She had seen many men like him Chicago. And she knew that he was listening.

As Tilly's eyes fixed themselves on her son, her heart broke. She knew his spirit had been crushed, and she wasn't sure it could ever be mended. Perhaps she should have stayed in Africa as Naomi had suggested. Her pain from the loss of Adam had caused her to forget the racial inequality in America.

Breathing a prayer before she replied, she began, "Andrew, do you remember how we talked about the law of the jungle? In Africa you watched as the animals learned to survive around each other. When we were there, almost everyone looked like us. But in America there are different kinds of people. And even though God's Word teaches that He 'created them male and female and blessed them and called them mankind,' some people still believe that we colored people are not of their kind. Some white folks even think they're better."

Andrew interrupted, "Are they?"

Tilly wrapped her arms around her handsome, intelligent son and whispered, "No. But if they think they are, then they will fight against what they see as being different. For now, just imagine that we've moved to another part of the jungle, and now we must learn to survive in our new surroundings. The man was right. You don't look a white woman in the eye. And when you're walking down the street and white people are coming toward you, you must step out of their way. You have to look for the "White Only" signs by water fountains, restrooms, swimming holes, and restaurants. Keep your head down, your voice respectful, and you won't get into any trouble."

Tilly glanced up at the distinguished-looking colored gentleman seated across from her, and she thought she saw tears glistening in his eyes. She directed her attention back to Andrew and said, "Who knows, Andrew, maybe one day you will be able to help people think differently. We need to keep praying because God can do anything."

Andrew didn't speak, but it was obvious that his mind was overrun with questions. He would be a grown man before he repeated the conversation he had with his mother that April day in 1887.

When the train slowed to a stop in Ralston, Meredith was already standing in the stairwell of the doorway waiting for it to open. Jerris held her back so she wouldn't step down too soon. They both rushed up to the ticket agent and Meredith inquired, "Excuse me, sir, I am looking for a woman with three children who would have arrived here about three hours ago."

The bald agent didn't take his eyes off his papers. The green visor he wore on his head hid his face. He asked, "What did they look like?"

Meredith described, "The woman is of slight built. She had an eleven-year-old son and twin girls."

"I make a habit of remembering everyone who comes and goes off these trains," the agent said proudly. "It's kind of a game I play. I'm not too good on names, but I remember a face, and no one like the family you described came through here today."

Jerris stated, "Surely you're mistaken, sir. We saw them standing on the platform as our train left the station. She's a beautiful colored woman."

"Did you say 'colored'?"

"Yes."

Jerris and Meredith saw the top of the man's head as he went back to his papers. "I don't waste my time remembering colored people. They all look the same."

"That's absurd!" stormed Meredith.

The agent put his pencil down. With one finger he pushed his glasses up close to his nose and glared at Meredith asking, "You two wouldn't happen to be nigger lovers, would you?"

Meredith started to respond, but Jerris put his arm firmly around her and led her out the door and onto the platform.

"What are you doing?" asked Meredith.

"We're leaving, Meredith. The man doesn't know and doesn't care what happened to Tilly."

"Then let's go into town and see if we can find her."

"Where would we start?" asked Jerris. "No, darling, we missed her and now we must be on to your Aunt Beatrice's house. There will be another time for the two of you to be together."

Once they were on their way to Sommersville, Meredith said to Jerris, "I saw something for the first time today. I now realize what a blessing it was Tilly and I were separated at ten years old."

"What do you mean?" inquired Jerris.

"We could have never remained friends. My father is a devoted husband, a faithful friend, and has been a loving father to me. But his view of colored people is skewed, and I'm sure my grandfather had a lot to do with it. People like my father and that ticket agent would have made sure I started to see Tilly the way they do. It's like God placed our friendship inside an airtight jar, sealed it, and didn't allow it to get rotten. I will be forever grateful to Him for that."

They didn't speak again for the rest of the trip. Meredith kept remembering in her mind the sight of Tilly standing on that platform with her three precious children. She also remembered

the promise she'd made to Tilly to make a difference in the condition of her people when she was grown. *Unfortunately, I've
become distracted in my everyday activities. Now,* Meredith
decided, *that is about to change.*

18

When Tilly reached Waynesboro, the afternoon shadows were lengthening into darkness. She hastened to inquire about a place to sleep for the night and was directed to a guesthouse for colored people which was located just two blocks away. The children were exhausted. She would have been, too, if she hadn't been their mother.

Waynesboro was a pretty town. The city hall could be seen from the train station. A park adjoined the station, and several elderly citizens relaxed on the benches chatting with each other. A small white church was a stone's throw away, and it was a comforting sight.

Tilly herded the children toward the guesthouse and swung open the white picket gate. The house was old but tidy, and the proprietor, Edna, was a jolly old lady who cheerfully welcomed them in. Her worn furniture was covered with white doilies, and pictures of folks, whom Tilly assumed to be family members, covered the walls. The house had a faint smell of mothballs combined with musty old furniture. Edna led them to their room at the back of the house and lit a candle. She left for a moment then brought back clean towels and soap.

"Will ya be needin' anyt'ing else, Mis' "?

Tilly answered, "Please call me Tilly. My name is Tilly Jensen."

The warm smile on Edna's face faded. She dropped her head slightly, looked over the top of her glasses and quietly responded, "Well, all right, Tilly. Will ya be needin' anyt'ing else?"

"No, Edna, but you've been very kind."

As Edna turned to leave the room, Tilly said, "Oh, I'm sorry there is one more thing. I've come to find my aunt, Hannah Richardson. Do you know her?"

Edna abruptly said, "No, I don' know no Hannah Richardson. An'," she added, "if she lived in des parts I would, 'cause I makes it my business to know everybody."

"Are you sure? My mother told me she lived in this town."

"I'm very sho'" replied Edna, hurriedly leaving the room.

Tilly sat on the bed in the dimly lit room where the children lay sleeping. She rested her head in the palm of her hand and began to sob as she thought about Adam, of missing Meri by so few minutes, and of the humiliating experience that had happened to Andrew. It was a quiet, aching cry. It was the kind of heartache that comes when sorrow leaves and despair takes its place.

Tilly was surprised to discover it was nine o'clock when she awakened—extremely late for an early riser. She'd been more exhausted than she'd thought, but now she woke up feeling refreshed. As she found her way to the front of the house, she began looking at the many pictures hanging on the walls. The sepia-colored photographs were of babies and families. Tilly stopped at one particular picture. It was of two elderly women. One of the women was seated and holding a cane. It was clear she was blind by the dark glasses she wore. A serious but pleasant-looking woman stood beside her.

Tilly was studying the picture when Edna came through the front door and greeted Tilly. Edna said, "Ya like those old pictures? Let me show you this one ovah heah. It's of my mother an' father."

When Tilly asked her about the picture she was looking at, Edna identified them as two of the town's people who Tilly wouldn't know. Edna gave her a tour of her photo collections and then said she was about to fix breakfast. But before she left for the kitchen, Edna stated, "Tilly, I'm awful sorry to tell you dat I'm goin' to be needin' yo' room tonight for some peoples who made plans a long time ago to be heah. So I hope ya find yo' aunt dis mornin'. Othahwise, ya'll be needin' to take de train dis afternoon. Dis is de only restin' place for coloreds in dis town."

Tilly got the children ready, fed them breakfast, and started out to find Aunt Hannah. As she walked up the street, a woman sweeping the sidewalk in front of her small house glanced at Tilly then hurried inside. It also appeared that some other people were purposely turning aside or going in the opposite direction. She decided her mind was playing tricks on her as she walked into the local colored barbershop.

The barber was busy cutting a man's hair. The customer had his eyes closed and appeared to be taking a nap.

"Excuse me, sir. I'm looking for a Hannah Richardson. Do you know her?"

The barber stopped the swift snipping of his scissors and responded, "Nope. No one by dat name in dees here parts."

Everyone Tilly stopped to speak to gave her the same answer. Actually there seemed to be very few people around at all. By noon, Tilly decided to return to Edna's to gather up their things. She must have misunderstood her mother when she'd told her the name of the town Aunt Hannah was from. Everybody couldn't be wrong.

After saying her goodbyes, Tilly and the children headed toward the train station. The sum of money that the African church had raised to help her and the children get settled in America would soon run out. If she couldn't find Aunt Hannah, she would to have head north.

Tilly had already checked, and a train for Chicago was leaving at five o'clock. She walked the children to the station, purchased their tickets, and sat down on a bench just outside the front door. She swatted at a fly as she began looking around. She glanced to her left and saw the little white church. The tiny bell in its tower had just rung four times. For some reason, the sound resonated inside her and, since the train wouldn't be leaving for almost an hour, she decided to walk over to the churchyard. She rounded up the children and headed toward the sanctuary.

Tilly saw a colored woman bent over a flower garden pulling up weeds and asked her whether the church was for colored people. The lady stood up, wiped her brow with the back of her hand, and nodded.

Tilly opened the church door and went inside. There was something about being in a church that had always affected her in a powerful way. Something inside her seemed to stir and come alive. Tilly directed the children to a pew halfway down the aisle and sat down. For the first time in months, she felt a sense of peace.

"You must be Tilly," said a voice behind her.

Tilly turned with a start and placed her hand over her heart. "Oh my!" she exclaimed. "You frightened me."

A man walked toward her and apologized. He introduced himself as Pastor Green.

"How do you know my name?" asked Tilly.

"In a town dis small, word gets around quickly."

The gray-haired preacher looked at Tilly's suitcases and questioned, "Are you leaving?"

"Yes, I came to find my aunt, Hannah Richardson, but no one in town has heard of her. So we're on our way to Chicago."

The preacher looked amazed and responded, "Well, I be. Dees folks are about to run you off with a lie. I t'ank the Lawd you stopped by the church befo' gittin' on dat train."

"I don't understand," said Tilly.

"Yo' aunt was a well-known and respected member of our community. She was sixty-five when she died two years ago."

"But why would everyone say . . . ?"

Pastor Green sat in the pew in front of Tilly and turned around to face her. " 'Cause Edna Murphy told dem to tell you dat there was no Hannah Richardson. She must have gone from house to house. Most of de people in town are related to Edna in one way or another, and those who aren't related have been victims of her gossiping tongue. I think she has something on everyone here except me."

Tilly looked at the pastor in amazement and asked, "But why would she do that?"

Pastor Green glanced up at the stained-glass windows and then back to Tilly. "Because de house she lives in belongs to you."

He continued the story. After the slaves were set free, Hannah had continued to work for Master Richardson and had saved her money. She'd saved every dime and several years later she had purchased the old house on Regent Street. When she died, her next of kin couldn't be found. So Edna, her close friend, took ownership of the house by saying she was her distant cousin. There were hardly any records kept on slaves, so with the help of some of her relatives who vouched for her, the courts took her at her word.

Tilly sat in stunned silence. Finally the pastor interrupted her thoughts, "Come wid me, I have somet'in' I'd like to show you."

Tilly gathered the children and they followed him out the door. He turned toward the garden where the woman was still bent over, hard at work. As Tilly looked closer she realized it wasn't a garden but a graveyard.

Pastor Green raised has hand in greeting to the woman, who stood up and smiled. Tilly followed him along the small grave-yard path. Finally he stopped and she saw the simple wooden marker, "Hannah Richardson. May she rest in peace."

Tilly stared at the marker as if she could see more than what was there. Pastor Green recaptured her attention when he said, "Der is somet'in' else I'd like you to see." He moved to the next grave. The marker read, "Sadie Douglas. To God be the glory."

Tilly looked at the pastor and asked, "Was this put here in honor of my mother?" Then she paused and stated, "No, that can't be. Aunt Hannah wouldn't have known my mother's name."

"No, Tilly, dis is yo' mother's grave."

"My mother?"

Pastor Green stood next to Tilly and put his arm around her shoulder as if he knew she would need the extra support. "Yes, yo' mother. Some people who worked with de Underground Railroad brought her to dis town. Dey had found her on de rivahbank. At first dey thought she was dead, but dey soon discovered she was still alive. Dey helped nurse her back to health. She didn' know how she lost huh sight. She thought dat a log might have struck huh while she was still in de water because she woke up unable to see.

Tilly remembered the photograph hanging on Edna's wall. She turned to the pastor and asked, "What happened to her?"

Pastor Green explained that Sadie had become one of the most faithful members in his church. "She had the prettiest voice I've ever heard—in fact, its beauty even surprised huh. Hannah thought she'd died and gone to heaven when Sadie came to live with her. She was a doting sister and dey would sit for hours stitching quilts and humming old songs. Hannah died a year after yo' mother. I don't know why yo' mother died; I guess she jes' come to de end of her time."

After a few moments of brushing away her tears, Tilly looked at her children and said, "This is Grandma Sadie's grave. She was my mother, and she was a very great woman."

Tilly knelt by the marker and ran her hand over the grass covering the grave. She hummed a tune her mother had taught her in the dark cellar, when they had huddled together waiting for the night to come. Sadie had told her it was a song she and Araba had sung in Africa. An unfinished chapter came to a close in Tilly's heart that spring afternoon in Waynesboro, and she smiled to herself.

When Tilly stood up the pastor asked, "What are you going to do now?"

Tilly kept her eyes on the graves and answered, "I don't know." Tilly did know one thing she would do soon, however. She would write Gus a letter and let him know he wasn't responsible for her mother's death. Ruby had been so right when she'd said, "God is always by yo' side."

When Edna opened the door, Tilly was standing on the porch. The children weren't with her.

Edna breathed a sigh of relief, then lifted her eyes toward heaven saying, "T'ank de Lawd! Please, please come in."

Tilly was rather confused by the greeting and decided to wait and hear what Edna had to say before delivering the speech she had prepared. Edna asked if she could get Tilly something to drink. When Tilly said no, they both took a seat in the living room.

Edna seemed to be sitting on pins and needles. She squirmed in her chair with her eyes cast toward the floor. Finally she began by saying, "I'm so happy ya came back, Tilly. I tried to catch ya at the train station but it had jes' left. As I watched it go down de train tracks I was sho' I'd nevah have de chance to make t'ings right.

Tilly came right to the point, "Why did you lie to me?"

A single tear began to roll down Edna's cheek. She rubbed her hand across the top of her head and looked at the ceiling. Taking a deep breath, Tilly could tell she was trying hard to hold back a floodgate of tears.

"I lied to ya Tilly, 'cause I was 'fraid. I did know ya Aunt Hannah. She and I wuz close friends fo' ovah forty years. When she died . . ."

Tilly abruptly cut off Edna's explanation and stated, "I know what happened, Edna. I just want to know why you didn't tell me the truth. What were you afraid of?"

Edna was so jittery that she seemed ready to explode. She started talking quickly, and Tilly asked her to slow down. Edna continued, "Well, when it was clear dat yo' aunt's next of kin couldn't be found, I claimed de house as her cousin. I didn't want to see it go back to de city. She worked so hard to git it. I promised myse'f I'd keep it 'til her relative was found . . . well dats what I tol' myself. But den I had a long run of bad luck—ain't seen my own chil'ren in years, and mine is po'. When you showed up heah, I got scared of what ya would do when ya found out I had been livin' in ya hous'. I'm not a young woman, Tilly, an' I don't know where I would go. So I lied and left early next mo'nin' to tell de townspeople to say dey didn't know Hannah. I felt so bad after you left."

With a degree of pride Edna announced, "People say I'm a gossip but I'm no liar! I tried to find ya so I could tell de truth. I'm sorry, Tilly."

Tilly rested her head back against the chair and closed her eyes. She didn't open them when she responded to Edna. "When I found out you lied to me, I was planning to have you thrown out in the street." Tilly sighed and then continued, "But I understand what it feels like to be afraid. There have been many days recently when I didn't know what to do, either."

Tilly got up and walked to the hallway where the picture of Hannah and her mother hung. She ran her fingers over the figure of her mother and stared at it until Edna spoke again. "So, Tilly, whut are ya goin' to do?"

Tilly returned to the chair, facing Edna. "When I left Ralston, I searched my heart, and I knew even before I arrived here that I wanted to return to Chicago. I want my children to be educated in the north. I also feel led to practice my nursing there. After hearing your explanation, I've decided to let you stay here—but I want to make sure this house is left to my children upon your death. Once the paperwork is finished, I'll be leaving."

Edna's eyes filled as she replied, "I will fo'ever be beholdin' to ya, Tilly."

Tilly responded, "There is one more thing."

"Whut is dat?"

"I want you to tell me everything you remember about Aunt Hannah and my mother."

Edna looked relieved and answered, "Well now, dat would be the greatest privilege of all. Let's go to the kitchen and make some tea. By de way, where are ya chil'ren?"

"I left them with Pastor Green. I didn't know what I would be facing when I came back here."

Edna gave a nod of understanding. For the next two hours, Tilly was immersed in the precious memories of her aunt and mother. Slowly her despair was replaced with an unabashed joy, and she felt encouraged to embark upon the next leg of her journey.

"Meredith, I've always treated my coloreds well, but I also made sure they knew their place. I can't allow you to do this! It has nothing to do with cost and everything to do with my good name. Why, I'll be the laughingstock of everyone in the county. I'm sorry, but the answer is no!"

Aunt Beatrice had recovered well enough for the family to return home within a week. Meredith was sitting opposite her father-in-law in his study. His collection of animal heads hung on the mahogany walls. The moose looked extremely sad, and the buffalo appeared dangerously hostile.

Solomon Hunter had turned beet red. Anyone else would have been intimidated by his outburst. But Meredith was determined. As far as she was concerned, Solomon could hang his head among the other stuffed animals on the wall. There was no way she was turning back.

When her father-in-law realized she wouldn't be swayed by his anger, he decided to change the nature of his appeal. He got up from the chair behind his desk and walked around to the front of it. He leaned against the desk, folded his arms, and spoke softly, "Meredith, be reasonable. What you're asking just isn't done in this part of the country. Colored children don't want to learn. They want to work with their parents in the fields. That's just the way they are. This idea of starting a school doesn't make sense. Their families need them to work."

"Then we'll start with Saturday or Sunday school," Meredith replied.

Solomon continued, "You don't know what you're asking. Anyway, who would teach the children?"

"I've already decided to put an ad in the classified section of the newspaper. Someone will respond."

Solomon pounded his fist on the desk and shouted, "No, you won't! Everyone I know will see it in the paper."

Meredith spoke in a deliberate tone, "You owe me, Solomon Hunter."

Solomon looked stunned. He knew she was referring to the incident with Carter. This was the first time she had ever mentioned it. A stuttering Solomon answered, "Now . . . now . . . Meredith, don't try using that on me. It won't work."

Meredith stood up and squared off with Solomon. "Yes, it will work. I've chosen the spot where I want the school erected. I'll speak with your foreman and give him the necessary instructions. Good day, Solomon."

Solomon watched Meredith leave the room and heard her hoop skirt swish from side to side as she walked down his marble hallway. Even though he was very upset, his meeting with Meredith deepened his admiration for her.

Tilly was sure Nurse Taylor would not be home when she and the children arrived. It was only one o'clock, and she usually didn't return until seven or eight in the evening. But after indecisively standing on the porch a while, Tilly decided to knock anyway. She was surprised when someone answered the door. Tilly introduced herself and asked for Nurse Taylor. The kind-looking woman invited her in and introduced herself as Mable, Nurse Taylor's sister. Tilly remembered Nurse Taylor speaking of her sister who lived in Memphis.

Mable told Tilly to take a load off her feet and went to the kitchen to get her and the children something to drink. When she returned she said, "Clare is resting upstairs. It seems to me that the only thing she talks about is you. She's going to be so glad you're here."

"What's wrong with her?"

Mable replied, "It started out as a bad cold and progressed into pneumonia. There was no one to care for her so I came to help her. The only problem is, I have to leave in two days. Until you arrived, there was no one I knew who could tend to her."

Tilly was already walking toward the stairs when Mable called out to her, "Please, tell me you're staying."

Slightly turning her head to answer, Tilly replied, "I'll be here as long as she'll have me."

Mable responded, "Well then, that will be forever."

Nurse Taylor was asleep when Tilly walked into her room and took a seat next to her bed. She could see the illness had taken quite a toll. Her full cheeks were sunken, and her body looked angular and gaunt beneath the sheet. Almost as if someone had shaken her, Nurse Taylor opened her eyes and tried to focus them. She closed them again and hesitantly said, "Tilly?" She coughed and asked again, "Is that you, Tilly, or am I in heaven?"

"Yes, it's me and you're still in Chicago. I've come to take care of you."

"Then I know I'll be fine." Nurse Taylor faintly smiled then asked, "Where's Adam? I want to see him."

Tilly fought off the lump in her throat and answered, "Adam has gone to be with the Lord. I mailed you a letter, but you must not have received it yet."

Nurse Taylor searched Tilly's face and whispered, "I'm so very sorry, Tilly. I know how deeply you loved him. He was a good man."

Tilly reached over to stroke Nurse Taylor's hair and said, "No, he was a *very* good man."

After a moment Tilly excused herself. "I don't want you to talk right now. I need to go back downstairs and talk with Mable."

Tilly discovered that Nurse Taylor had been ill for over three months. The doctor said it appeared to him that her lungs had been permanently damaged. He recommended that she remain very quiet because rest would have to be her medicine. There was little else he could do.

Two days later Tilly drove Mable to the train station, and then returned to apply every ounce of nursing skill she had acquired to Nurse Taylor. She continued to pray under her breath as she worked on her patient. The first time Nurse Taylor heard her pray, she smiled to herself and marveled at God's faithfulness.

Two months later, Tilly was watching the children play in the living room and was grateful they had adjusted to their new surroundings so well. Andrew liked Chicago—especially the fact they lived in a predominantly colored section of town. He didn't have to worry about reading signs that told him what he couldn't do and where he couldn't go. His fears began to subside.

Andrew was also quite helpful with the twins as his mother tended to Momma Clare, the name the children gave to Nurse Taylor. Tilly laughed when they first called her by that name. From that day forward she would be officially known as Momma Clare.

Clare smiled and her eyes twinkled. She knew that Tilly was the best medicine God could have ever prescribed for her. She had missed her so, and as the days rolled by she observed how much Tilly had changed. Clare was sad that Adam had died, but she was grateful for the impact he'd had on Tilly's life. She was a changed woman. Gone was the wall that kept people at a distance. And she was beginning to see a side of humor in Tilly that hadn't been apparent when she'd stayed with her as a young girl.

Within three weeks, Momma Clare was able to sit up in the bed and feed herself. Although it would be another month before she could make an attempt to get out of bed, her progress was continuous. Before long, Momma Clare was taking short walks outside. Her strength grew daily. As she carefully made her way up the street, her neighbors waved at her. She had tended to many of them, and they loved her.

One morning, as Tilly walked arm in arm with her toward their apartment, Momma Clare spoke up. "Tilly, it's time for you to return to nursing."

Tilly smiled and said, "What do you think I've been doing with you?"

Momma Clare chuckled, looked down at Tilly, and replied, "I'm getting better now and there are a lot of people who need you. I'll tend the children while you take care of the needy. I will ask the Lord to send you an assistant."

A wave of apprehension swept over Tilly when she thought about being away from Andrew and the twins. The four of them had never been apart—and yet she knew that what Momma Clare said was true.

Tilly started out working just a couple of hours a day, but the time continued to increase as the demand for medical help grew. Andrew started school, and Momma Clare watched the four-year-old twins during the day. Tilly was amazed that she could keep up with them, and they loved her dearly.

After working for just over six months, on a frigid winter day at the home of an elderly lady, she met Dr. Robert Ryan. The short, slight man entered the tiny bedroom of Tilly's patient. Colored doctors were few and far between. The cost of being that well educated was too great for most people. Tilly was relieved when he came in carrying his black doctor's bag. She knew her patient was dying, and Tilly had done all she could do.

Dr. Ryan acknowledged Tilly's presence by nodding his head in her direction as he approached the bed. His voice was filled with compassion when he spoke to the sick woman. Dr. Ryan's hands moved gently yet confidently across the patient's body, searching for the source of her pain. A tender spot caused her to wince. After the examination was completed, the doctor beckoned Tilly into the hallway.

"Good day, nurse. My name is Dr. Robert Ryan."

"Hello, doctor, I'm Nurse Jensen. It's a pleasure meeting you."

"This woman needs to be taken to the hospital. She'll die if she stays here."

Tilly looked around the run-down apartment building, knowing all too well that the aged widow could not afford a hospital stay. Dr. Ryan saw the distressed look on Tilly's face and answered her unexpressed concern.

"I know what you're thinking Nurse Jensen. I'll make arrangements at the hospital and will pay for her care myself."

Tilly studied the doctor in amazement. His was a common face, but it was handsome in its kindness. She said, "You must be a very poor man, Dr. Ryan."

"And why is that, Nurse Jensen?"

"Because hospital care is expensive. If you make it a common practice to pay your patients' hospital bills, you must be a very poor man."

"Oh, trust me, I can't do it for everyone. But every now and then I feel impressed to help a certain patient. God has been kind to me so I try to pass that on to others."

Tilly returned to her patient to prepare her for the trip to the hospital. At first the woman adamantly refused to cooperate until Tilly explained that Dr. Ryan would be paying for her medical treatment. When the woman asked her why, Tilly simply repeated what the doctor had said to her.

As the medical transport left for the hospital with the elderly woman inside, Dr. Ryan and Tilly stood on the steps watching its departure.

Dr. Ryan looked at Tilly and asked, "How long have you been with this patient today?"

"Since early this morning."

"Well, you look like you could use a cup of tea."

The thought of sipping a hot beverage came as a welcome relief to Tilly. As they walked to the nearest diner, Dr. Ryan told her a little about his past. He was from New York City, where his father and mother were educators. He had experienced an affluent lifestyle and had decided to become a doctor when his mother died. For years he had believed that she would still be alive if her doctor had administered a different type of treatment.

He and Tilly talked about some of the medical cases that had faced her in recent weeks, and she was able to acquire valuable information from Dr. Ryan as suggested treatments. When she briefly mentioned her time in Africa, he became immensely interested about her experiences there.

Two hours had passed before Tilly checked her watch. She jumped up and apologized for rushing off, but she needed to get home to her children. "I am sure you have a family that needs you, too, Dr. Ryan."

The doctor smiled slightly and responded, "Unfortunately, up to this point, medicine has been my family."

"Well then, how long has it been since you've had a home-cooked meal?"

Dr. Ryan replied, "It's been a very, very long time."

With a smile Tilly added, "Perhaps sometime in the future I can change that." She stretched forth her hand to Dr. Ryan. "Good day, and thank you for having tea with me," she smiled at her new friend. "I've enjoy talking with you very much."

19

*M*eredith watched as the sign was lifted above the schoolhouse door and nailed firmly in place. It read, "Tilly Douglas Elementary School."

The simple one-room schoolhouse had been painted red. Meredith walked inside to inspect the classroom: at the front stood a desk with a blackboard behind it. To the right was a pot-bellied stove, ready to be used during the cold winters. Thirty desks filled the empty floorspace, and on each one paper and books had been placed.

Meredith felt a sense of anticipation as she walked outside into the bright autumn sun. School would start the next day— even though no teacher had applied. This was of no concern to Meredith because she had decided she would teach the class herself if necessary. She had made many trips to the share-cropper's shanties informing them of the Saturday school. Class would start at three o'clock, which would allow children to help in the fields. It would end at five-thirty. Meredith knew it was a very limited period of time, but she had decided to start slowly.

At first the colored people had looked at her with mistrust but it wasn't long before the word was spread that she had helped her slave escape through the Underground Railroad. Soon Meredith felt at home in the presence of these hard-working families, and she was utterly excited about the first day of school.

On September 14, the Tilly Douglas Elementary School held its first class. Meredith rang the school bell at two fifty-five, and when she walked out onto the school porch, she saw children coming from every direction—fifty-eight students in all! There weren't enough desks so the extra children sat on the floor. They ranged in age from five to fifteen years old, and Meredith was grateful they were so well behaved.

Bobby Carson, a seven-year-old, sat at Meredith's feet as she taught. He never took his eyes off her face the entire time. When class was almost over, he said in a loud voice, "My daddy say ya gonna teach me tuh read!" His grin revealed his missing front teeth.

Meredith looked down at Bobby's expectant face. "Your father is right. Do you want to learn how to read?"

Bobby nodded his head and continued, "My daddy say when I learns to read den I gonna really be free."

Once the students had left, Meredith collapsed in her chair and rested her weary head in her hands. She kept reprimanding herself over and over again, telling herself *What are you doing? Why did you think this would succeed? You're not a teacher!*

She didn't hear the approaching footsteps and was startled when she heard a voice say, "I understand you're looking for a teacher." A woman was standing on the school porch. The bright setting sun blocked Meredith's vision; however, she didn't have to see. She would have known that voice anywhere.

"Miss Martha!"

Meredith ran up through the row of desks and threw her arms around Miss Martha's neck.

No one could have convinced Meredith when she was ten years old that she would one day be elated to see Miss Martha, but her old teacher was a most welcome sight. Martha turned to the man standing quietly next to her, and Meredith apologetically said, "Oh, forgive me, sir. I didn't see you. Please, please both of you come in."

Meredith led them into the schoolhouse. Martha gave the room a quick look of approval, then focused her attention on Meredith. "I'm sorry I couldn't come sooner. I saw your ad but needed to get some things in order at home before I made the trip."

Turning again to the tall, robust man next to her, Martha stated, "This is Paul, my husband. He comes with the package. He's a handyman by trade, and he can fix whatever is broken."

A surprised Meredith shook Paul's hand as she invited the two of them to sit down. Martha explained to Meredith the impact that Tilly's ability to read had made on her life over the years. Up until then she had believed the lie that slaves were incapable of learning. Fortunately, Martha had been able to secure a teaching position soon after she left the Douglas' employ. And since her next employer did not share the same opinion as Meredith's father, her own bias had been both challenged and changed. She'd had the opportunity to teach the colored children on the plantation and had found them to be eager to learn, attentive, and bright.

Martha explained, "When I saw the ad in the newspaper, I wondered if Meredith Hunter was once Meredith Douglas. You were no more than ten years old the last time I saw you. But I thought to myself, *No one else would be this bold!*

Meredith laughed as Martha continued, "You wouldn't know it, but your bravery helped me face some painful situations in my life. I thought if a little girl like you could stand in the face of adversity the way you did with Tilly, then perhaps I should do the same. There were some obstacles I had to overcome before I could even consider getting married, but, as you can see, I've worked through them."

Martha looked at her husband and asked, "Isn't that right, Paul?"

Paul nodded and smiled.

Before they left, Meredith went over some details with Martha. As Meredith climbed wearily into her wagon that evening, she looked back over her shoulder at the little red schoolhouse and thought it would make a wonderful painting. She would begin in the morning.

≈ ≈ ≈

Tilly rode in the ambulance to the hospital with the eight-year-old girl. The slum area where the child lived was infested with rodents and, two days earlier, she had been bitten in the leg by a rat as she slept. Now infection had begun to spread through her little body, and she shivered underneath the blanket.

The ambulance stopped in front of the emergency door, and the young girl was whisked into an overcrowded hallway. Tilly was walking next to the gurney as they rounded the corner when she heard her name being called. The medical assistants stopped and pushed the rolling bed against the wall until a doctor was available.

"Nurse Jensen," called the voice again.

She turned to see Dr. Ryan standing next to her.

"Oh, doctor, thank goodness you're here! This is Georgia, and she has an infected rat bite."

Dr. Ryan lifted the eyelids of the frightened girl and checked her pupils. After a few further observations, he gave instructions to the emergency nurse, who moved quickly to fulfill his order.

Facing Tilly, whose eyes were still on Georgia, Dr. Ryan said, "She'll be fine, Nurse Jensen. You brought her in time. Now, come with me."

Dr. Ryan put his hand under her elbow and began walking Tilly down the hall.

"Where are we going?" she asked.

At that moment, Dr. Ryan stopped in front of the nurse's station and laid his clipboard and pencil down. Leaving instructions with the head nurse, he once again began leading Tilly up the hallway.

"Nurse Jensen, it has been my intention for several weeks to contact you. I'm sorry to say that my schedule took control of me, and I have not done so. But there is no way I'm going to let you go until we've had a chance to sit down and talk for a while."

Dr. Ryan extended his hand as they approached an open doorway, and Tilly walked into the doctors' lounge area. Two other doctors were drinking coffee there and acknowledged Dr. Ryan's presence when he entered. The clean, sterile-looking room had two tables, each with four chairs, a stove, and a counter area. Dr. Ryan pulled out a chair for Tilly at the empty table, then took down two cups from the cupboard above the sink and poured coffee into them.

There was a pencil stuck behind his right ear and a stethoscope hung around his neck. Tilly thought he looked weary. Of course she understood why—she had seen the large numbers of people waiting to be treated. The colored section of the hospital was understaffed and poorly equipped to handle the immense patient load.

"So tell me, Nurse Jensen, what have you been doing since we last talked?"

At first Tilly felt uncomfortable at their impromptu meeting. She had thought about Dr. Ryan several times since their shared cup of tea that past winter, and she had wondered about his well being. For a few moments her words felt forced, but gradually she began to loosen up as she told him about some of her medical adventures.

"Dr. Ryan," said a nurse standing in the doorway, "you're needed in room one. A man just came in and his situation is very bad."

Standing up quickly, Dr. Ryan apologized, "I'm sorry, Nurse Jensen, I'd better go. But I was wondering—does that dinner invitation still stand?"

For an instant Tilly didn't remember what he meant. But then she hastened to say, "Of course!"

"When?"

"Well, how about Sunday at three?" Tilly stammered. "I'll leave my address at the nurses' station."

By then Dr. Ryan had reached the door. His farewell wave was also his sign of acceptance. When he finished with the male patient, he picked up the message left for him and read the directions. Then he looked at her name and said softly, "Tilly."

≈ ≈ ≈

Meredith rolled over as Jerris opened their bedroom shutters. The autumn-morning sun flooded the room as she pulled the blanket over her head. Her husband was the morning person, but she knew, too, that it was time to get up. She had only a few more touches to make on her painting of the red schoolhouse, which she hoped would be finished by the end of that beautiful Saturday morning.

The school was going so well that Martha had decided to extend the days from Friday to Sunday. Meredith loved sitting in on the class. Bobby Carson had proved to be the star student. She should have known when he spoke up the first day of school—he was outgoing and very intelligent. It almost seemed that he had been born to learn. The children's parents worked extra hard to free their children up to attend school. The boys and girls would arrive at three and the class finished at six.

Once classes got underway, Meredith was pleased to see a couple of her neighbors volunteering their time to assist Martha. It continued to be the talk of the town, however, and the general feelings were disgust and contempt.

Jerris got back into bed and Meredith snuggled her head on his chest. He stroked her hair then reminded her it was time to get up. Stretching like a contented cat, Meredith sighed, then said, "Jerris, I've been thinking about something a lot lately."

He looked interested, so she continued, "I want to go and visit Tilly. I know it's quite a train ride, but so much time has passed. In her last letter Tilly expressed her own desire to get together with me. Perhaps we could meet halfway. What do you think?"

Jerris was silent for a moment, then he answered, "You can go on one condition."

"What is that?"

"I want to go with you."

An urgent knocking on the door made them both sit up in the bed with a start. Jerris recognized Clyde's voice calling "Mr. Hunter, please come quick!"

Jerris jumped up and pulled on his robe. Throwing open the door, he asked, "What is it, Clyde?"

"Der's a man outside de house dat say he got to see ya!"

Jerris rushed down the stairs with Meredith following closely at his heels. As they ran out on the front porch, Meredith recognized him immediately. It was Bobby's father, R.C.

Jerry had rolled his wheelchair out onto his bedroom balcony, which overlooked the front yard, so he was able to hear the colored man's conversation with his parents.

With hat in hand, R.C. said, "Mr. Hunter, Mrs. Hunter, I has some bad news."

"What is it?" Jerris asked.

"It's de school, suh. It's on fire. We been tryin' to put it out, but it's bad, suh."

Jerry turned his wheelchair and looked to the west. Thick black smoke was rising from behind the trees. Rushing into the house, Jerris and Meredith quickly dressed and raced to the schoolhouse on their horses. There were about forty colored men, women, and children standing back, watching the schoolhouse burn. The flames leaped high in the air. Meredith saw Bobby sitting at a distance under a tree, his head buried in his hands.

Walking up to the young boy, Meredith sat down and took him into her arms. She looked at the burning building, then back down at Bobby. Kissing the top of his head she said, "Don't worry, Bobby. You'll have another schoolhouse."

Bobby looked in her face and asked, "Why did dis happen?"

Meredith knew the reason but just shook her head in response.

Just then two men rode up, surveyed what was left of the schoolhouse, and headed in Meredith's direction. She recognized Dick Farvis and his son as they came closer. Stopping in front of her, they looked down from their horses.

"Mrs. Hunter, we sure are sorry 'bout what happened here today."

"Thank you, Dick."

"Maybe now the colored children will go back to doing what they were born for."

Meredith cut him off, "And just what is that, Dick?"

"Why, workin' the fields, ma'am. As a matter of fact, I came over here to round up my people so they can get back to work. Well, like I say, I'm sorry. But it's for the best."

"For whose best?"

Dick tipped his hat and said, "Well, ours, ma'am, of course."

Meredith was so angry she wanted to strike out, but she knew that wasn't ladylike, so she resisted the urge.

Just then R.C. approached and reached down to pick up his son, who buried his face in his father's neck. Looking down at Meredith he said, "Mrs. Hunter, if you get the material, we'll build another schoolhouse."

With the fire finally under control, Jerris and Meredith returned to the house and found Paul and Martha waiting for them in the parlor. She could tell Martha had been crying. Clyde brought in some tea and they sat opposite her.

"It's just awful!" Martha began. "Why would anyone want to burn down a schoolhouse?"

"We all know why," answered Jerris.

"But what are we going to do?" asked Martha.

Meredith spoke with cool determination. "We'll build again. And if they burn it down, we'll build again."

Martha looked at Paul and dabbed her eyes, "But what will I do until it's finished? Winter is almost here, and a new school-house couldn't be ready until spring."

A voice behind them spoke up, "Then we will go to the children." Jerry was wheeling himself toward them in his chair.

Meredith questioned, "What do you mean, Jerry?"

"I mean, we'll go to their homes and teach the children there. As many as can fit into a house."

"But, but . . ." stammered Martha, "what do you mean 'we'?"

"I mean you and me, Miss Martha. There's no reason I can't teach."

Meredith hated the thought of the schoolhouse burning down, but she loved the fire it had ignited in her son's heart. The last time she had seen that kind of expression on his face was the day he'd won the victory over Jackson at the horse race. Their meeting went on for hours, and the conclusion was clear-cut: Paul would supervise the reconstruction of the schoolhouse while Martha and Jerry conducted home-schools until it was built.

The next morning, bright and early, Jerry was about to get into the wagon on his way to his new job. Meredith tenderly put her arms around him and whispered, "Go turn the light on in someone's life, my son."

When Dr. Ryan spent Sunday evening with them, Clare found him to be delightful. Andrew, who had just turned eleven, enjoyed talking with him about school. The four-year-old twins found him amusing. Meanwhile, Tilly sat quietly and watched the scene unfold before her. She had already determined that Dr. Ryan was by nature a quiet man. Although he entered into any conversation comfortably, it was easy to see he was a man of deep thought.

As the evening wound down, Tilly got the doctor his hat and walked him outside. It was dusk, and she could hear a mother calling her children in from playing outside. Her neighbor sitting on the front porch across the street smiled and waved. Tilly called out to her, "Hello, Mrs. Granger! How are you feeling this evening?"

The elderly woman answered with a nod, "All is well."

Dr. Ryan's eyes were full of admiration when Tilly looked at him.

"Why are you looking at me like that?"

"Because I think you're an incredible woman."

"How could you think that? You hardly know me."

"You'd be surprised how much I know about you."

"Tell me."

Dr. Ryan leaned against the balcony railing on the front porch. "Well, you're a devoted mother and friend, as evidenced by your children and Clare. From the few things you have told me about your past marriage, you were also devoted to and deeply loved by your husband. You're committed to helping the unfortunate, and you snore while you're sleeping."

Tilly was so taken aback by his last statement that she burst into laughter.

Dr. Ryan continued, "And you have the most contagious laugh I have ever heard. By the way, did I mention you are pretty?"

Tilly's relaxed posture stiffened. Dr. Ryan sensed he had gone too far and stood up.

"I've offended you."

"No, no, not at all. I'm just wondering why you're saying all these things to me," replied Tilly.

Taking her hand in his, Dr. Ryan asked, "Do you mind if I call you Tilly?"

She shook her head.

"I'm saying all these things because I am terribly fond of you. I've met a lot of people in my lifetime but none as charming and admirable as you. Would you mind if I called on you again?"

Tilly stopped staring at the ground and focused her attention on his face. "No, Robert, I wouldn't mind."

Andrew, Lydia, Rachael, and Clare had rushed back to their chairs by the time Tilly came back into the house. They had been at the window overlooking the porch, pushing at each other so they could get a good look at the unfolding events.

Clare cleared her throat then said, "Nice young man, your Dr. Ryan."

"My Dr. Ryan?" Tilly responded with one eyebrow raised.

The twins chimed in, "No, our Dr. Ryan." Everyone laughed, including Tilly.

20

Seven years later

The invitation arrived on a Wednesday morning in June, when summer was just lifting its winsome head. Clyde brought the envelope into the parlor and presented it to Jerris, who was reading a history book while Becky flipped through the latest fashion magazine and Jerry worked on a model boat he had been building for three months. Meredith looked up from her needlepoint in curiosity, waiting until Jerris read its contents.

Jerris smiled and then announced:

> Ralph and Elizabeth Evans
> announce the engagement of
> Jackson Solomon Hunter
> to
> Candace Nicole Evans
> Engagement party
> Sunday, June 12
> 1 p.m. to 4 p.m.
> Evans Estate
> Your presence is requested

Jerris looked up from the invitation and laughed. "My dear Meredith, your mouth is hanging wide open."

Becky and Jerry also laughed, and Meredith joined in when she realized he was right. She responded, "Please forgive me, darling. It's just that it took me by such surprise. But it's wonderful news. Jackson is twenty-six years old, and I think that's a perfect age for a man to get married."

Responding to her statement, Jerris added, "If my memory serves me right, I was twenty-six years old when I married you."

Meredith smiled coyly. "Precisely, dear."

Chiming in Becky said, "Can I go? Can I go?" At fourteen years old, Becky possessed a youthful charm that was infectious.

"Of course you can go," her father replied. "I'm sure you'll find an appropriate dress in that fancy magazine you've been looking at all day."

"Really? Oh, Daddy, I adore you!" Becky said as she bounced out of the room in delight, already designing her party attire.

Jerris quietly read the invitation again with a sense of relief. In the years since Jackson had confronted his parents about Agatha's letter, their relationship with him had gone up and down. They could never determine his mood. Meredith hated to admit it, but she had felt a great sense of relief when Jackson had decided to move into his own residence a year after the incident.

Even now one moment Jackson would be warm and jovial, and the next moment sarcastic and cruel. Meredith knew there was a war going on within him, but only he could fight the emotional villain who was trying to destroy his soul. When they were together at social affairs, he was polite but distant. Meredith grieved the loss of her son's friendship and recalled the last time they were together. It had been just six months earlier. Their family had just arrived at the Norton's ball when Meredith saw Jackson getting punch. It had been only two weeks since she had seen him at church, where he had been most delightful to her.

Walking toward Jackson, she was almost sure he'd seen her walking toward him because he turned abruptly and went through the motions of pouring more punch into an already full cup.

"Hello, Jackson, it's so good to see you! Next to your father, you are the most handsome man at the ball. I noticed the young ladies staring at you—and I don't blame them. You'll make some fortunate young lady a wonderful husband."

Lowering his cup Jackson had replied, "That will probably never happen, Mother."

"And why would that be, Son?"

Jackson answered with a smirk, "You probably won't understand this, but I have a profound mistrust of women."

Jackson's words stung, and Meredith fought back the tears. She struggled to control her emotions and replied, "Jackson, the peace I have concerning our relationship comes from the knowledge that if you do not discover the truth on earth, we will be together forever in eternity. If I have to wait until then, so be it."

Jackson took a sip of his punch and, with a chilling look, vowed, "Trust me, Mother, you will have to wait." With that, he turned to warmly greet a man and his wife who had just approached the refreshment table. Meredith made her way back to Jerris.

"I see our son is in rare form again," he acknowledged.

Meredith asked, "What do you mean?"

"I saw the expression on your face while he was talking to you. I knew he was stabbing you with his verbal daggers. Would you like to leave?"

Meredith extended her hands to Jerris, "Absolutely not! I haven't danced with the man of my dreams yet."

"You amaze me, Meredith Hunter! Have I told you lately that I'm happy you're my wife?"

"Does this morning count?" Meredith asked as he pulled her close, and together they waltzed around the room.

That had been the past. Now they had received the engagement invitation. Meredith was thrilled with Jackson's change of heart. Priscilla walked in as they were discussing the news and inquired, "So what is all this excitement?"

Under his breath, Jerry said, "Uh, oh."

Jerris handed Priscilla the invitation. She read it matter-of-factly then returned it to him. She made no comment before leaving the room.

Giving each other an understanding look, Jerris and Meredith watched her walk out. When Jackson first became resentful toward his parents, he had also transferred those feelings to his siblings. Priscilla had been too young to understand, so she'd felt abandoned by her oldest brother. Once she came of age, Jerris had explained the details of the severed relationship.

Priscilla didn't understand what all the confusion had to do with her and developed an overwhelming bitterness toward Jackson. She was a beautiful twenty-year-old, but seemed older than her years because she took everything to heart. She was visiting her parents with her husband, Ralph—and they had proudly announced the night before at dinner the expected arrival of their first baby.

Meredith sighed as Jerris got up, walked over to her, and placed his hand on her shoulder. He bent down and kissed her cheek, reminding her that the truth always has a way of exposing itself.

"Anyway, who knows? Maybe Candace will have as great an effect on Jackson as you've had on me."

Meredith appreciated his kind words. But, at the same time, she was praying that God would heal her hurting heart.

The weather for Jackson and Candace's engagement festivities reminded Meredith of his eighteenth birthday party. It was perfect. The back lawn of the Evans estate was decorated in royal splendor, and everyone was dressed in elegant garden attire. The orchestra serenaded them with soft music, and the guests awaited the appearance of Jackson and Candace with great anticipation.

Jerris and Meredith were seated at the head table. When the trumpet sounded, the guests arose in honor of the newly engaged couple. They looked stunning. Candace's wavy, jet-black hair was swept up with small, dainty flowers running through it. Her warm, dark eyes and beautiful smile greeted the crowd.

As they drew closer Jerris heard Meredith gasp. He quickly understood why: Candace was wearing the single strand of pearls with the diamond clasp. Jerris was grateful he was standing behind Meredith so that he could put his hands on her waist to steady her. He leaned forward and whispered in her ear, "Be strong, my love."

Jackson acknowledged the crowd with a wave of his hand, and seated his fiancée at his right. Before taking his seat, he leaned over and kissed his mother on the cheek and acknowledged Jerris' presence.

"You look lovely indeed, Mother."

Forcing a smile, Meredith replied, "Thank you."

The guests approached the head table throughout the afternoon. When some of the guests commented on Candace's beautiful necklace, Jackson was quick to add that he had presented it to her as an engagement present.

Meredith's father and Diane came forward to congratulate the engaged couple, and Jack was stunned when he realized what Jackson had done. He glanced at his daughter and could immediately see that the appearance of the pearls had taken its toll.

Meredith didn't remember anything else that happened that day. As they rode home in the carriage, Jerris and Jerry took her hands and squeezed them with gentle consolation. Meredith glanced over at each of them, trying to force a smile.

Jerris spoke softly, "Remember, Meredith, you've often told me that unless my challenge is bigger than Jesus dying on the cross and being raised from the dead, then God can handle it."

Meredith laid her head on Jerris' shoulder and responded, "I know, Jerris, I know."

≈ ≈ ≈

Tilly sat in her favorite chair by the fireplace holding a pad in her hand. There was one line in her poem that just wouldn't flow properly. Leaning her head against the back of the chair she stared at the ceiling. As she lowered her gaze, her eyes fell on the oil painting hanging over the hearth. It was a picture of the little red schoolhouse with the words "Tilly Douglas Elementary School," written across the portal. Standing in the doorway was Miss Martha and sitting nearby was Jerry in his wheelchair. Meredith had told Tilly that she'd added them to the picture when the second schoolhouse was built.

Tilly's mind drifted to Meredith, because she was the central theme of the poem entitled, "What if?" It read,

> What if I had never met you?
> What if our lives had not been intertwined?
> Would I not have been the loser
> of a relationship divine?
>
> What if we had never parted?
> What if life had kept us bound?
> Would we have remained forever faithful
> to
>
> What if you had grown cold?
> What if I had not forgiven?
> Would we not have missed our loved ones
> and our dreams never risen.
>
> What if we never again see each other?
> What if somehow time just leaves?
> Would you meet me on the other side
> where joy lives and not grief?

Tilly reflected on the second stanza and couldn't come up with the words she needed to complete the poem. She then focused on the line that said, "What if we never again see each other?"

Looking back up at the little red schoolhouse, she stared at it for a long time. After making her decision, she put her notebook down, deciding to return to it the next day and try again. Making her way down the hallway, she walked past the living room and saw Robert reading to the twins. They were eighteen now, both full-time students at the university. Lydia was studying law while Rachael preferred accounting. Robert had had a tremendous influence on Andrew, and in just three months her handsome son would be receiving his doctorate in medicine.

The twins noticed their mother in the doorway. Lydia spoke up, "Momma, please come sit down. You'll be pleased to know that we're reading from your book of poems."

Tilly still felt a little embarrassed that some of her works had been published. When she and Robert had been married five years earlier, he had presented a book of her poems to her as a wedding present. She was still trying to figure out how the children had known where she kept her writings so they could be put into the book. Tilly was also quite amazed at how the poems were received by others and by the opportunities that had presented themselves for her to do readings as far away as New York.

Tilly took a seat as Robert continued to read her poems softly, melodically. She wondered if she could do it as well. Looking around the room she admired its beauty. Never in her wildest imagination would she have ever dreamed of living in such a beautiful place. The two-story English Tudor home had been left to Robert by his parents. Fortunately he had allowed her to completely redecorate it, and the furnishings were elegantly simple but warm.

When Robert finished reading, he removed his glasses and smiled. Looking at Tilly he said, "Mrs. Ryan, your poetry is a work of art. It's almost as if you're painting a picture with words."

Tilly cleared her throat and leaned forward in her chair. "As always, my dear Dr. Ryan, you flatter me with the kindness of your words."

"Flattery it is not, my love, for that word applies to commendations given that are not true. My statement concerning your writing falls short of what I truly feel."

Smiling, the twins looked at each other and simultaneously said, "Oh, how sweet!"

Tilly laughed and then became somber. "Robert, I've been thinking. I'd like to go see Meri."

"That's an excellent idea. When will you leave?"

Tilly should have known that his response would be positive. He was supportive of almost anything she wanted to do. "I'd like to go when the children are out of school for the summer so they can all go with me."

"Well you can forget about Andrew going," Rachael quipped. "He said the next time he saw the South he would be looking at it from heaven. There's is no way he's going back down there!"

Sighing, Tilly said, "I'll talk to Andrew. I think it's important for him to visit the places that have great meaning in our family's history. Plus the fact I'm sure things have gotten better over the years."

Robert raised one eyebrow as he tapped his pipe against the ashtray. "Don't be too sure about that, Tilly. I'm assuming you'll be traveling by train so you can go straight to and from your destination. That way there will probably be little to worry about."

Talking to her son later, Tilly realized that Rachael had been right—Andrew had put up quite a fuss about returning to the South, but Tilly had prevailed. Later, Andrew wondered why he had even tried to disagree with his mother. She had a way of putting things that made him want to do something even though every ounce of his being said no.

Tilly and her children stood at the Chicago train station saying their goodbyes to Robert. They would only make one stop after they crossed into the South—and that was in Ralston. Just hearing the name of that town invoked a myriad of emotions in

Andrew, but fortunately they would only be there for fifteen minutes to pick up passengers.

Waving to Robert from their window, the train pulled out of the station. Tilly relaxed in her seat. She was grateful that the car was only half full of passengers. As they continued on their journey she smiled often as her children actively debated about several issues. *How can I have three children who think so differently?* Tilly wondered. *And yet I'm so thankful they are intelligent and able to effectively communicate their ideas with one another.*

The train ride was long and at one point they had all fallen asleep leaning against one another. The conductor seemed to be standing directly over Tilly when he announced loudly, "Next stop, Ralston!"

Jumping around like a young school girl, Meredith shared with Jerris the telegram announcing Tilly's arrival. He knew it was one of the happiest days of her life, and he had to admit that he was quite delighted himself. The whole household was excited!

It seemed like Patience hadn't stopped humming since she'd gotten the news. She spent a considerable amount of time preparing the rooms where Tilly and her children would be staying. The servants didn't know what to make of it. They had never waited on a colored person before, and many conversations ensued as they discussed their perceptions of what it would be like.

But now the day had arrived and Meredith knew Tilly was going to be thrilled when she stepped off the train and saw how many people were waiting to greet her.

"Hurry, Bobby, or we'll be late!" called Meredith. Bobby Carson appeared in the doorway of the red schoolhouse, holding a piece of paper in his hand. She was sure it was his speech. Meredith continued helping Miss Martha load the children into the wagons that would take them to the train station to meet

Tilly and her family. Everyone was so excited! Meredith had been preparing them for weeks. She had shared stories with the children about her relationship with Tilly. It seemed they couldn't get enough, and they were eagerly looking forward to meeting Mrs. Hunter's best friend.

The hot, humid day didn't dampen anyone's excitement as they made their way to the station. Meredith had planned it so that they would arrive about fifteen minutes early.

Stepping down from the train, Tilly and the children were relieved to be able to stretch their legs. Andrew looked around and was amazed at how uncomfortable he felt. *You're a grown man now,* he repeated to himself. He noticed that the "White Only" sign was still hanging over the water fountain. There were quite a few coloreds at the station, and they began loading the train. Taking a drink from the "Colored Only" fountain, Andrew straightened and noticed his mother waving him toward the train.

"You'll have to go to the last car," said the stoic-looking conductor, who was standing next to the entrance of their train car.

"There must be some mistake. This is the car we came in," Tilly replied,

"Well, that's too bad. This car is reserved for whites only on this leg of the trip. The last car is for coloreds."

Looking down the tracks at the last car, Tilly could see the people were packed into the seats and standing in the aisle.

"But, sir, there isn't enough room for me and my children. Why, I would barely fit in there myself. Our tickets show that we're to sit in this car."

"There's no room," replied the blue-uniformed conductor.

Tilly looked at the empty seats where she and the children had sat during the train ride to Ralston.

"But sir…"

"All aboard!" he announced.

"There's nowhere to sit—and our bags are in *this* car."

"Well, you've got one minute to get them off because this train is pulling out. If you don't hurry, your bags will be going without you."

Andrew and the girls rushed past the conductor and quickly pulled out their luggage. They stepped to the platform just as the train released its brake. The four of them stood in stunned silence as it began to move down the track. It seemed all the colored people in the last section were staring at them. One mean-looking woman yelled out the window, "Jes' 'cause ya got dem fancy clothes on don' mean ya are bettah dan us an' kin ride on de white man's train." Several of the people around her laughed.

Lydia whined, "Momma, what are we going to do?"

Tilly tried to collect her thoughts and was hoping she was not wearing her true emotions on her face. Andrew thought he had never seen a calmer person. Tilly made her way to the ticket counter where a bald white man had his head down looking at some papers. His green visor hid his face.

"Excuse me, sir," said Tilly, "I need to get to Kensington."

Without looking up, the agent replied, "The next train leaves in two days at the same time."

"Well, could you tell me where we can stay the night?"

Andrew whispered, "Momma, two days. We can't stay here two days!"

Tilly raised her hand to hush his comments and then continued, "Please direct us to the colored hotel."

"Ain't no colored hotel. This town hardly has people. The colored section is five miles up the road. Somebody will take you in."

"Is there a taxi?"

At that point he put his pencil down and looked up. "Did you say taxi?" He burst into laughter and the old white man sitting at the end of the counter joined him. The agent took his glasses off and wiped away a tear and answered, "No, I don't think you'll be finding a taxi. You'll have to walk."

"Walk?" questioned Rachael. "But what will we do with our luggage?"

The agent picked up his pencil and as he returned to his first position she heard him say, "That's your problem."

Tilly's heart sank. She herded the children onto the front porch of the train station and looked around the town. The buildings were scattered and there were very few people in sight. She thought that was understandable given the unbearable heat. She could see a sign on the outside of one of the buildings with peeled paint which read, "Duncan's General Store."

Once again Lydia asked, "Momma, what are we going to do?"

Tilly sat down on a bench and replied, "The first thing we're going to do is sit down. Then Andrew will walk over to that general store and buy us something to drink. The key is not to panic. I've taught you all your life that there is a solution to every problem if you just calm yourself down and take the time to think."

Andrew hesitated at first but then began walking toward the store. Two white men were sitting on the front steps of the store and neither of them moved when Andrew approached. He stepped around them and went into the hot, stifling store. A young, thin woman with her brown hair pulled back in a ponytail was dusting off some cans which were stacked on the shelves. Her white cotton apron was tied around her paisley-print dress.

"Can I help you?" she asked Andrew.

"Yes, I would like to buy some drinks."

She pointed to a cooler against the wall. There was a large block of ice in the bottom of it and the bottles felt cold. He also picked up a couple of white handkerchiefs, returned to the counter, and asked how much it cost. Then he counted out the correct change.

"I've never seen you around here," observed the clerk.

Andrew wrapped his hand around the top of the paper bag and replied, "That's because I'm from Chicago. We just missed our train so I thought I'd pick up some cool drinks."

The young woman smiled and said, "You talk funny."

Andrew responded, "How is that?"

"Oh, I don't know. Like somebody who's smart. I never heard a colored person talk like you."

Andrew smiled, "Well, I'm studying to be a doctor."

"Fancy that! I always wanted to be a nurse and work at a big hospital."

"You remind me of a nurse that works at the hospital where I'm taking some of my studies."

The young lady replied, "Is she pretty like me?"

Andrew laughed and she joined in. Just then a big white man emerged from behind a checkered cloth hanging across a doorway and looked intently at Andrew.

"What's so funny?" he asked.

Andrew froze. He had seen that look before.

The young lady hastened to say, "Nothing, Pa. This here man says he's going to be a doctor one day. That's all."

By now another man came out of the back. Andrew thought he looked to be the older man's son.

Picking up the brown paper bag, Andrew said, "Good day." As he left he overheard the younger man ask, "What was that all about?"

Tilly saw her son leave the store and immediately knew something was wrong. Andrew was trying to walk calmly, but he could hardly hear himself think over the pounding of his heart. This was just like the nightmares he'd had off and on throughout his life since his last experience in Ralston. He was halfway to his mother when the girl's father stepped onto the porch of the general store, raised something over his head and shouted, "Hey you!"

Andrew turned around and saw the old man and his son. The two men who had been sitting on the stairs stood and looked in his direction. Andrew dropped his bag and started to run.

"Oh no," whispered Tilly. "Andrew, don't run!" she shouted.

But it was too late. Andrew ran past her and his sisters, across the platform and alongside the railway track. The white man and his son ran toward him, and as Andrew tried to step across the train tracks his foot got caught and he fell to the ground crying out in agony. When Tilly reached him he was reaching for his leg. She dropped down beside him and soon after that the two men from the store were standing over her and Andrew.

Huffing, the older man said, "What's wrong with you boy? I was just trying to give you your handkerchiefs. You forgot them." Throwing the white cloths next to Tilly the man turned and walked away shaking his head. Andrew overheard the son snicker and say, "That boy ran like he thought we were going to lynch him." His father laughed.

Tilly pulled Andrew away from the train tracks and took a look at his leg. There was no doubt it was broken. Fortunately, the ticket agent was accommodating in gathering together some supplies that would help her set the fracture.

As Tilly wrapped the last tape around his leg, Andrew grabbed her arm and said, "Momma, please promise you'll take me home on the next train."

"But Andrew, you're in no shape to travel. You'll be in too much pain.

Andrew looked in her eyes and pleaded, "Momma, please!"

Tilly nodded. After making Andrew comfortable, she purchased return tickets to Chicago. Two hours later they were headed home. Before leaving, Tilly sent a telegram to Meredith hoping she would get it before she went to the train station.

As the "iron horse" made it's way back to Chicago, Tilly pondered on how Adam's fear—not the ill-fated attempt to escape—had caused the accident. Then she realized that fear, whether real or imagined, becomes a person's reality. She repented of her decision to bring Andrew. *I wonder if I'll ever see Meri again,* she thought to herself.

As the last person stepped down from the colored train car, Meredith looked at Jerris despondently and asked, "What could have happened? Why didn't she notify me that she wasn't coming?"

Everyone got ready to leave, their heads hanging down in disappointment. As Jerris helped Meredith into the wagon, Garrett, from the telegraph office, came running toward them.

"Good day, Mrs. Hunter. I thought I saw you come into town. This is for you," he said, handing her a telegram. It read:

> MRS. MEREDITH HUNTER STOP ANDREW HAD AN ACCIDENT STOP IT DEMANDED WE RETURN TO CHICAGO STOP I AM SO SORRY STOP TILLY

Meredith handed the telegram to Jerris and cried, "Why can't Tilly and I get together? Oh, Jerris, I am so disappointed I could just spit!"

Jerris looked at Meredith with amusement in his eyes. Even she couldn't help but laugh.

Clyde noticed Meredith sitting motionless in the atrium, staring out the window as if in a daze. Even when he stood beside the chair and gently called her name she didn't move. Then slowly she lifted her head and looked at him as he handed her a letter. Walking away, Clyde heard her mumble, "Thank you."

God, my heart is so heavy that not even a letter from Tilly lifts my spirits, Meredith whispered when she recognized her friend's handwriting. *I miss her so much, and it doesn't seem fair that we couldn't get together again.*

Unfolding the letter, Meredith began reading, and her heart grew heavier as Tilly related what had happened in Ralston.

How could this happen to dear, sweet Andrew? Meri asked herself.

Tilly had ended the letter with a poem entitled, "What If?" and Meredith read it again and again before setting it on the end table. Her eyes misted over as she wondered how long it would take before the division between the races would be over. Meredith's distant stare returned when she admitted to herself that it would probably be a long, long time. . . .

21

Many years later

obby Carson stood at the pulpit, staring at a roomful of white faces. Through the church windows he could see hundreds of colored people standing outside. No black man had ever walked into this sanctuary before—except to clean it—and Bobby understood the magnitude of the moment.

Picking up the glass of water that sat on the podium, Bobby took a drink. As he drank out of a glass intended only for a white person, he saw the look of disgust on Dick Farvis' face. He took one more swallow before beginning.

"Meredith Douglas Hunter was my friend and, I might add, a friend to all colored people. I am grateful to her family members who have asked me to speak about her today. There is a song that says, 'Jesus loves the little children, all the children of the world, red, and yellow, black and white, they are precious in His sight, Jesus loves the little children of the world.' Meredith Hunter believed the words of that song."

Jerris blew his nose, Jerry wiped tears from his eyes, and Becky had laid her head on Priscilla's shoulder. Jackson shifted nervously in his seat.

Bobby continued, "God does love the little children, and we are all just little children grown up. He still considers us His children. God used this woman to help educate hundreds of colored children in this community. Some have gone on to become teachers, doctors, lawyers, and more. I went on to become the principal of the Tilly Douglas Elementary School. Some people say a man should pull himself up by his own bootstraps, but we didn't have any boots until Misses Hunter gave them to us! Meredith gave us love, she gave us understanding, but most of all—through knowledge—she gave us our freedom."

When Bobby was finished he stepped down from the pulpit and headed up the church aisle toward the front door. Knowing he wouldn't be allowed to stay in the sanctuary after completing his words of eulogy, he exited the building.

Tilly gasped for air. No matter how hard she tried to breathe, there just didn't seem to be enough air to fill her lungs. It took every ounce of her strength to simply breathe in and out. Tilly's gray hair was spread on the pillow. She opened her eyes, turning her head to the side.

Andrew was seated next to the bed with his wife, Earlean. Robert stood at the end of the bed with the twins, Lydia and Rachael, beside him. Tilly smiled as she thought how appropriate that sight was. Ever since the day Tilly had first brought Dr. Robert Ryan home for dinner, the twins seemed to always be at his side.

Rachael's husband sat next to the beveled-glass window, watching some of their children running in the backyard. Evening was quickly approaching, and their playtime was almost over. Tilly looked at Lydia, who had decided marriage would be a distraction to her career as an attorney. It seemed, however, that her friend Matthew had almost convinced her otherwise

Tilly thought Andrew looked wonderfully handsome. She'd never forget the day they had called his name at the graduation service for his doctorate. Now he had a booming medical practice. Andrew laid the Bible he had been reading to his mother on the nightstand. Tilly watched him place it on top of her book of poems.

Tilly's grandchildren were downstairs. All seven of them had been up earlier to give Grandma Tilly a hug and kiss. Even six-month-old Joshua had put his arms around her neck and drooled on her face. For some reason their affection felt different to Tilly that day. As a matter of fact, everything appeared different—even her large bedroom, which she dearly loved. She had decorated it with romance in mind. A beautiful, white eyelet bedspread with matching pillowcases covered her intricately carved mahogany bed. The mirrors on the armoire reflected the fine furnishings and light fixtures in the room. An imported lace cloth was draped softly across the lamp nearest her bed, casting a soft glow.

A knock at the door startled everyone. Lydia walked over to open it. Tilly tried to focus her eyes. For a moment she thought she was dreaming that she was standing on the platform of the train station waving to her friend Meri. *Who are these women? One of them looks so much like Meri. . . .* Lydia exchanged words with the strange women and then led them to the bed. As the first lady drew closer, Tilly saw the silver locket around her neck. Andrew and Earlean arose, offering their chairs to the visitors. Tilly stretched her hand toward the locket. The woman leaned forward until it rested in her hand.

"Hello, Tilly. My name is Priscilla Hunter-Stewart, and this is my sister, Becky."

Tilly mouthed their names while searching their faces. Becky was the very image of her mother.

Priscilla lifted the chain holding the locket over her head placing it in Tilly's hand. "Mother asked that I bring this to you."

Tilly fought to get out the words, "Your father sent me word about your mother. I was too sick to come to the funeral."

Meredith's daughter nodded and smiled, then continued, "One of her last requests was that we come visit you. Mother said she always thought she would see you again, and she couldn't believe the years had denied her that privilege. She said that each time the two of you made plans to get together something would interfere. Either Jerry would get sick or something would happen at the school. I believe that you once even came down with the chicken pox, not to mention the incident at Ralston. I watched her frustration on a number of occasions when those plans were denied."

"Isn't it strange," Tilly whispered, "we were born in the same year and now . . ."

Tilly had always thought she and Meri would be together again one day. But time had a strange way of escaping, even when you were looking right at it.

Priscilla leaned forward and opened the locket. Tilly tried to fix her vision long enough to see the image of Meredith's beautiful mother. She remembered the day they exchanged the locket and the smooth black stone in Meredith's bedroom.

Tilly summoned Lydia with her finger and said the word, "Letters."

Priscilla didn't understand what Tilly had just whispered. But Lydia had spent countless hours tending to her mother's medical needs, and she understood the old woman's every word. Lydia pulled out the bottom drawer on the chest of drawers and took out two boxes full of letters. Tilly pointed in Priscilla's direction, and, again, Lydia understood.

Lydia said to Priscilla, "My mother wants me to give these to you. They are letters written to her by your mother over the years. I have read them all, and I feel as if I know you and your mother. She was a very special woman."

At the mention of her mother, Priscilla became choked up and couldn't speak.

Becky took Tilly's hand and recounted, "My father said you would have been proud of my mother's funeral. It seemed every colored person within fifty miles attended. She wrote to you about Bobby. Remember the little boy who attended the first day in her class? Well, he's the principal of your school now, and he gave a eulogy. That caused quite a stir in town."

Priscilla gave Becky a reprimanding look. Looking uncomfortable, Becky tried to rephrase her statement, "Well, what I mean is that for some people . . . well, they never saw a colored man speak in a white church."

Priscilla rolled her eyes and said quietly yet firmly, "Becky, please! What she's trying to say, Tilly, is that mother was loved by everyone. Dad said you would be pleased to know that."

Even in Tilly's poor state of health she found Becky utterly refreshing. She was just like her mother—forthright and unpredictable.

Priscilla continued to talk, but Tilly could no longer hear her words. And yet there seemed to be sounds all around her. At first the sounds were indistinguishable, but then they became sweetly clear. Familiar voices. Music.

All of a sudden Tilly sat up in bed, extended her hand with the locket in it, and exclaimed, "Meri!"

Each person in the room glanced over to look at what Tilly saw. There was no one there. And when they turned back around, Tilly lay peacefully on the pillow, the silver locket resting against her heart.

After their return home, Priscilla spent weeks pouring over the letters written by her mother and by Tilly. One day she reached for a red ribbon and tied three particular envelopes together.

It had been raining all day, and the evening's darkness fell like a warm comforter. Jackson was finishing dinner with his wife and three children when he saw his butler heading for the door. He wondered who would be out on such a wretched night. The butler entered the dining room and said, "Miss Priscilla is waiting in the entry. She refuses to come in but wants to see you in private."

Jackson hastened to the front door and found his sister there, soaked with rain. She was holding a package wrapped in oilskin. She didn't say a word. Priscilla simply lifted up her small bundle and placed it in Jackson's hands. Then she turned quickly and retreated into the darkness.

Jackson was too stunned to even ask her if she wanted a ride. He put the rain-drenched package on the floor and removed the outer covering. Inside was a box full of letters, and on the top were three of them tied with a red ribbon. Jackson picked up the envelopes and took them to his study. Sitting at his desk he untied the ribbon and noticed his mother's faded handwriting. His eyes strained to read the date. He quickly recognized it as being the day after his father had died. The words seemed to peel off the letter and affix themselves to his soul. It was a letter to Tilly describing in detail the events that took place the previous day.

Jackson remembered his mother's account to him the day he challenged her in her bedroom. This account was identical. As he continued to read, he felt not only the agony of his mother's pain, but also the deep love she had for his father, Carter. The second letter was also written to Tilly shortly after his mother's marriage to Jerris. Her words cried out for consolation as she had made the choice to marry a man she did not love so that she could protect the name of her unborn child.

Jackson could hardly see through the tears pouring from his eyes. The last letter was written by Tilly. The depth of her friendship flowed through the warm expressions of sympathy and shared grief. At the end of the letter was a poem entitled *Night Come Swiftly*. Jackson read it slowly and carefully:

Night Come Swiftly

Terror chased me by day
And so I prayed,
Night come swiftly.

Evil wanted me to fall
And so I called,
Night come swiftly.

My friend was robbed
And so I sobbed,
Night come swiftly.

Night hide my friend
And cover her shame,
Hold her till she's without blame.

And deliver her safely
To face the sun's ray,
Of a bright and glorious day.

Tilly and Meredith had written in their wills their desire to be buried side by side. Tilly's body had been brought to the Hunter estate to be put to rest. Andrew overcame his fears and he and the twins had stopped to visit the Douglas Plantation on the way to the funeral. They viewed the mansion where their grandmother and mother had lived, and even saw the grave markers of Bertha and her son, Ben. Their mother had told them that out of the 200,000 colored soldiers who had fought in the Civil War, only twenty-one men had received the Congressional Medal of Honor—and Ben was one of them.

Now Jackson stood next to Andrew at the gravesite. They had both failed to realize just how much they knew about each other until they were face-to-face. There was an unspoken bond that neither could explain.

Jerris had his arm around Jackson's shoulder as he wept bitterly. Andrew overheard Jackson saying over and over again, "Mother, I'm sorry."

Jerris comforted Jackson by saying, "She forgave you long ago, and she saw this day coming through the eyes of faith. Let's spend the rest of our lives remembering her love and kindness. Teach it to your children, so they will call her blessed."

A single, large marble tombstone was placed over the double grave. It read

Meredith Douglas Hunter
Tilly Douglas Jensen Ryan
1851–1921
"Love is stronger than death"

Jackson's oldest daughter, Laura, trailed behind him and her grandfather as they slowly made their way from the gravesite. She looked at her mother and noticed that something was different about her. Then she realized that she was not wearing the single-strand pearl necklace with the diamond clasp that she'd always worn. Laura never saw the necklace again, and somehow knew that it should never be mentioned.

The word had gotten around quickly in town, not only among the whites, but the coloreds also, that Jackson Hunter had entertained some colored people for dinner at his house. In fact, he had hosted them in the formal dining room, no less. After that supper, Andrew, Lydia, and Rachael had read from their mother's book of poems while Jerris, Jackson, Jerry, Priscilla, and Becky listened intently.

When they left the next morning, Jackson sat by his fireplace admiring his new painting. After reading her letters, he had rummaged around in his mother's art studio and had brought down her last artistic effort. It was a self-portrait. He'd had it framed and prominently hung. He was amazed at the unexplainable peace in her eyes that seemed to fill the entire room. Jackson thought back on his earlier days with his mother and realized at that moment that her peace was not unexplainable at all. She had gone to great lengths to explain it to him—and to demonstrate its source.

About the Author

P. B. Wilson is the author of *The Master's Degree, Knight in Shining Armor, Liberated Through Submission,* and *Betrayal's Baby.* She and her husband of more than 20 years, well-known author, songwriter and record producer Frank E. Wilson, conduct marriage and family seminars across America.

Other Books by P.B. Wilson

≈ ≈ ≈

Betrayal's Baby
Knight In Shining Armor
Liberated Through Submission
The Master's Degree by Frank & P.B. Wilson
7 Secrets Women Want To Know